What Happened to th Party?

The Grand Old Party—once moderate and even magnanimous—has fallen into a prison of its own making when it comes to presidential politics. Republicans may be having a heyday in the Congress, but their prospects for the 2016 presidential election aren't great—and won't improve unless and until they break out of their intellectual and ideological straightjackets and start speaking to where the American public lives: geographically, culturally, and politically.

John Kenneth White is a Professor of Politics at the Catholic University of America and the author of several books on political parties and the U.S. presidency.

What Happened to the Republican Party?

And What It Means for American Presidential Politics

John Kenneth White

Routledge
Taylor & Francis Group

NEW YORK AND LONDON

First published 2016
by Routledge
711 Third Avenue, New York, NY 10017

and by Routledge
2 Park Square, Milton Park, Abingdon, Oxon, OX14 4RN

Routledge is an imprint of the Taylor & Francis Group, an Informa business

© 2016 Taylor & Francis

Library of Congress Cataloging-in-Publication Data
A catalog record for this book has been requested

ISBN: 978-1-61205-921-1 (hbk)
ISBN: 978-1-61205-922-8 (pbk)
ISBN: 978-1-315-67529-9 (ebk)

Typeset in Sabon
by Apex CoVantage, LLC

For Everett Carll Ladd (1937–1999), a mentor who continues to inspire, and for Matthew R. Kerbel, another colleague, mentor, and friend whose insights helped shape this book.

Contents

Acknowledgments

During the writing of this volume, I have incurred more than the usual number of obligations. I am deeply indebted to Jennifer Knerr, Vice President and Associate Publisher, at Paradigm Publishers for believing in this work and helping to shape it. My colleagues, Matthew R. Kerbel at Villanova University and William Crotty at Northeastern University, copiously read several drafts of the manuscript and offered valuable insights. I am deeply grateful to them. I am also beholden to my students at the Catholic University of America, who heard several versions of the arguments presented here and helped me to refine my thesis. I also owe a great thanks to Anne Lesher, reference librarian at Mullen Library at the Catholic University of America, for her prompt responses to my many requests.

In many ways, this work relies on prior assistance I received for previous works. In particular, I owe a great debt to the late Richard B. Wirthlin, pollster for Ronald Reagan. Our many conversations about the Republican Party during the Reagan years are reflected in this book. The late Everett C. Ladd at the University of Connecticut taught me a great deal about the utility of polling data and that political science should be accessible to every interested reader. I hope that is reflected in this work. As always, my family remains a constant support.

Preface
Why Republicans?

Some years ago, in a book titled *The Losing Parties*, Philip A. Klinkner maintained that minority parties matter because the means they use to extricate themselves from their difficulties shapes the future discourse of American politics: "[P]arties out of power merit observation because an election loss may exert a strong influence on their ensuing behavior. For example, losing parties are more likely than winning parties to innovate and reform themselves and the party system and to raise new issues. Defeat provides them with a powerful motivation for changing their personnel, organizational structure, internal party procedures, and platforms since past methods have failed to achieve victory. In-parties, following both the need for consistency and the adage 'if it ain't broke, don't fix it,' seem less disposed to change themselves."[1] Indeed, the significant role of the minority party has long been recognized by political scientists. In 1950, the American Political Science Association advocated an enhanced role for the out-party: "*[T]he opposition party acts as the critic of the party in power, developing, defining, and presenting the policy alternatives which are necessary for a true choice in reaching public decisions. . . . [D]*emocratic government is greatly influenced by the character of the opposition party. . . . When there are two parties identifiable by the kinds of action they propose, the voters have an actual choice" [italics in original].[2]

From this vantage point, it makes sense to focus on the Republican Party, which is today's minority party in *presidential politics*. Since 1992, no Republican candidate has garnered more than 300 electoral votes, or won more than 51 percent of the popular vote. Moreover, the only Republican president to serve since Bill Clinton—George W. Bush—is an anathema to many Americans. Even now, years after leaving the White House, George W. Bush remains unpopular, as several recent polls illustrate:

- 69 percent blame Bush for the current economic problems facing the United States;[3]
- 61 percent say that Bush's decision to wage war in Iraq was the "wrong thing" to do;[4]

- 56 percent disapprove of the way Bush handled his job as president;[5]
- 51 percent blame Bush for "the situation in Iraq," as the Iraqi government has failed to find a sustaining coalition to help keep the country from breaking apart;[6]
- 47 percent answer "a lot" when asked if the Bush administration was to blame "for the difficulties the middle class has faced in the past decade";[7]
- 43 percent believe Bush will be viewed by historians as either a "below average" or "poor" president.[8]

In a presidential nation such as ours, presidents become public faces of the parties they represent.[9] One illustration: back in 1986 pollster William Hamilton played the "word association game," asking voters to name those individuals they most associated with the Democratic and Republican parties. The most frequent answers: 54 percent linked the GOP to Ronald Reagan; 46 percent connected the Democratic Party to John F. Kennedy.[10] Since Reagan, Republicans have not only had a hard time winning the presidency, they have been unable to find a successful president who can help restore their tattered image. Today, only one out of three voters has a positive image of the Republican Party, and only one out of five approve of the job Republicans are doing in the U.S. Congress.[11] In the coming 2016 presidential contest, the word "Republican" is likely to be a drag upon the party's standard-bearer. Rand Paul, one of the GOP presidential contenders, recently stated, "The Republican Party brand sucks."[12]

Any reader of this book will surely ask: Aren't Democrats torn apart by internal dissensions? Don't they have an unpopular president who is tarnishing their image? The answer to both questions is undeniably yes. A rising populism—best symbolized by Massachusetts U.S. senator Elizabeth Warren—opposes the business-friendly "third way" politics of the Bill Clinton years. Seeking the presidency, Clinton labeled himself a "New Democrat"— one whose first reliance would *not* be on the federal government but would focus instead on giving "people the tools they need to make the most of their lives."[13] The 1992 party platform crystallized the party's new thinking:

> We offer a new social contract based neither on callous, do-nothing Republican neglect, nor an outdated faith in programs as the solution to every problem. We favor a third way beyond the old approaches—to put government back on the side of citizens who play by the rules. We believe that by what it says and how it conducts its business, government must once again make responsibility an instrument of national purpose. Our future as a nation depends upon the daily assumption of personal responsibility by millions of Americans from all walks of life—for the religious faiths they follow, the ethics they practice, the values they instill, and the pride they take in their work.[14]

Toward those ends, Clinton signed onto deficit reduction even as he lamented doing so: "I hope you're all aware we're all Eisenhower Republicans. We're Eisenhower Republicans here, and we are fighting the Reagan Republicans. . . . Isn't that great?"[15] Despite such outbursts, Clinton stuck to his "New Democrats" formulation—the obvious inference being, of course, that there were old Democrats stuck in the rigid bureaucracies of the New Deal past.

Critics derided the so-called "New Democrat philosophy" as not being a philosophy at all. Historians James MacGregor Burns and Georgia J. Sorenson argued that Clinton's never-ending pursuit of Reagan Democrats left the Democratic Party philosophically bereft.[16] Today, New Democrats have taken a back seat to party activists who want government to do more in the wake of the 2008 financial collapse and the Great Recession that followed. Populists, like Elizabeth Warren, see government as a necessary corrective force to big businesses and the "too-big-to-fail" banks that ran roughshod over too-timid (or nonexistent) federal regulations. Says Warren:

> Today the game is rigged—rigged to work for those who have money and power. Big corporations hire armies of lobbyists to get billion-dollar loopholes into the tax system and persuade their friends in Congress to support laws that keep the playing field in their favor. Meanwhile, hardworking families are told that they'll just have to live with smaller dreams for their children.[17]

These internal Democratic divisions are compounded by the party's inability to exert unified control over the federal government. For Republicans, the long-term gift of their 2010 and 2014 landslides was that it extended beyond Congress to state governorships and state legislatures. Because the Democratic "shellacking" (Obama's characterization of his party's 2010 loss) happened in a census year, Republicans were able to redraw U.S. House districts to ensure their majorities for the remainder of the decade. The contortions they constructed were in the spirit of the salamander-style district once approved by the famed Massachusetts Democrat Elbridge Gerry. (The term "gerrymander" is named in Gerry's honor.)

Another problem for the Democrats is Barack Obama. In the sixth year of his presidency, Obama is at a low point. His job approval rating is stuck in the very low forties (even dipping into the thirties in some places). A recent poll found Obama inhabiting George W. Bush territory as the *worst* president since World War Two: 33 percent chose Obama; 28 percent selected Bush.[18] While Obama raised substantial cash for Democratic candidates in 2014, few wanted to appear by his side. Kentucky Democratic senate candidate Alison Lundergan Grimes even refused to disclose how she voted for president in 2008 and 2012. Worse still, 54 percent view Obama as unable to lead the country and get the job done.[19]

This is a long way from 2008. Back then, Obama ran hoping to be a *transformational president*. Comparing himself to Ronald Reagan, Obama told the editorial board of the *Reno Gazette-Journal*: "I think Ronald Reagan changed the trajectory of America in a way that Richard Nixon did not and in a way that Bill Clinton did not. He put us on a fundamentally different path because the country was ready for it. . . . He just tapped into what people were already feeling, which was we want clarity, we want optimism, we want a return to that sense of dynamism and entrepreneurship that had been missing."[20] Obama's chief rival that year, Hillary Clinton, took umbrage at Obama's unfavorable comparison to her husband and promised to be a *transactional president*, someone who, like Lyndon B. Johnson, could pass landmark legislation. As Clinton told a reporter: "Dr. King's dream began to be realized when President Johnson passed the Civil Rights Act. It took a president to get it done."[21] While it is far too early to place a historical marker on the Obama presidency, Americans are disappointed. Obama's entrance onto the national stage was marked by a promise that he could be the kind of transformational leader who could lift the country out its partisan morass. Speaking before the 2004 Democratic National Convention, Obama struck a theme that he would pursue for most (but not all) of his presidency:

> There's not a liberal America and a conservative America; there's the United States of America. There's not a black America and white America and Latino America and Asian America; there's the United States of America. The pundits like to slice and dice our country into red states and blue states; red states for Republicans, blue states for Democrats. But I've got news for them, too. We worship an awesome God in the blue states, and we don't like federal agents poking around our libraries in red states. We coach Little League in the blue states and, yes, we've got some gay friends in the red states. There are patriots who opposed the war in Iraq, and there are patriots who supported the war in Iraq. We are all one people, all of us pledging allegiance to the stars and stripes, all of us defending the United States of America.[22]

Today, Obama's quest to restore our motto of "*E Pluribus Unum*" has morphed into "*E Pluribus Duo*"—out of many, two partisan and distinct nations that are at odds over culture, values, and policy. Governing such a divided nation is nearly impossible, and by his second term Obama was reduced to signing executive orders and issuing federal regulations in order to bypass first a divided Congress and now a GOP-controlled Congress. Republicans seem perfectly happy to be engaged in a death match with Obama—making sure they bring his poll numbers down, even if that means they lose broad public support.

A reader of this book may also wonder, "If both parties are in trouble, why not have a new party?" It's an idea most Americans love at first sight. A recent poll found 64 percent answering, "Yes!" when asked if they would consider voting for a third-party presidential candidate in 2016.[23] But when a follow-up question is posed, "Do you think a qualified third party candidate has a reasonable chance of winning the next presidential election?" 58 percent say "No!"[24] As these mercurial numbers illustrate, third parties act as a kind of Rorschach test: they are loved until they come up with actual candidates and ideas. The long history of U.S. politics tells us that third parties are rarities, and although they can burn brightly once in a while, they flame out when their attractive ideas are appropriated by one or both major parties. Ross Perot is the latest example. Having captured 19 percent of the vote in 1992—the best showing for a third-party candidate since Theodore Roosevelt in 1912—Perot's Reform Party has gone the way of the Whigs, as both parties seized on Perot's main issue: controlling the federal deficit. Today, concern about the deficit has reemerged, but it animates the Tea Party (which itself is not a third party but an activist wing within the Republican Party). While there may be a billionaire or two who would like to run for president as an independent (Donald Trump, anyone?), there is no present movement to form a third party to challenge the institutional dominance of the Democrats and Republicans.

It is the Republicans, I argue, that hold the keys to the future of American politics. Throughout history, what the minority party does in presidential politics matters a great deal. The dialogue, issues, and candidates the party chooses to elevate not only shapes our politics but determines the difference between victory and defeat; the difference between a closely divided country and one that suddenly—and decisively—makes a determination to go in a different direction.

History is replete with examples of Republicans doing just that. Back in 1936, Democrat Franklin D. Roosevelt vanquished Republican Alf Landon in a historic landslide. Landon was a conservative who lashed out against the "folly" of Roosevelt's New Deal, citing Social Security as an example of government "bungling and waste" that would intrude upon a citizen's right to privacy:

> Imagine the vast army of clerks which will be necessary to keep these records. Another army of field investigators will be necessary to check up on the people whose records are not clear, or regarding whom current information is not coming in. And so bureaucracy will grow and grow, and Federal snooping will flourish.[25]

Landon saw the forthcoming vote in apoplectic terms:

> America is in peril. The welfare of the American men and women and the future of our youth are at stake. We dedicate ourselves to the preservation of their political liberty, their individual opportunity, and their character as free citizens, which today for the first time are threatened by government itself.[26]

By 1940, Republicans dramatically changed course and nominated Wendell Willkie. Willkie was a startling choice: he had been a delegate to the 1924 Democratic convention; voted for Franklin D. Roosevelt in 1932; and was a registered Democrat until two years prior to his nomination. Far from undoing Roosevelt's New Deal (especially his prized Social Security program), Willkie wanted to conserve it. This was a very different direction for the Republican Party, and it resulted in an improved performance: Willkie gained five million votes over Landon, and FDR had the smallest victory for an incumbent president since Woodrow Wilson in 1916. There is a famous scene recreated by historian James MacGregor Burns on that tense 1940 Election Night. As the Roosevelts gathered in Hyde Park to listen to the returns, FDR did not like what he saw, broke out into a cold sweat, and banished the family from the dining room where they gathered to celebrate. Later, as the clock approached midnight, the big city votes swung FDR's way and an unprecedented third term was guaranteed.[27] Four years later, Roosevelt and Willkie plotted to create two very different parties: a liberal Democratic party that would be purged of recalcitrant southern Democrats and a conservative Republican party whose remaining progressives would leave to join the Democrats. The idea, however, came to naught as Willkie was overtaken by death and Roosevelt was consumed by World War Two.[28]

By 1952, the internal Republican struggle came to a head in a climactic showdown between Dwight D. Eisenhower and Robert Taft. Eisenhower wanted to modernize the Republican Party by accepting broad elements of the New Deal. Eisenhower's opponent that year, Robert A. Taft, was rightfully dubbed "Mr. Republican," and his vision for his beloved party was far different from Eisenhower's. Taft proposed a substantial reduction in the federal budget, and he argued that the powers of the presidency in foreign affairs had been badly abused by Harry S. Truman. Eisenhower disagreed, saying: "I'm running because Taft is an isolationist. His election would be a disaster."[29]

By choosing Eisenhower, Republicans remade their party into a sturdy presidential vehicle. A twenty-year saga that began in 1932 (and encompassed candidacies ranging from Alf Landon to Dwight D. Eisenhower) came to a close. Its conclusion altered both the tone and tempo of politics. For the next thirty-six years, Republicans won seven of ten presidential victories—five of them by landslide margins (1952, 1956, 1972, 1980, and 1984).

With the passage of time, Republicans made even more strategic choices. During the Eisenhower years, conservatives bemoaned Ike's accommodations with Democrats and derided his Modern Republicanism as nothing more than Democratic "me-tooism." Barry Goldwater led the charge, and in 1964 he came away with the presidential nomination in that strange year. Ronald Reagan took up Goldwater's banner, and his presidency not only remade the Republican Party into a conservative bastion but relocated it, too: away from the Northeast (which had been a power center for Modern Republicanism) and into a rising South and West.

Out-of-power Democrats have also made strategic choices. It is fair to say that following Ronald Reagan's twin landslides, Democrats determined that the New Deal was over (at least for the moment), and the party would have to recalibrate if it wanted to win back the White House. The rise of Third Way thinking—along with intellectual and political organizations to support it such as the Progressive Policy Institute and the Democratic Leadership Council—were undeniably helpful in Bill Clinton's ascent to the presidency. Clinton later claimed that he could have never won without these entities—both of which he played a leading role in creating as a potential candidate and utilizing once he became president.

Today's Republican story is compelling for two reasons: (1) how the GOP descended from the Reagan era is an intriguing journey that says much about our present-day politics; and (2) while the pathway forward to winning the White House may seem clear, the titanic struggle over whether to even choose a victorious path is still to come. Indeed, the fight ahead promises to be loud and long. Equally unclear is whether Republicans will chose to put Ronald Reagan behind them and accommodate themselves to a new demography, or whether they will construct a twenty-first century ideas factory that will give future nominees some ideological flexibility. The election of 2016 surely will provide some clues about the path Republicans will ultimately take, but that election is likely to be one more battle in an ongoing war.

It is typical for parties to struggle for years after crippling defeats. Democrats took a dozen years after Reagan's 1980 triumph to conclude they had more than merely a candidate problem, they had a party problem—and Republicans appear destined to follow the same path. To paraphrase Hillary Clinton, the "hard choices" the GOP has to make still lie ahead—and those choices will say much about the tone and direction of our politics for years to come.[30]

Notes

1 Philip A. Klinkner, *The Losing Parties: Out-Party National Committees, 1956–1963* (New Haven: Yale University Press, 1994), 1.
2 Committee on Political Parties, *Toward a More Responsible Two-Party System* (New York: Rinehart Books, 1950), 18–19.
3 Gallup poll, June 20–24, 2013. Text of question: "Thinking about the economic problems currently facing the United States, how much do you blame George W. Bush for these—a great deal, a moderate amount, not much, or not at all?" A great deal, 32 percent; a moderate amount, 37 percent; not much, 22 percent; not at all, 8 percent; no opinion, 1 percent.
4 Quinnipiac University, poll, June 24–30, 2014. Text of question: "Do you think going to war with Iraq in 2003 was the right thing for the United States to do or

the wrong thing?" Right thing, 32 percent; wrong thing, 61 percent; don't know/ no answer, 7 percent.

5 CNN/Opinion Research Corporation, poll, November 18–20, 2013. Text of question: "From what you have heard, read, or remember about some of our past presidents, please tell me if you approve or disapprove of the way each of the following handled their job as president? George W. Bush, who was president from 2001 to 2009." Approve, 42 percent; disapprove, 56 percent; no opinion, 2 percent.

6 Quinnipiac University, poll, June 24–30, 2014. Text of question: "Who do you blame more for the situation in Iraq, President Barack Obama or former President George W. Bush?" Obama, 27 percent; Bush, 51 percent; neither (volunteered), 11 percent; both (volunteered), 5 percent; don't know/no answer, 5 percent.

7 Princeton Survey Research Associates, poll, July 16–26, 2012. Text of question: "How much do you blame the Bush administration for the difficulties the middle class has faced in the past ten years? Do you blame the Bush administration a lot, a little, or not at all?" A lot, 47 percent; a little, 35 percent; not at all, 16 percent; don't know/refused, 2 percent.

8 Gallup poll, November 7–10, 2013. Text of question: "How do you think each of the following presidents will go down in history—as an outstanding president, above average, average, below average, or poor? George W. Bush, president from 2001–2009." Outstanding, 3 percent; above average, 18 percent; average, 36 percent; below average, 20 percent; poor, 23 percent; no opinion, 1 percent.

9 See, for example, Joseph Califano, *A Presidential Nation* (New York: W. W. Norton, 1975).

10 Survey conducted by William R. Hamilton and Staff for Larry Sabato and AMPAC, cited in *The Polling Report*, October 20, 1986, 3.

11 See NBC News/*Wall Street Journal*, poll, June 11–14, 2014. Text of question: "Now I'm going to read you the names of several public figures and groups, and I'd like you to rate your feelings toward each one as very positive, somewhat positive, neutral, somewhat negative, or very negative. . . . The Republican party." Very positive, 6 percent; somewhat positive, 23 percent; neutral, 24 percent; somewhat negative, 22 percent; very negative, 23 percent; don't know/not sure, 2 percent. See Quinnipiac University, poll, March 26–31, 2014. Text of question: "Do you approve or disapprove of the way Republicans in Congress are handling their job?" Approve, 18 percent; disapprove, 73 percent; unsure, 9 percent.

12 Quoted in Dana Milbank, "Can Rand Paul Save the GOP?," *Washington Post*, November 2, 2014.

13 Democratic Party Platform, 1996 (Washington, D.C.: Democratic National Committee, 1996), 17.

14 Democratic Party Platform, 1992 (Washington, D.C.: Democratic National Committee, 1992), 7.

15 Quoted in Bob Woodward, *The Agenda: Inside the Clinton White House* (New York: Simon and Schuster, 1994), 165.

16 James MacGregor Burns and Georgia J. Sorenson, *Dead Center: Clinton-Gore Leadership and the Perils of Moderation* (New York: Scribner, 1999).

17 Elizabeth Warren, *A Fighting Chance* (New York: Henry Holt and Company, 2014), 2.

18 Quinnipiac University, poll, June 24–30, 2014. Text of question: "Which of these twelve presidents we have had since World War Two would you consider the worst president: Harry Truman, Dwight Eisenhower, John Kennedy, Lyndon

Johnson, Richard Nixon, Gerald Ford, Jimmy Carter, Ronald Reagan, George Bush Senior, Bill Clinton, George W. Bush, or Barack Obama?" Dwight Eisenhower, 1 percent; Lyndon Johnson, 3 percent; Richard Nixon, 13 percent; Gerald Ford, 2 percent; Jimmy Carter, 8 percent; Ronald Reagan, 3 percent; George Bush Senior, 2 percent; Bill Clinton, 3 percent; George W. Bush, 28 percent; Barack Obama, 33 percent; don't know/no answer, 4 percent.

19 NBC News/*Wall Street Journal*, poll, June 11–15, 2014. Text of question: "Thinking about the rest of Obama's term as president, do you think he can lead the country and get the job done or do you no longer feel that he is able to lead the country and get the job done?" Lead the country and get the job done, 42 percent; cannot lead the country and get the job done, 54 percent; depends (volunteered), 2 percent; not sure, 2 percent.

20 Quoted in Chuck Todd, *The Stranger: Barack Obama in the White House* (New York: Little Brown and Company, 2014), 14.

21 Quoted in John Heilemann and Mark Halperin, *Game Change: Obama and the Clintons, McCain and Palin, and the Race of a Lifetime* (New York: Harper Collins, 2010), 185.

22 Barack Obama, Keynote Address, Democratic National Convention, Boston, Massachusetts, July 27, 2004.

23 Fox News, poll, October 20–22, 2013. Text of question: "In the next election, would you consider voting for a third party presidential candidate?" Yes, 64 percent; no, 30 percent; don't know, 6 percent.

24 Fox News, poll, October 20–22, 2013. Text of question: "Do you think a qualified third party candidate has a reasonable chance of winning the next presidential election, or not?" Yes, 37 percent; no, 58 percent; don't know, 5 percent.

25 Alfred M. Landon, "Text of Governor Landon's Milwaukee Address on Social Security," Milwaukee, Wisconsin, September 27, 1936. Quoted in John Kenneth White, *The Values Divide: American Politics and Culture in Transition* (Washington, D.C.: CQ Press, 2003), 81.

26 Quoted in Kirk H. Porter and Donald Bruce Johnson, *National Party Platforms: 1840–1968* (Urbana: University of Illinois Press, 1970), 365–366.

27 James MacGregor Burns, *Roosevelt: The Lion and the Fox* (New York: Harcourt, Brace, and World, 1956), 452.

28 Ibid., 466.

29 Quoted in Robert A. Divine, *Foreign Policy and U.S. Presidential Elections, 1952–1960* (New York: New Viewpoints, 1974), 31.

30 Hillary Rodham Clinton, *Hard Choices* (New York: Simon and Schuster, 2014).

"I Can't Sell My Kids On This Party"

"I can't sell my kids on this party."
Moderate Republican in Colorado Springs, Colorado

At its peak during the Ronald Reagan years, *The McLaughlin Group* featured host John McLaughlin, who would regularly ask panelists at the end of his program—using his staccato-style, rapid-fire delivery—to make their political predictions for the coming week. Once uttered, the pundits' prognostications disappeared into the ether of the cathode ray tubes that most televisions featured in those days. Making predictions about politics—especially those concerning the future of any political party—is extremely hazardous. In 1980, political scientist Everett Carll Ladd wrote in the pages of *Fortune* magazine that Jimmy Carter would "probably win," noting that Ronald Reagan's "candidacy is in trouble, in spite of Carter's manifest weaknesses, because he has not persuaded the electorate that he would do a better job than Carter."[1] Nearly a dozen years later, on the eve of Bill Clinton's surprising 1992 victory, author Peter Brown published a book titled *Minority Party: Why Democrats Face Defeat in 1992 and Beyond.* In it, Brown claimed that the Democrats were a new and permanent presidential minority. Having lost three straight elections by landslide margins, Brown argued that the Democrats could no longer assemble an electoral college majority. He was hardly alone in his thinking, as even many Democrats held similar views. Former Arizona governor Bruce Babbitt, who would later become interior secretary in the Clinton administration, believed Democrats had not learned their lessons from the stinging defeats inflicted upon them by Ronald Reagan and George H. W. Bush: "As we cross into the next century, we are looking potentially, in the absence of some serious change, at an unbroken string of Republican presidencies. A lock on the presidency."[2]

But one year after publication of *Minority Party*, the Republican lock was broken, and the Democrats led by Bill Clinton began their own White House winning streak. In the six presidential elections encompassing the years 1992 to 2012, Democrats carried the popular vote in five of them.[3]

Moreover, Barack Obama is the first president since Dwight D. Eisenhower to capture 51 percent of the popular vote in two straight presidential elections, and the first Democrat to do so since Franklin D. Roosevelt.

Parties are elastic organizations, and their ability to "bounce back" after major defeats often surprises both pundits and academics alike. Shortly after Lyndon B. Johnson overwhelmed Barry Goldwater in 1964, political scientist Nelson Polsby declared that the much-heralded U.S. two-party system had morphed into a "one-and-a-half party system," with Republicans serving in the unenviable role of being the nation's "half-party."[4] "Will the GOP Survive?" became a common theme, as columnists bemused themselves by writing political obituaries with titles such as "The Party That Lost Its Head."[5] Yet a mere four years after Goldwater's landslide loss, Republican Richard Nixon was walking triumphantly into the White House—a victory made even more astounding by Nixon's famous declaration to the press corps after losing the California governorship in 1962, "You won't have Nixon to kick around anymore."[6] A few days after his exiting the political arena, ABC television ran a half-hour program titled *The Political Obituary of Richard Nixon*—just one more reminder that political prognosticators must beware of climbing out too far on a limb.[7]

Politics never cease to surprise. Just when it seems that we have a clear view of the political landscape, a fog descends and we are amazed by what we see when it lifts. In many respects, our current view has been shaped by a Republican hold on the presidency that goes back to Dwight Eisenhower's win in 1952. In the ten presidential elections held from 1952 to 1988, Republicans won seven of them.[8] The GOP electoral lock seemed impregnable, and it shaped the governing rules of politics. For example, it was famously said that the "real majority" in U.S. politics was composed of those who were *"un-young, un-poor, and un-black."*[9] One could add that most voters were married suburbanites, faithful church attendees, and had kids under the age of eighteen living at home. These middle-class citizens often cast Republican ballots—at least in presidential politics. Once part of Franklin D. Roosevelt's vaunted New Deal coalition, they drifted away from the Democratic party to become reliable supporters of Republican presidential candidates—especially Dwight D. Eisenhower, Richard M. Nixon, and Ronald Reagan—who conjured memories of a happier, more orderly era. James Q. Wilson once described the requisite "Sunday Afternoon Drive" in suburban Reagan country as looking "around" at homes to see "how much it cost, how well it was cared for, how good a lawn had been coaxed into uncertain life, and how tastefully plants and shrubs had been set out."[10]

This portrait of a tidy, suburbanized, mostly white, and reliably Republican presidential electorate has been upset by present-day realities. Today, it is the Republican Party that has lost its presidential majority. In a country divided into red states (Republican) and blue states (Democratic), it is the Democrats who have constructed a seemingly impregnable blue wall.

In the past six presidential contests, eighteen blue states plus the District of Columbia have voted straight Democratic and have cast a total of 242 electoral votes. The red wall—thirteen states that have voted Republican in the past six elections—is more akin to a small stone fence, producing a mere 102 electoral votes.[11] In a game where 270 votes are needed to win, Democrats have a huge head start.

Adding to the GOP dilemma is a once-orderly party now being rendered asunder and challenged by Tea Party insurgents. Tea Party adherents differ from the GOP establishment in terms of where they live, how much exposure to higher education they have received, their income, what they read and watch on television, and with whom they associate. These divisions are demographic, cultural, and above all political. As Table 1.1 indicates, Tea Party Republicans have a very different worldview from both establishment Republicans and the rest of the country. Political analyst Sean Trende writes that these very different perspectives are the basis for ongoing battles between these two opposite wings of the Republican Party:

> The Republican base is furious with the Republican establishment, especially over the Bush years. From the point of view of conservatives I have spoken with, the early-to-mid-2000s look like this: Voters gave Republicans control of the Congress and the presidency for the longest stretch since the 1920s.
>
> And what do Republicans have to show for it? Temporary tax cuts, No Child Left Behind, the Medicare prescription drug benefit, a new

Table 1.1 Tea Party vs. Non-Tea Party Republicans vs. the United States

Issue	Republican Tea Party Supporters	Non-Tea Party Republicans	United States at Large
Does immigration help or hurt the United States? (percentage answering "hurt")	68	47	47
Support or oppose the Common Core? (percentage answering "oppose")	53	42	31
Approve or disapprove of proposal to reduce greenhouse gases (percentage answering "disapprove")	74	47	39
What to do about climate change? (percentage answering "global warming is unwarranted")	38	7	13

Source: Chuck Todd, Mark Murray, and Carrie Dann, "There's the Tea Party—And Then There's Everyone Else," *First Read*, June 19, 2014. Based on the NBC News/*Wall Street Journal* poll, June 11–20, 2014.

cabinet department, increased federal spending, TARP [the Troubled Asset Relief Program], and repeated attempts at immigration reform. Basically, despite a historic opportunity to shrink government, almost everything that the GOP establishment achieved during that time moved the needle leftward on domestic policy.[12]

This Tea Party vs. non-Tea Party division within the GOP ranks is also upending other political axioms. It is often said that people will bring their feelings about a political party in line with how they intend to vote. After the tragedies of September 11, 2001, many Americans were favorably disposed to George W. Bush and his Republican Party. Bush had a job approval rating of 90 percent—the highest in the history of the Gallup poll, whose job approval question dates back to Franklin D. Roosevelt.[13] At the same time, 54 percent were also warmly disposed to the Republican Party.[14] And in 2002, the GOP made midterm gains, as voters cast "belated ballots" for George W. Bush (ballots Bush could have used in the disputed 2000 contest with Al Gore) when making their congressional decisions.

Today, things are very different. In the Republican sweeps of 2010 and 2014, Americans voted for a party they *didn't like.*[15] In 2010, an astonishing 53 percent held negative views of the Republican Party; in 2014, 54 percent.[16] As House Speaker-elect John Boehner wisely noted in 2010, "This is not a time for celebration," adding, "What I got out of the election is not so much that we [the Republicans] won but they [the Democrats] lost."[17] Since 2010, opinions of the Republican Party have *worsened.* After the government shutdown in 2013, only 22 percent expressed a favorable opinion of the Republican Party.[18] Those figures have hardly improved since. As in 2010, victories by Republican candidates in 2014 happened *despite* their party label—not because of it. In 2014, 59 percent said they were either disappointed or angry with Republican leaders in Congress.[19]

Ironically, it is these victories that are making the GOP dilemma *worse.* When focusing on their presidential losses, many Republicans assume a facial expression that all but asks, "What, me worry?" "What problem," they reply, "does the GOP have?" And, in one sense, they are right. To wit: Republicans have substantial majorities in both the House and Senate; Democratic control of state governorships and state legislative seats is *the lowest since the Civil War*; and Barack Obama is suffering from a severe case of second-term blues, with job approval ratings mired in the low forties and an ever-growing number who say that the forty-fourth president is "so yesterday."

Nevertheless, Americans worry about replacing Obama with a Republican president in 2016. Is the GOP ready to govern? What new ideas animate conservative thought? What activity in the conservative think tanks in Washington, D.C., will invigorate a new Republican administration? The answers are hardly encouraging. Only 23 percent say they trust the Republican Party "to govern more responsibly" than Democrats. (Democrats fare only a little better with 31 percent trusting them.)[20] As the GOP becomes captive to conservative pressure groups, radio talk show hosts, and hucksters (e.g., Rush Limbaugh, Bill O'Reilly, Sean Hannity, Glenn Beck, and Donald Trump) who have little interest in winning elections and every interest in providing entertainment, the party's ability to reach out to moderates has become limited. On Election Day 2012, only 41 percent of self-described moderates supported Mitt Romney, while 56 percent backed Barack Obama.[21] Even in the landslide year of 2014, just 45 percent of moderates voted Republican.[22] Former California governor Arnold Schwarzenegger argues Republicans must jettison those purists who have little interest in winning elections:

> [I]n the current climate, the extreme right wing of the party is targeting anyone who doesn't meet its strict criteria. Its new and narrow litmus test for party membership doesn't allow compromise. . . . Being a Republican used to mean finding solutions for the American people that worked for everyone. It used to mean having big ideas that moved the country forward. It can mean that again, but big ideas don't often come from small tents.[23]

Rather than facing up to the hard choices ahead, Republicans are focused on process—not ideas. After Mitt Romney's defeat in 2012, Republican National Chairman Reince Priebus commissioned an autopsy. According to the study, many of Romney's difficulties were due to rules designed to increase exposure of the 2012 Republican field. Among its recommendations were to limit televised debates (to fewer than the twenty that occurred in 2012); have the Republican National Committee choose the debate moderators; begin the primary season later rather than earlier; space out the primaries and caucuses so states are not tripping over each other to go first; improve data-gathering and metrics (something the report notes the Obama campaign excelled in); convene Republican poll-takers to discuss problems related to sampling and gathering reliable polling data; and hold the party's convention sometime during the early summer months. (The 2016 Republican convention is scheduled for July.) Some of these complaints are bipartisan: Democrats agree that an out-of-control primary calendar must be tamed, and concerns about polling techniques in an age of cell phones are universally held by pundits and polling experts alike.[24]

But the problems facing the GOP go beyond mere procedural reforms. What does conservatism mean in a new century? Where will the Republicans find a potentially popular president who can recast the party's tattered image? When will Republicans finally bid farewell to Ronald Reagan, who died in 2004 and left behind a millennial generation that only knows him as a *historical* figure? It is worth noting that in 2016 a person aged 18 was born a decade *after* Reagan left the White House.

As this book points out, the problems the GOP faces are multifaceted and not easily solved. Today's Republican Party finds itself *outmanned* by a Democratic Party whose reliance on non-whites seems well-placed—as these former minorities are rapidly becoming new majorities. By 2050, whites will be a minority throughout the United States, as the American face changes from white to some form of beige.[25] All of this is upending old rules that were once considered inviolable, including the one that said winning the white vote is tantamount to winning the presidency. Consider: in 1980, Ronald Reagan captured 56 percent of whites.[26] Thirty-two years later, Mitt Romney did even better, winning 59 percent.[27] But for the first time ever in 2012, a candidate with so large a percentage of white votes *lost*. The reason for upending this old political axiom became clear when exit poll data showed Obama beating Romney by an astounding *63 points* among non-whites.[28]

Democrats are also succeeding with "non-traditional" families, as the once aptly named nuclear family (a term that originated during the Cold War) that consisted of a mom, dad, and kids has become something of an anachronism.[29] Today 41 percent of U.S. children are born outside of marriage, and the percentage living with two married parents has fallen from 88 percent in 1960, to 66 percent in 2010.[30] Thus while 54 percent of married voters with children backed Mitt Romney in 2012 (an impressive score), they constituted only 27 percent of the electorate. Those who were not married with kids supported Obama by a margin of 53 percent to 45 percent.[31] Conservative analyst David Frum writes that "the GOP is rapidly becoming the party of yesterday's America."[32]

The demographic challenges the Republican Party faces are significant. Yet they are compounded by an infrastructure the GOP built during the past half century that once seemed impregnable. This infrastructure included several think tanks (e.g., the American Enterprise Institute, Heritage Foundation, Cato Institute); conservative talk radio (whose premier host is Rush Limbaugh); fund-raising super political action committees (e.g., Crossroads America and Crossroads GPS); and the premier gem, Fox News, whose nightly audiences reach into the millions. Today, that vaunted political machinery is rapidly transforming into a GOP prison from which the party finds it hard to escape. One small example: as Fox News and Tea Party leaders denounce immigration reform—calling any path to citizenship for the approximately 11 million illegals in the U.S. "amnesty"—the proliferation of that term ties the hands of more moderate, pragmatic Republicans who see the rapidly emerging demographic future of the United States and want their party to be part of it. But woe to those who support "amnesty," as many Republicans have found themselves subjected to primary challenges led by Tea Party-inspired candidates.

In 2014, Eric Cantor became the first-ever majority leader to lose an intraparty primary, in part because he both favored the DREAM Act (which would enable illegal immigrants to qualify for in-state college tuition rates) and announced that he would develop a GOP immigration measure that, according to one report, "would provide a pathway to citizenship for young immigrants."[33] Tea Party Republicans were furious. Jamie Radtke, cofounder of the Virginia Tea Party Federation, said of Cantor, "He made an enemy of his friends."[34] Conservative radio talk show host Laura Ingraham also denounced the majority leader:

> Who do you think Barack Obama and Nancy Pelosi want to win this primary? Why do they want Eric Cantor to win? They want Eric Cantor to win because Eric Cantor is an ally . . . [in] the fight for immigration amnesty.[35]

Cantor's defeat immobilized Republicans who once saw immigration reform as a political necessity. In 2008, John McCain won a mere 31 percent of the Hispanic vote; four years later, Mitt Romney did *even worse*, capturing just 27 percent.[36] Obama's dominance among Hispanics allowed him to carry once-reliably Republican states in the Southwest—including Nevada, Colorado, and New Mexico.[37] Even formerly deep-red Virginia fell into Obama's hands thanks to his winning 65 percent of the Hispanic vote.[38] The same thing happened in Florida—a must-win GOP state—where Obama won 60 percent Hispanic support.[39] After Romney's loss, the Republican National Committee declared that the GOP "must embrace and champion comprehensive immigration reform. If we do not," the committee warned, "our Party's appeal will continue to shrink to its core constituencies only."[40] But Cantor's defeat meant that what was once a top priority on the GOP's "to-do list" has been shunted aside, leaving Republicans ill-equipped to compete for Hispanic votes in 2016 and reduced to their "core constituencies" of whites, evangelicals, rural voters, and assorted Tea Party types.

Ironically, Democrats do not have high favorable ratings among Hispanics, and critics of Barack Obama have labeled him the "deporter-in-chief." But when forced to make a choice, overwhelming majorities of Hispanics choose Democratic candidates because they sense that Republicans fear their increased presence will negatively alter the future of the country. The problem is further inflamed by incendiary comments made by GOP officeholders who are more interested in appealing to their local base of overwhelmingly white supporters at the expense of the national party. Iowa congressman Steve King, for one, characterized his opposition to the DREAM Act by hurling Hispanic racial epithets: "For [every one] who's a valedictorian, there's a 100 out there that weigh 130 pounds, and they've got calves the size of cantaloupes because they're hauling 75 pounds of marijuana across the desert."[41] Former House Majority Leader (and Tea Party activist) Dick Armey notes: "You can't call someone ugly and expect them to go to the prom with you. We've chased the Hispanic voter out of his natural home."[42]

Despite these admonitions, Democratic pollster Stanley Greenberg and his partner, former Clinton strategist James Carville, find that evangelicals and Tea Party members (who comprise 70 percent of the GOP base) remain firmly opposed to immigration reform. A sampling from their focus groups:

> Don't come here and make me speak your language. Don't fly your flag. You're on American soil. You're American. You come to our country, you need to learn our language. Why should I put "press 1" if I want to speak in English? You know, everything—every politically correct machine out there says, "Press 1 for English. Press 2 for Spanish."
>
> (Evangelical man, Roanoke)

> There's so much of the electorate in those groups that Democrats are going to take every time because they've been on the rolls of the government their entire lives. They don't know better.
>
> (Tea Party man, Raleigh)[43]

It is attitudes like these that prompted one moderate Republican to declare, "I can't sell my kids on this party."[44] The inability of the GOP to make the sale to a broad swath of Americans has long-term implications for our politics because—however much Democrats deride today's Republican Party and take pleasure in its present troubles—having a vibrant and thoughtful Republican Party is *necessary*. One reason is that it is the job of the out-of-power party to pick and choose the issues upon which it will contest elections. In so doing, political scientist E. E. Schattschneider maintained an opposition party necessarily exercises discernment because its electoral coalition is so diverse:

> A large party must be supported by a great variety of interests sufficiently tolerant of each other to collaborate, held together by compromise and concession, and the discovery of certain common interest, and so on, and bearing in mind that a major party has only one competitor and that party managers *need not meet every demand by every interest* [emphasis in original].[45]

The result is a "moderate" opposition even though, Schattschneider conceded, "the language of politics is usually immoderate."[46]

Today's political language is hardly moderate in part because the Republican base is motivated by its ideological homogeneity and virulent opposition to Barack Obama. In 2009, Republican congressman Joe Wilson made headlines when he yelled the words "You lie!" to President Obama as he was addressing a joint session of Congress on healthcare reform. Wilson's impudence was unprecedented in the history of personal presidential addresses to Congress. Many were disturbed, including Wilson's wife, who called her husband on his cell phone to inquire who was "that nut" who shouted at the president.[47] But Wilson's outburst appealed to the Republican base, and he raised $1 million in campaign contributions as a direct result.[48] Wilson is hardly alone. In 2012, former White House chief of staff John Sununu denounced Obama, saying, "I wish this president would learn to be an American."[49]

The notion that Obama was somehow "un-American" took root in the Republican base and led it to become ever more disconnected from reality. In 2010, more than 50 percent of Republicans surveyed thought it was "definitely true" or "probably true" that Obama "sympathized with the goals of fundamentalists who want to impose Islamic law around the world." Nearly 25 percent of Republicans said that they thought Obama was a Muslim, up from 13 percent in 2008, and more than 33 percent believed he wasn't born in the United States.[50] Author Jonathan Alter has described this phenomena as "Obama Derangement Syndrome," noting:

> Bit by bit many Republicans were not just losing contact with the country beyond their echo chamber; they were entering a fantasyland of self-delusion. Obama Derangement Syndrome was a symptom of a deeper disturbance on the American right that would eventually help, not hurt, the president.[51]

Former congressman Barney Frank, a pugnacious Democrat from Massachusetts, captured the GOP dilemma by placing a bumper sticker on his car reading, "We're Not Perfect, But They're Nuts."[52]

A vivacious conservative vision is needed, in part to give expression to Thomas Jefferson's long-held view that freedom must be paired with local civic virtue in order to make the former work. So-called Jeffersonian localism has historically found a home in one of the major parties—the Democrats espoused it during the "states' rights" era of the late nineteenth century, and Ronald Reagan gave it renewed expression in the late twentieth century. Its counterpart, Hamiltonian nationalism—the belief that freedom must be bridled by a strong central government acting on behalf of the nation as a whole—has also historically found a home in one of the major parties: Abraham Lincoln's Republican Party of the 1860s and thereafter, and Franklin D. Roosevelt's Democratic Party, where it still resides today.[53]

These competing visions matter because they help frame the political debate and ensure the stability of the two-party system. More than a century ago, former president and party enthusiast Martin Van Buren celebrated partisan differences as necessary elements of a vibrant democracy:

> The two great parties of this country, with occasional changes in name only, have for the principal part of a century, occupied antagonistic positions upon all important political questions. They have maintained

an unbroken succession, and have, throughout, been composed respectively of men agreeing in their party passion, and preferences, and entertaining, with rare exceptions, similar views on the subject of government and its administration.[54]

It remains essential that the Republican Party undertake the hard work needed to rectify its current dilemmas in order to ensure truly competitive elections and make it ready to govern when the opportunity, once again, will surely present itself.

This book describes how we got to this place. Chapter 1 describes the heyday of the Ronald Reagan era when the GOP was at a zenith with a popular president who cared deeply about remaking the Republican Party in his conservative image. Chapter 2 tells the story of how a wily Bill Clinton *outmaneuvered* the Republican Party by "dishing the Whigs"—a phrase meaning stealing the other fellow's clothes while he is swimming. In Clinton's case that meant stealing Ronald Reagan's values strategy and angering Republicans to the point that they pursued Clinton's impeachment. Chapter 3 describes the making of a new political demography that Barack Obama understood and has translated into two presidential majorities (with more Democratic victories to come if left unchallenged). Chapter 4 describes how once-vibrant conservative-minded intellectuals have created their own orthodoxy that has become something of a prison that pragmatic, reform-minded Republicans cannot escape. Finally, Chapter 5 describes why a vibrant Republican Party is necessary for the nation's political health. The central question that remains is, can the Republican Party escape from its self-imposed prison to thrive once more?

Notes

1 Everett Carll Ladd, "Why Carter Will Probably Win," *Fortune*, July 28, 1980, 89.
2 Quoted in Peter Brown, *Minority Party: Why Democrats Face Defeat in 1992 and Beyond* (Washington, D.C.: Regnery Gateway, 1991), 334–335.
3 The exception was in 2004 when an incumbent president, George W. Bush, won a second term. In 2000, Al Gore beat George W. Bush in the popular vote by 627,398 votes.
4 Cited in Yanek Mieczleoski, *Gerald Ford and the Challenges of the 1970s* (Lexington: University Press of Kentucky, 2005), 348.
5 Patrick J. Buchanan, *The Greatest Comeback: How Richard Nixon Rose from Defeat to Create the New Majority* (New York: Crown Forum, 2014), 19.
6 Quoted in Richard M. Nixon, *RN: The Memoirs of Richard Nixon* (New York: Grosset and Dunlap, 1978), 245.
7 Ibid., 246.
8 The exceptions were John F. Kennedy in 1960, Lyndon B. Johnson in 1964, and Jimmy Carter in 1976.
9 Richard M. Scammon and Ben J. Wattenberg, *The Real Majority* (New York: Coward-McCann, Inc., 1970), 45–71.

10 James Q. Wilson, "A Guide to Reagan Country," *Commentary*, May 1, 1967, 40.

11 The Democratic blue states are California, Connecticut, District of Columbia, Delaware, Hawaii, Illinois, Maine, Maryland, Massachusetts, Michigan, Minnesota, New Jersey, New York, Oregon, Pennsylvania, Rhode Island, Vermont, Washington, and Wisconsin. The Republican red states are Alabama, Alaska, Kansas, Idaho, Mississippi, Nebraska, North Dakota, Oklahoma, South Carolina, South Dakota, Texas, Utah, and Wyoming.

12 Quoted in David Frum, "Crashing the Party: Why the GOP Must Modernize to Win," *Foreign Affairs*, September/October 2014.

13 Gallup poll, September 21–22, 2001. Text of question: "Do you approve or disapprove of the way George W. Bush is handling his job as president?" Approve, 90 percent; disapprove, 6 percent; no opinion, 4 percent.

14 Gallup poll, November 8–10, 2001. Text of question: "Please tell me whether you have a favorable or unfavorable opinion of each of the following parties. How about the Republican party?" Favorable, 54 percent; unfavorable, 38 percent; no opinion, 8 percent.

15 In 1946, Republicans gained 55 House seats and 12 Senate seats; in 2010, Republicans added 63 House seats and 7 Senate seats.

16 Edison Media Research and Mitofsky International, exit poll, November 2, 2010, and Edison Media Research, exit poll, November 4, 2014.

17 Quoted in Adam Aigner-Treworgy, "GOP's Cantor: 'We Have to Deliver,'" CNN.com, November 3, 2010. Quoted in Peter J. Boyer, "House Rule: Will John Boehner Control the Tea Party Congress?" *The New Yorker*, December 13, 2010.

18 NBC News/*Wall Street Journal*, poll, October 25–28, 2013.

19 Edison Media Research, exit poll, November 4, 2014. Text of question: "Which comes closest to your feelings about Republican leaders in Congress?" Enthusiastic, 7 percent; satisfied, but not enthusiastic, 32 percent; dissatisfied, but not angry, 37 percent; angry, 22 percent.

20 NSON Opinion Strategy, poll, March 24–April 9, 2011. Text of question: "Which political party do you trust more to govern responsibly? The Democratic party, the Republican party, some other party, neither?" Democrats, 31 percent; Republicans, 23 percent; some other party, 3 percent; neither, 35 percent; both/all about the same (volunteered), 4 percent; don't know/no response, 4 percent.

21 Edison Research, exit poll, November 6, 2012.

22 Edison Research, exit poll, November 4, 2014.

23 Arnold Schwarzenegger, "Schwarzenegger: GOP Take Down That Small Tent," *LATimes.com*, May 6, 2012.

24 Republican National Committee, *Growth and Opportunity Project* (Washington, D.C.: Republican National Committee, December 2012).

25 See Jeffrey S. Passel and D'Vera Cohn, *U.S. Populations Projections: 2005–2050*, Pew Research Center report, February 11, 2008, 9, and Sam Roberts, "A Generation Away, Minorities May Become the Majority in U.S.," *New York Times*, August 14, 2008.

26 CBS News/*New York Times*, exit poll, November 4, 1980.

27 Edison Research, exit poll, November 6, 2012.

28 Edison Research, exit poll, November 6, 2012.

29 University of Minnesota professor Elaine Tyler May maintains that the 1950s-style nuclear family with its homemaker mom and working dad was a "glamorized, professionalized, and eroticized" symbol of American superiority during the Cold War. See John Kenneth White, *Still Seeing Red: How the Cold War Shapes the New American Politics* (Boulder: Westview Press, 1997), 5.

30 W. Bradford Wilcox, ed., *The State of Our Unions: Marriage in America, 2011* (Charlottesville, VA: National Marriage Project, 2011), 16, 102.

31 Edison Research, exit poll, November 6, 2012.

32 David Frum, *Why Romney Lost (And What the GOP Can Do About It)*, Newsweek ebook, published online 2012.

33 Matt Fuller, "Obama Calls Cantor After Day of Immigration Sparring," *Roll Call*, April 16, 2014.

34 David A. Fahrenthold, Rosalind S. Helderman, and Jenna Portnoy, "What Went Wrong for Eric Cantor?" *Washington Post*, June 11, 2014.

35 Ibid.

36 Edison Media Research and Mitofsky International, exit poll, November 4, 2008, and Edison Research, exit poll, November 6, 2012.

37 Edison Research, exit poll, November 6, 2012.

38 Edison Research, Virginia exit poll, November 6, 2012.

39 Edison Research, Florida exit poll, November 6, 2012. Among Cuban Hispanics in Florida, Obama won 49 percent to Romney's 47 percent. Among non-Cuban Hispanics, the vote was more lopsided: Obama, 66 percent; Romney, 34 percent.

40 Republican National Committee, *Growth and Opportunity Project*, 8.

41 "Steve King: Most Dreamers Are Hauling 75 Pounds of Marijuana Across the Desert," *Huffington Post*, July 23, 2013. The Republican House Speaker denounced King for his comments, calling him an "asshole." See Tom Kludt, "Boehner Thought Steve King Was an 'Asshole' for 'Cantaloupes' Comment," *Talking Points Memo*, January 17, 2014.

42 Quoted in Republican National Committee, *Growth and Opportunity Project*, 8.

43 Stanley Greenberg and James Carville, memo, "Inside the GOP: Why Boehner Is Halting Immigration Reform," February 2, 2014.

44 Ibid.

45 E.E. Schattschneider, *Party Government* (New York: Rinehart and Company, 1942), 85.

46 Ibid.

47 Quoted in Jonathan Alter, *The Promise: President Obama, Year One* (New York: Simon and Schuster, 2010), 402.

48 "Wilson Funds Reach $1 Million after 'You Lie' Cry, Aide Says," CNN.com, September 12, 2009.

49 Frum, *Why Romney Lost*.

50 Cited in Jonathan Alter, *The Center Holds: Obama and His Enemies* (New York: Simon and Schuster, 2013), 31.

51 Ibid., 43.

52 Ibid.

53 For more on this see John Kenneth White and Matthew R. Kerbel, *Party On! Political Parties from Hamilton and Jefferson to Today's Networked Age* (New York: Oxford University Press, 2012).

54 Quoted in A. James Reichley, "Party Politics in a Federal Polity," in John Kenneth White and Jerome M. Mileur, eds., *Challenges to Party Government* (Carbondale: Southern Illinois University Press, 1992), 43.

Chapter I

Zenith

Reagan's Triumph

"I can call spirits from the vasty deep."
William Shakespeare, *King Henry IV*

July 4, 1986. That evening found Ronald Reagan aboard the USS *John F. Kennedy*, stationed in New York Harbor. The president had come to New York for a two-day "Liberty Weekend" whose highlight was the rededication of the one-hundred-year-old Statue of Liberty. Millions of spectators lined the New York streets as 250 sailing vessels from thirty countries set sail in the harbor.[1] Naval guns boomed. Fighter planes screamed overhead. Stately windjammers paraded. Bells rang.[2] Earlier in the day, 27,000 new Americans took their citizenship oaths as Reagan celebrated the immigrant story, highlighting his recent nomination of Italo-American Antonin Scalia, a son of immigrants, to the U.S. Supreme Court.[3] When Reagan bestrode the decks of the USS *Kennedy* accompanied by his wife, Nancy, he received a thunderous ovation from thousands of sailors in stands on the bow of the ship.[4] It was the height of Reagan's presidency. His overall job approval rating stood at 68 percent, with 82 percent of those under the age of twenty-four expressing support.[5] And these high numbers translated into a string of congressional successes. At the dedication ceremony, Reagan noted that prospects of the passage of his tax reform measure had "put a smile on the face of our Statue of Liberty."[6] Similarly, a recent controversial House vote endorsing aid to the Nicaraguan Contras made Reagan "feel proud that on this Independence Day weekend, America has embraced these brave men and women and their independent struggle."[7]

At sunset, with Miss Liberty watching over Reagan's shoulder, the president delivered a short Fourth of July address from the deck of the USS *Kennedy*. The words were not particularly memorable (unlike other Reagan speeches)—but the setting was unforgettable.[8] Famed producer David Wolper attended to the details—including weekend appearances by John Denver, Melissa Manchester, Barry Manilow, Johnny Cash, Elizabeth Taylor, Frank Sinatra, and Whitney Houston—with every image crafted for the

ABC television mega-event that was broadcast to forty countries around the world. On cue, as Reagan ended his speech with the words, "Now, let's have some fun—let the celebration begin!"[9] laser lights enveloped the newly refurbished statue and 40,000 pyrotechnics set off from thirty barges began a nonstop twenty-eight minute spectacular. The beauty of the televised images of the largest-ever fireworks display in history was captured in the *Washington Post*: "Incandescent rainbows, splinters of gold and silver, sizzling stars of light reflected off the windows of Wall Street skyscrapers."[10] Stretching from the East River, around the tip of Manhattan, up into the Hudson River, and around the Statue of Liberty and Ellis Island, the production required an estimated 220 miles of wires; 777,000 pounds of mortar tubes (through which aerial shells were launched); 30,000 pounds of equipment; and 100 pyro-technicians.[11]

Viewers were mesmerized. Even newly appointed Soviet ambassador Yuri Dubinin—gaily decked out in his wife's rumpled Khaki hat and sporting a brightly striped shirt—exclaimed: "We have every respect for the celebration as a national holiday of the United States. It is a very good statue, a very good statue."[12] When asked how he enjoyed the event, an exuberant Reagan responded, "It was great, just great."[13] On that unforgettable Fourth of July, there was a merging of the man, the president, patriotic pride, and a renewal of the timeless American values of family, work, neighborhood, peace, and freedom. Speaking from the decks of the *Kennedy*, Reagan declared that Americans were "known around the world as a confident and happy people."[14] Writing in *Time* magazine, Lance Morrow proclaimed Reagan to be "a Prospero of American memories, a magician who carries a bright, ideal America like a holography in his mind and projects its image in the air."[15] Ronald Reagan was at his zenith.

The most remarkable event of that particular July 4 is that it happened at all. A decade earlier (almost to the day) Ronald Reagan challenged incumbent president Gerald R. Ford to a near draw in the Republican nominating contest. After a bitter convention floor fight, Ford won by a whisker, and Reagan withdrew, leaving with the words of an Irish ballad: "I will lay me down and bleed a while. Though I am wounded, I am not slain. I shall rise and fight again."[16] Despite Reagan's promise of a political resurrection, his defeat was viewed by many as a last hurrah. The former California governor was discounted as a washed-up, ex-Hollywood actor who was intellectually lazy, spoke only from cue cards, and showed little grasp of policy. Gerald Ford disparaged him as "one of the few political leaders I have ever met whose public speeches revealed more than his private conversations,"[17] and not "technically competent." Said Ford: "[H]is knowledge of the budget, his knowledge of foreign policy—it was not up to the standards of either Democrat or Republican presidents. . . . I've talked to several foreign leaders who were shocked at his lack of detailed information."[18] Clark Clifford, who served on Harry Truman's White House staff and later was

Lyndon B. Johnson's defense secretary, memorably called Reagan an "amiable dunce."[19] Even some Hollywood types thought Reagan was politically miscast. One movie mogul famously dismissed him, saying: "No, Jimmy Stewart for Governor. Reagan for best friend."[20]

Reagan's intellectual laziness was highlighted by his repeating essentially the same speech that he began delivering to General Electric workers in the late 1950s. "The Speech," as it came to be called, was filled with antigovernment bromides, including: "Our natural, unalienable rights are now considered to be a dispensation of government, and freedom has never been so fragile, so close to slipping from our grasp as it is this moment."[21]

While some thought Ronald Reagan could do no harm as president—thanks to his intellectual laziness and his dependence on staff for support—others thought he posed a serious danger. Even some Republicans castigated Reagan as a divisive figure whose vehement anticommunism and bombastic statements would create a foreign policy debacle should he enter the Oval Office. In his 1976 primary fight with Ford, Reagan asserted that the Soviet Union "out-guns us, out-tanks us, and out-subs us."[22] Reagan warned that, unless there were huge increases in defense spending, "our nation is in great danger, and the danger grows with each passing day."[23] Ford responded with a television advertisement in which a somber female voice warned: "Governor Reagan couldn't start a war. President Reagan could."[24] Another pro-Ford commercial was imbued with a sense of urgency:

> When the Hot Line rings, who do you want to answer? And what do you want him to say? Do you want someone who talks like he wants to start a war, or someone who'll stop one? Think about it. You've got 'til Tuesday.[25]

Hamilton Jordan, Jimmy Carter's chief of staff, believed Reagan's bellicosity would haunt him in the general election, and so he cheered Reagan's rise. In his diary, Jordan confided: "I thought Reagan's very strength—his hold on the right wing of the Republican party—was also his vulnerability."[26] Republican pollster Richard Wirthlin advised Reagan that "Jimmy Carter practices piranha politics—he eats his opponents alive." Unseating Carter, Wirthlin warned, "will be extremely difficult, even unlikely."[27]

Reagan's Rise

Jimmy Carter made Ronald Reagan's presidency possible. Carter had narrowly beaten Ford in 1976, partly by inventing something he called the "misery index"—a combination of unemployment and inflation rates. In 1976, the misery index stood at 12.5 percent; four years later it had risen to 20 percent.[28] Given these dismal figures, it was impossible for Carter to run on his record. Instead, his only hope was to frame the contest as a choice between a president with few achievements and an unprepared opponent who frightened people. For his part, Reagan was having none of it. Accepting the Republican nomination, he declared:

> Can anyone look at the record of this administration and say, "Well done?" Can anyone compare the state of our economy when the Carter administration took office with where we are today and say, "Keep up the good work?" Can anyone look at our reduced standing in the world today and say, "Let's have four more years of this?"[29]

Even Patrick Caddell, Carter's chief pollster, conceded that "there was no way we could survive if we allowed [the election] to become a referendum on the first three years of the Carter administration."[30]

Jimmy Carter helped make that referendum happen. In July 1979, Carter gave what became known as his "malaise speech." In it, he proclaimed a "crisis of confidence":

> What you see too often in Washington and elsewhere around the country is a system of government that seems incapable of action. You see a Congress twisted and pulled in every direction by hundreds of well-financed and powerful special interests. You see every extreme position defended to the last vote, almost to the last breath by one unyielding group or another. You often see a balanced and fair approach that demands sacrifice, a little sacrifice from everyone, abandoned like an orphan without support and without friends.[31]

Ronald Reagan profoundly disagreed. Announcing his candidacy a few months later, he declared:

> There are those in our land today . . . who would have us believe that the United States, like other great civilizations of the past, has reached the zenith of its power; that we are weak, fearful, reduced to bickering with each other and no longer possessed of the will to cope with our problems. Much of this talk has come from leaders who claim that our problems are too difficult to handle. We are supposed to meekly accept their failures as the most which humanly can be done. They tell us we must learn to live with less, and teach our children that their lives will be less full and prosperous than ours have been; that the America of the coming years will be a place where—because of our past excesses—it will be impossible to dream and make those dreams come true. I don't believe that. And I don't believe you do either. That is why I am seeking the presidency. I cannot and will not stand by and see this great country destroy itself.[32]

Richard Wirthlin saw the speech as providing an unprecedented opportunity: if Carter projected an image of listlessness, Wirthlin counseled his candidate should "convey the clearest possible message that Reagan stands for leadership and control. The prevailing view in America is that no one is in control; the prevailing impression given by the White House is that no one can be in control; and the prevailing view abroad is that the will to be in control is gone."[33]

Jimmy Carter's ineffectiveness was dramatized by the taking of hostages at the U.S. embassy in Tehran, Iran. The hostages were seized on November 4, 1979—exactly one year to the day before the 1980 balloting. A failed rescue mission in April 1980 only added to the country's disillusionment. As time went on, the Reagan campaign tried to prepare the country for a successful rescue by calling any such action an "October surprise." (Wirthlin calculated that such a mission could add as much as ten points to Carter's sagging polls.[34]) But the last-minute deliverance that so many Carter Democrats hoped would happen—and so many Reagan Republicans feared—failed to materialize. In fact, the Iranian government would hold the U.S. hostages for the remainder of the Carter presidency, freeing them only minutes after Reagan took the presidential oath.

For much of 1980, voters shared the commonly held views of the Fourth Estate regarding Reagan's personal and political inadequacies. The Reagan-Carter race seesawed back and forth, as Americans debated amongst themselves the wisdom of putting Reagan in Carter's place. The Reagan campaign's initial forays did little to diffuse public uneasiness about a Reagan presidency. Set loose on the campaign trail, the newly minted Republican nominee declared the Vietnam War to be a "noble cause"; doubted the theory of evolution; voiced pro-Taiwan views that threatened the U.S. relationship with China; and claimed that trees caused as much pollution as automobiles[35] (leading one protestor to hold a sign reading "Cut me down before I kill again"[36]). Hamilton Jordan noted, "For two weeks it was delicious, watching Reagan on the news each night stumble from one controversy to another, doing what we had thought we'd have to do—making him, not the President, the issue."[37] Even the campaign's launch at the Neshoba County State Fair in Philadelphia, Mississippi, and Reagan's call for "states' rights" there, was jarring, as it was the place where three civil rights workers were slain in 1964 for registering African-Americans to vote. *The Washington Post* ran an editorial with the incendiary headline: "Chilling Words in Neshoba County—Is Reagan Saying That He Intends to Do Everything He Can to Turn the Clock Back to the Mississippi Justice of 1964?"[38]

But Reagan quickly found his footing (thanks to a staff shake-up on the campaign plane). Most importantly, a last-minute presidential debate worked in Reagan's favor. Reagan's prowess in debates was well known. After besting Robert Kennedy in a 1967 debate, the New York senator reportedly asked, "Who the f— got me into this?"[39] Jesse Unruh, a California Democrat who Reagan beat in the 1970 gubernatorial election, warned the Carter team not to

> make the same mistake that every person in this room has made at one time or another and underestimate Ronald Reagan. You may think he's too old or too much of a right-winger or just a grade-B movie actor. He's all of those things, but above everything else Ronald Reagan is an excellent communicator. You can argue with him or debate and think you've got him cornered, then he'll say something folksy, shrug his shoulders, and he's gone.[40]

When Carter attacked Reagan's conservative record and his opposition to Medicare, Reagan gave an aw-shucks grin, saying, "There you go again." Reagan's parting words became among the most memorable in presidential debate history:

> Next Tuesday all of you will go to the polls, will stand there in the polling place and make a decision. I think when you make that decision, it might be well if you would ask yourself: Are you better off than you were four years ago? Is it easier for you to go and buy things in the stores than it was four years ago? Is there more or less unemployment in the country than there was four years ago? Is America as respected throughout the world as it was? Do you feel that our security is as safe, that we're as strong as we were four years ago? And if you answer all of those questions yes, why then, I think your choice is very obvious as to whom you will vote for. If you don't agree, if you don't think that this course that we've been on for the last four years is what you would like to see us follow for the next four, then I could suggest another choice that you have.[41]

Overnight, what was supposed to be a nail-biter became a landslide. Reagan won 50.75 percent of the popular vote and forty-four states. Carter took just 41.01 percent and six states—the worst drubbing for an incumbent president since Franklin D. Roosevelt vanquished Herbert Hoover in the midst of the Great Depression.[42] Reagan's triumph was even more amazing considering that Richard Wirthlin's surveys found that only 30 percent of voters called themselves Republicans, while a majority—51 percent—said they were Democrats.[43] To overcome the odds, Reagan had to woo independents and disaffected Democrats. It was a herculean task, but 56 percent of independents ultimately sided with Reagan, as did one in four Democrats.[44]

Still, many dismissed Reagan's victory as a personal, not a partisan, triumph. Indeed, there was no question that Reagan was likeable. Near the conclusion of his presidency, an astounding 79 percent approved of Reagan as a person.[45] House Speaker Tip O'Neill saw this close-up. Encountering an ex-construction worker who lost his job after suffering a spinal cord injury, the man expressed his anger over proposals to tax workmen's compensation benefits. When O'Neill pointed out that it was the Reagan administration that initiated the proposal, the injured man cried out: "Not the president. He's got nothing to do with it. It's the people around him."[46] Pollsters took note and began to devise questions that tried to separate liking Reagan from approving his policies. According to a 1988 survey, the public was closely divided on Reagan's conservative approach to governance, even as it overwhelmingly liked him as a person: 38 percent liked Reagan personally and approved of most of his policies; 29 percent liked Reagan, but disapproved of his policies; 10 percent disliked Reagan but approved of his policies; and 21 percent disliked Reagan and disapproved of his policies.[47]

This closely divided support for (48 percent) and against (50 percent) Reagan's policies gave credence to a prevailing view that Reagan had little impact on his party's fortunes. Added to this is the fact that Reagan left the White House with *fewer* Republicans in both houses of Congress than when he entered.[48] Political scientists maintained that Reagan and his immediate predecessors had created a presidency by plebiscite, which replaced the partisan presidents of the nineteenth century. The late Everett Carll Ladd described this best, calling Reagan's success a "brittle mandate"—meaning that Reagan's electoral coalition could easily splinter apart if he failed to deliver.[49] Senate Majority Leader Howard Baker agreed, calling Reagan's plan to revive the economy through tax cuts and spending cuts a "riverboat gamble."[50] In short order, the idea of "plebiscitary presidents," whose personas (not loyalty to their respective parties) were responsible for their victories, took hold.[51] In Reagan's case, the election was all about his charming personality and dissatisfaction with Carter—and little else.

Indeed, it was the very weaknesses of political parties that allowed presidents to dominate politics. John F. Kennedy refused to wait his turn and defied the Democratic Party establishment to win the nomination in 1960.[52] Lyndon B. Johnson ran in 1964 as an anti-party candidate in whom the national interest dictated that the country be saved from a dangerous warmonger in the person of Barry Goldwater. George S. McGovern upended the party establishment and rewrote the nomination rules (for both parties) that gave an enhanced role to primaries and caucuses, which only accentuated the politics of persona. On the Republican side, Richard M. Nixon distanced himself from the GOP by forming the ill-named Committee to Reelect the President (with the horrendous acronym CREEP). The word "Republican" was banished from Nixon's television advertisements, and the dreaded R-word never emanated from the presidential lips. Nixon later complained that Republicans lacked "the ability to *think* like a majority party, to take risks, to exhibit the kind of confidence the Democrats had because of their sheer numbers."[53] Avoiding risks became a hallmark of

Gerald R. Ford's 1976 campaign, as he was advised to become a stealth candidate when it came to making a case for the Republican Party:

> The President must not campaign for GOP candidates. This will seriously erode his support among independents and ticket-splitters. The President should not attend any party fundraisers. Any *support* given to a GOP candidate must be done in a manner to *avoid* national attention.[54]

A warning delivered decades earlier by the American Political Science Association about an all-too-powerful president at the expense of political parties seemed prescient:

> When the president's program actually is the sole program, either his party becomes a flock of sheep or the party falls apart. This concept of the presidency disposes of the party system by making the president reach directly for the support of a majority of voters. It favors a president who exploits skillfully the arts of demagoguery, who uses the whole country as his political backyard, and who does not mind turning into the embodiment of personal government.[55]

Ronald Reagan was different. For decades, he had argued against "me-too Republicanism," saying he wanted his party to present "bold colors" and not be a party of "pale pastels." At the midpoint of his presidency, Reagan told a reporter: "A political party isn't a fraternity. It isn't something like the old school tie you wear. You band together in a political party because of certain beliefs of what government should be."[56] GOP platform writers heeded Reagan's advice, writing in 1980:

> For too many years, the political debate in America has been conducted in terms dictated by the Democrats. They believe that every time new problems arise beyond the power of men and women as individuals to solve, it becomes the duty of government to solve them. A defense of the individual against government was never more needed and we will continue to mount it.[57]

Unlike his immediate predecessors, Reagan cared deeply about the fortunes of the Republican Party. In 1980, he joined his fellow GOP congressional candidates on the steps of the Capitol to promise a "new beginning." During his presidency, Reagan sought to build the Republican Party at every turn. He especially relished what became known as "naturalization ceremonies," when Democratic officeholders—many from the South—would come to the White House and change their party registrations, just as Reagan himself had done in 1962.[58] For Reagan, it was not enough to have a personal triumph. At age sixty-nine, his aim was larger: to remake the Republican

Party in his own conservative image. Reagan's former image-maker Michael Deaver put it well when he noted that Reagan marched to "a different drummer."[59]

Reaganism's Rise

Those who study history like to bemuse themselves with the question, "What would history be like if, say, Abraham Lincoln had been elected president in 1852 instead of 1860?" Of course, we will never truly know the answer to that query, but the meaning behind it is clear: at key junctures in the American story, the person and the moment converge. Ronald Reagan was just such a person, and 1980 was just such a moment. Demographically, the United States had changed along lines suitable to Reagan's political interests. In 1970, the U.S. Census Bureau found that a majority of Americans were living in the suburbs—a historical first. The "un-young, un-poor, and un-black" Real Majority—famously described by Richard M. Scammon and Ben J. Wattenberg in their book by the same name—had come to their burgeoning suburban communities from the New Deal-era big cities.[60] Indeed, it was the very success of Franklin D. Roosevelt's New Deal—turning a 1930s generation of "have-nots" into a 1960s generation of "have-mores"—that made such a move possible. The mostly white suburbs—replete with their station wagons and cookie-cutter homes occupied by middle-class families—were famously depicted in Ronald Reagan's 1984 reelection commercial titled "Morning in America." In a series of iconic images, the advertisement depicted an idealized version of American life much as Reagan himself envisioned it: a briefcase-toting dad climbs into a station wagon headed for work; a kid on a bike tosses the morning paper onto his front porch; a pair of young newlyweds leaves church and kisses as a set of grandparents looks on approvingly; Mom, Dad, and kids haul in their latest acquisition (a carpet) into their suburban home complete with a white picket fence; and a police officer hoists an American flag. The voice-over concludes with a pitch that Reagan had restored pride and patriotism to their rightful places in the civic culture:

> It's morning again in America. Today more men and women will go to work than ever before in our country's history. With interest rates at about half the record highs of 1980, nearly 2,000 families today will buy new homes, more than at any time in the past four years. This afternoon 6,500 young men and women will be married, and with inflation at less than half of what it was just four years ago, they can look forward with confidence to the future. It's morning again in America, and under the leadership of President Reagan, our country is prouder and stronger and better. Why would we ever want to return to where we were less than four short years ago?[61]

But underlying these happy images was a politics of resentment. As newly minted suburbanites settled into their Levittown-style homes, there grew a dislike toward government. During the New Deal, many saw themselves as government's *beneficiaries*. By the 1980s, that sentiment had changed, and many suburbanites saw themselves as *taxpayers*. In 1978, Howard Jarvis began his Proposition 13 movement in California, which proposed strict limits on property taxes—a measure approved by 63 percent of California voters. Adding to the resentment was a growing concern over the nation's changing moral values. In 1980, James Q. Wilson defined "Reaganism" as opposed to those who would

> legalize marijuana, abortions, and pornography and tolerate or encourage draft resistance, all in the name of personal freedom, and who would support court-ordered school busing, bans on gun ownership, affirmative action, and racial quotas, all in the name of rationalizing and perfecting society. Indeed, Reaganism is based on a profound conviction that the opposite policies are more nearly correct. . . .[62]

In 1979, Richard Wirthlin discovered that a rapid erosion of the country's values was creating an era of personal anomie. Among his most revealing data were these:

- Two-thirds agreed "everything changes so quickly these days that I often have trouble deciding which are the rights rules to follow."
- A majority said we were "better off in the old days when everyone knew just how they were expected to act."
- Seventy-one percent felt "many things our parents stood for are going to ruin right before our eyes."
- Nearly eight in ten believed "what is lacking in the world today is the old kind of friendship that lasted for a lifetime."
- One in two described themselves as "left out of things going on around me."[63]

James Q. Wilson found Reaganism's adherents held firmly to the view that "the very virtues they have and practice are, in their eyes, conspicuously absent from society as a whole." He noted that Reagan's followers believed politics to be "corrupt," that it consisted of "deals" and catered to "selfish interests." Universities fell into the same category, as

> children don't act as if they appreciate what is being given them, they don't work hard, and they are lectured to by devious and wrongheaded professors. And above all, everywhere they look, somebody is trying to get "something for nothing," and succeeding.[64]

This resentment toward government combined with an emerging culture war recast Republicans into a party of the disaffected. In 1980, Democratic New York senator Daniel Patrick Moynihan saw the potency of Reagan's critique: "There is a movement to turn Republicans into Populists, a party of the People arrayed against a Democratic Party of the State."[65] Enervating the GOP was the idea that tax cuts would actually add more revenue to the federal coffers—a policy that became known as "supply-side economics" and was embraced by Reagan. The intellectual firepower behind these and other ideas led Republican National Chairman Bill Brock to boast that the Democratic Party's monopoly on new ideas was over:

> The notion of an activist federal government with an obligation to use its centralized powers "to meet new social programs with new social controls" was a new idea in the 1930s. . . . [Now] the Republican party finds itself in opposition . . . not only to a majority party that controls the machineries of government, but to the force of certain such ideas.[66]

The populist-like appeal of opposing big, impersonal institutions had been apparent for some time. Back in 1967, television talk show host Merv Griffin asked Robert F. Kennedy to explain why things were going so horribly wrong with "rioting," "labor unrest," and "young people revolting against the establishment." Kennedy's reply foreshadowed Reaganism's rise:

> I think [a] great problem within our country . . . is that everything has become so impersonal—everything is so large and so big you feel you don't play a role anymore, that you can't affect things. You can't affect what government does—it's so big, and so large, and so far away. It spends a great deal of money and you're a small cog. You have very little say in how a university is run, what you're being taught. And, again, you're just a number in a university or a school. You don't have a relationship with a teacher, for instance. . . . I think labor unions are so large and have become impersonal. And management is the same way.
>
> For the individual now, it's difficult for him to associate with anything, or with anybody, or any institution, and therefore we begin to move in perhaps a different direction. I think that's the explanation of the hippies. They've reached the conclusion that they can't affect their own lives, they can't affect society, and there's a lot of terrible things they see going on within our own country and perhaps around the world. This distresses them, and they can't see their ability to change the course of events. So they turn off, they pull the curtain down, and say we can't get off the Earth, but we'll leave it as much as we can. Perhaps the *major* problem we have within government—but a great problem all

of us have within society—is how all of us are going to come back to the idea that the individual is important, and that the society exists for him, and government exists for him, and just doesn't exist for the rest of us.[67]

The inability of Democrats to capture the populist anger "terrified" Daniel Patrick Moynihan, as the disorders of the 1960s and the disappointments of the 1970s put the Democratic Party on its heels.[68] One of the most astute observers of the Reagan coalition, Barack Obama, captured the essence of Reagan's charm:

> [A]s disturbed as I might have been by Ronald Reagan's election in 1980, as unconvinced as I might have been by his John Wayne, *Father Knows Best* pose, his policy by anecdote, and his gratuitous assaults on the poor, I understood his appeal. It was the same appeal that the military bases back in Hawaii had always held for me as a young boy, with their tidy streets and well-oiled machinery, the crisp uniforms and crisper salutes. It was related to the pleasure I still get from watching a well-played baseball game, or my wife gets from watching reruns of *The Dick Van Dyke Show*. Reagan spoke to America's longing for order, our need to believe that we are not simply subject to blind, impersonal forces but that we can shape our individual and collective destinies, so long as we rediscover the traditional virtues of hard work, patriotism, personal responsibility, optimism, and faith.[69]

It is this desire for order that lay at the heart of Reagan's appeal. For years, Reagan worried about the effects the women's rights and sexual revolutions were having on his idealized 1950s-era vision of the family. A letter written during his gubernatorial days is illustrative:

> I am deeply concerned with the wave of hedonism—the humanist philosophy so prevalent today—and believe this nation must have a spiritual rebirth, a rededication to the moral precepts which guided us for so much of our past, and we must have such a rebirth very soon.[70]

Even in his personal appearance, Ronald Reagan was a prototypical picture of the 1950s organization man—replete with a neatly folded handkerchief in his breast pocket, white shirt, knotted tie, dark blue suit, and polished black shoes. Reagan, the salesman, not only pitched himself as a reincarnation of Robert Young in his unforgettable leading role in *Father Knows Best*, but also sold the electorate on a Republican Party that would, in his words, "build a new consensus with all those across the land who share a community of values embodied in these words: family, work, neighborhood, peace, and freedom."[71] The 1980 platform elaborated on its standard-bearer's themes: "We will reemphasize those vital communities like the family, the neighborhood, the workplace, and others which are found at the center of our society between government and the individual."[72]

Ronald Reagan never deviated from that plank. He extolled

> parents who sacrifice long and hard so their children will know a better life than they've known; church and civic leaders who help to feed, clothe, nurse, and teach the needy; millions who've [sic] made our nation and our nation's destiny so very special—unsung heroes who may not have realized their own dream themselves but then who reinvest those dreams in their children.[73]

As president, he commemorated Mother's Day—calling the nation's moms "quiet, everyday heroes [from whom] we first learn about values and caring and the difference between right and wrong."[74] Radio listeners could have easily imagined that Reagan was describing the real Harriet Nelson, as portrayed in *The Adventures of Ozzie and Harriet*, or the mythical characters of June Cleaver and Betty Anderson of *Leave It to Beaver* and *Father Knows Best* fame.

And when real-life examples were not enough, Reagan resorted to telling stories. One particularly memorable occasion occurred in 1987, when a besieged Reagan left the nation's capital to escape the fury of the Iran-Contra affair. As Air Force One landed in the more friendly environs of West Lafayette, Indiana, the president told a large crowd about a letter he received concerning a boy named Billy. Reagan vividly described the scene: Billy nagged his father to oblige him in his sole pastime of playing baseball, while Billy's dad wanted to relax and read the Sunday newspaper. To stall the boy, Reagan described how Billy's father cut a newspaper map of the world into tiny pieces, and he asked Billy to Scotch-tape it together again. The two agreed that when Billy had successfully completed the task, both would go outside for a ball game. Reagan reported that after a mere seven minutes, Billy put the map together. When asked how he accomplished this seemingly impossible task so quickly, a proud Billy responded, "On the other side of the map there was a picture of the family, and I found that if you put the family together the world took care of itself."[75] At that, the crowd burst into applause. Few took Reagan's parable at face value, but everyone grasped its point: the importance of family. Nancy Reagan, who understood her husband's knack for reading audiences, said of him: "There's a certain cynicism in politics. You look back of a statement for what a man really means. But it takes people a while to realize that with Ronnie you don't have to look in back of anything."[76]

Speaking after the 1980 ballots were counted, Richard Wirthlin declared, "Durable coalitions do not just happen, they are built."[77] By 1984, construction of the Reagan coalition was complete. That year, Reagan won forty-nine states to Walter Mondale's one, his home state of Minnesota, and the District of Columbia. Taken together, the results of 1980 and 1984 gave Reagan an astounding 93 states; Carter-Mondale, 7. Indeed, the number of Reagan's statewide victories was larger than the number of states Democrats carried in the previous five presidential elections *combined*. The electoral college results were similar: Reagan, 1,014 electoral votes; Carter-Mondale, 62. If this were a ball game, the umpires surely would have called a halt.

A major reason for Reagan's 1984 success was his accomplishments. Seventy-two percent agreed Reagan was "effective in getting things done"; 69 percent thought he "has the strong leadership qualities this country needs"; 64 percent said he was "in touch and in charge"; and 63 percent believed he would "deal with the problems of the future effectively and boldly."[78] One reason for these high numbers was the fast start Reagan got off to in the early days of his administration by getting Congress to approve his budget and tax cuts. In 1981, Richard Wirthlin prepared a report for the newly inaugurated president that advised:

> How we begin will significantly determine how we govern. Certainly, the people and the pundits will start asking whether the Reagan Administration constitutes a juncture in American history when the role of the federal government was changed and a "new beginning" was commenced along the lines of Mr. Reagan's approach to governance.[79]

To Reagan's 1980 question, "Are you better off than you were four years ago?" 49 percent of 1984 voters said their financial situation had improved, and 84 percent of them backed Reagan.[80] As Wirthlin later noted, "Growth is the best alternative we can offer to the Democrats' state welfareisms."[81]

Another key to Reagan's success was young people. Among that group, Reagan improved his 1980 score by 16 percentage points to a record 65 percent of the vote.[82] But their support for Reagan did not end there: 54 percent of eighteen- to twenty-four-year-olds backed Republican congressional candidates.[83] And their party identifications became aligned with their votes: 46 percent called themselves Republicans; 37 percent were Democrats.[84] Lance Morrow noted that young voters had "binary vision"—Jimmy Carter means failure; Ronald Reagan means success—and concluded: "Just as Franklin Roosevelt's ideas set the style that would dominate the next four decades of American politics, Reagan—a zealous admirer of FDR's when young—wants the younger generation to complete the Reagan Revolution."[85] Democratic pollster Patrick Caddell warned that Democrats were sending the wrong message to young voters: "What I fear is that the signals have been that the party is anti-change, anti-growth, anti-participation, and primarily concerned with restoring the New Deal agenda and the primacy of the New Deal coalition members."[86] *New York Times* columnist Tom Wicker agreed, noting that Democrats had become *"a party of access"* in which "the voiceless find a voice," while Republicans "maintain enough coherence and unity to become *a party of government*."[87]

The South also proved to be another area of Reagan strength that reshaped the rules of politics. During the New Deal, the Solid South was a lynchpin for Franklin D. Roosevelt's election, with that one-party region giving FDR the greatest of landslides. In 1932, Roosevelt won 85 percent of the mostly all-white votes cast in Alabama. Fifty years later, Democratic poll-taker Peter D. Hart found among white Alabamians that Democratic loyalties still prevailed: Democrats, 53 percent; Republicans, 24 percent. But by Election Day 1984, white Alabamians had left the Democratic Party in the dust: Republicans, 41 percent; Democrats, 29 percent.[88] Other southern states showed similar results. For example, of the sixty-eight elected judgeships in Dallas County, Texas, Republicans won fifty-eight. Former Lyndon B. Johnson White House press secretary George Christian declared, "[Now it is] socially acceptable to be a Republican [in Texas]."[89] Pollster Peter Hart predicted a southern Republican realignment would have repercussions for years to come: "What you see five years from now is going to be very, very different. There are going to be a lot more Republicans."[90] Hart's prescient forecast proved correct: when Republicans took over the House in 1994, a majority of House members from Dixie, led by Newt Gingrich of Georgia, were Republican—a historic first.

Clearly, the twin Reagan landslides placed a final nail in the New Deal coffin. Shortly after the 1984 results were tallied, William Schneider wrote in *The New Republic*:

> Democrats are in the same position as the French aristocracy at the time of the Bourbon Restoration. We can pretend that nothing happened, but the *ancien regime* is dead. Things will never be the same. The problem for the Democrats is to avoid the fate of the Bourbons of whom Talleyrand said, "They learned nothing and they forgot nothing."[91]

Richard Nixon agreed:

> The Democrats face a traumatic dilemma. In 1972, they could excuse McGovern's loss by the fact that he was not a mainstream Democrat. Mondale, campaigning on traditional Democratic issues and appealing to the old Democratic coalition of minorities, labor, the disadvantaged, etc., which proved unbeatable for Roosevelt, Truman, and Johnson. What this election demonstrates is that there just aren't enough voters in those groups to make a majority.[92]

ABC News anchor Peter Jennings agreed, "The golden Democratic age of FDR will not come soon again."[93]

The tattered image of the Democratic Party stood in sharp contrast to an enhanced GOP one. By 1984, 31 percent had a better opinion of Republicans than they did four years earlier, and 56 percent thought they could better handle the country's most important problems.[94] But the advantages did not stop there: the GOP had a 31-point lead over the Democrats as the party best able to restore the nation's defenses; 17 points when it came to being better for prosperity; 17 points on handling U.S.-U.S.S.R. relations; 15 points on cutting drug use; 14 points on reducing unemployment; 13 points on controlling inflation; and 5 points on balancing the budget.[95] After Reagan's reelection, the historic Democratic partisan advantage had been wiped clean: Democratic identifiers, 42 percent; Republicans, 43 percent.[96] Democratic pollster Paul Maslin noted, "These are historic gains for a party that has traditionally been viewed as wedded to established interests, isolationist, and the cause of the [Great] Depression."[97] No longer would GOP presidential candidates have to run away from their party. Republican pollster Robert Teeter noted that Republican candidates "can use the name Republican [in their campaigns] for the first time in my political lifetime."[98] Or, as Reagan put it, "We're making the GOP stand for Grand Opportunity Party."[99]

An Enduring Image

A few days before his assassination, John F. Kennedy wrote a letter to Clinton Rossiter after the famed political scientist sent him the latest edition of his book, *The American Presidency*. Rossiter believed the presidency placed an enormous burden on its custodians. Thus, he began the manuscript with an epigraph taken from William Shakespeare's *Macbeth*: "Methought I heard a voice cry, 'Sleep no more.'" Kennedy thought other Shakespearean lines were "more appropriate." In *King Henry IV*, Part 1, Glendower boasts, "I can call spirits from the vasty deep," to which Hotspur replies:

> Why, so can I, or so can any man;
> But will they come when you do call for them?[100]

John F. Kennedy's proposed epigraph is apropos for the Reagan years. Reagan's ability to summon forth the "spirits from the vasty deep" helped Americans to renew their patriotism and create a renewed sense of faith in themselves. Such confidence building was salutary after the disasters of race riots, Vietnam, Watergate, and the malaise of the 1970s. By altering the nation's perception of itself from the "pitiful, helpless giant" once described by Richard Nixon, American self-esteem was restored.[101] This had consequences that reached into every home. Richard Wirthlin expressed it this way:

> In being the person who establishes a tone, a president has influence on every American—be it a young person entering the job market, an individual on the margin of deciding whether to study or whether to work, an entrepreneur trying to determine whether to invest in his own business or go to work for someone else.[102]

John Adams once said of George Washington,

> If he was not the greatest President, he was the best *Actor* of the Presidency
> we ever had. His address to the States when he left the Army: his solemn
> Leave taken of Congress . . . his Farewell Address to the people when he
> resigned the Presidency. These were all in a strain of Shakespearean and
> Garrickal excellence in Dramatic Exhibitions [emphasis added].[103]

Former New York governor Mario Cuomo—who was in attendance at
the 1986 Statue of Liberty rededication—described Reagan in a similar
vein: "By his personal conduct when he's shot, when he is told he has cancer, when he goes to Normandy—the way he's deported himself has been
a moral instruction to my children."[104] Near the conclusion of his presidency, ABC News anchor Peter Jennings remarked: "Reagan certainly held
us spellbound. I shall always wonder whether it just happened or if he calculated that it would happen."[105]

For Republicans, the images Reagan projected were both powerful and personal. Far from being just another GOP president in a long line of predecessors,
Reagan transformed his party into a defender of nationalism and traditional
American values. He had become the founder of a new, majority-minded, confident Republican Party whose continuance in power seemed assured. To pay
tribute, fervent supporters led by Republican activist Grover Norquist started
the Reagan Legacy Project in 1997—an effort to have something named for
Reagan in all 3,140 counties in the United States. The Reagan project has
had many successes: in Washington, D.C., National Airport was rechristened
in Reagan's name, as was the Ronald Reagan Building and International
Trade Center in the heart of the District. More than a decade after Reagan's
death, the GOP love affair with the late president shows no signs of abating.
Two-thirds of Republicans say Reagan is the best chief executive since World
War Two.[106] Perhaps even more astounding is the 52 percent of Republicans
who name Reagan as the best president *ever*—ahead of John F. Kennedy,
Abraham Lincoln, Franklin D. Roosevelt, and George Washington.[107]

Ronald Reagan's consummate acting skills left an enduring, almost indel-
ible, image upon the Republican Party. As *Time* reporter Lance Morrow
once wrote:

> Acting, when it achieves the right harmonics between performer and
> audience, is a work of almost intimate leadership. The actor enters into
> the minds of others and leads them through the drama, making them
> laugh or cry, making them feel exactly what he wants them to feel. It is
> a powerful and primitive transaction, a manipulation, but at its deepest
> level a form of tribal communion.[108]

The only president to summon some form of "tribal communion" prior
to Reagan was John F. Kennedy. Yet Reagan's achievement is even more

noteworthy, for Kennedy's "tribal communion," though powerful, came *after* his assassination.

But admiration for Reagan is one thing; having a death grasp on the Republican Party is another. Just as Democrats had to let go of Kennedy long after his demise, Republicans must do the same for Reagan. Today a generation of millennials has grown up and is entering the voting booths without ever knowing Ronald Reagan as president. He is, for them, a *historical* figure—much in the same way that Abraham Lincoln is a figure of history for all living Americans. Conservative commentator Jennifer Rubin writes, "The Republican party can remain a Ronald Reagan historical society, or it can try to endure as a force in national politics. But it can't do both."[109] Too many Republicans, however, want Reagan to remain encased in amber.

Today we are as far away from Reagan's 1980 election as Reagan was in 1980 when he supported Franklin D. Roosevelt for a fourth time as a Democrat! A person born in 1980 will be approaching middle age by the time Election Day arrives in 2016. As Henry Olsen and Peter Wehner of the conservative-minded Ethics and Public Policy Center presciently observe:

> The constant invocation of Reagan's name to bolster arguments for present-day policies (and present-day politicians) actually hinders our understanding of the substance of Reagan's legacy—and undermines the Republican party's ability to make a case for itself in the here-and-now.[110]

Time has marched on. But the images Reagan left behind for those who were alive to experience them still remain powerful ones. Undoubtedly, Reagan's triumph was a balm for a long-suffering Republican Party that endured five straight losses at the hands of Franklin D. Roosevelt and Harry S. Truman. It was a balm for a Republican Party that placed Dwight D. Eisenhower as its head, who always envisioned himself as a "nonpartisan" ("I Like Ike")—and whose preference was to set himself apart from the Republican Party (e.g., "Citizens for Eisenhower," never "Republicans for Eisenhower"). And it was a balm for a Republican Party that saw Richard M. Nixon resign the presidency in disgrace.

Ronald Reagan became the Republican whose name was synonymous with his party—and he liked it that way. It is a link that Republicans still refuse to cut; yet it is a link that is gradually and surely being severed with each passing year.

Notes

1 See Margot Hornblower, "Millions View Colorful Shower in Honor of Refurbished Statue," *Washington Post*, July 5, 1986, A-1.
2 See "For Liberty's 100th Year, the Biggest Party Ever," *New York Times*, July 6, 1986, E-1.

3 Bernard Weintraub, "Notebook: Reagan Amid 'All the Hoopla,'" *New York Times*, July 6, 1986, 16.

4 Bernard Weintraub, "For Ronald Reagan, the Ceremonies Stir Pride and Patriotism," *New York Times*, July 5, 1986, 1.

5 Gallup poll, July 1–2, 1986. Text of question: "Do you approve or disapprove of the way Ronald Reagan is handling his job as President?" Approve, 68 percent; disapprove, 23 percent; don't know, 10 percent.

6 Weintraub, "Notebook: Reagan Amid 'All the Hoopla.'"

7 Ibid.

8 The lack of memorable phrases reflected the departures of talented speechwriters Peggy Noonan and Bently Elliott from the White House. According to the *New York Times*, one White House official, when asked about Reagan's speech, "rolled his eyes and shook his head." See Weintraub, "Notebook: Reagan Amid 'All the Hoopla.'"

9 Ronald Reagan, Address to the Nation on Independence Day, New York Harbor, July 4, 1986.

10 Hornblower, "Millions View Colorful Shower in Honor of Refurbished Statue."

11 "Largest Fireworks in History." See http://usfireworks.biz/blog/2011/06/largest-fireworks-displays-in-history/

12 Quoted in Hornblower, "Millions View Colorful Shower in Honor of Refurbished Statue."

13 Quoted in Weintraub, "Notebook: Reagan Amid 'All the Hoopla.'"

14 Reagan, Address to the Nation on Independence Day.

15 Lance Morrow, "Yankee Doodle Magic: What Makes Reagan So Remarkably Popular a President?" *Time*, July 7, 1986, 12.

16 Ford received 1,187 delegate votes to Reagan's 1,070. Cited in Dick Wirthlin with Wynton C. Hall, *The Greatest Communicator: What Ronald Reagan Taught Me about Politics, Leadership, and Life* (New York: John Wiley and Sons, 2004), 32.

17 Gerald R. Ford, *A Time to Heal: The Autobiography of Gerald R. Ford* (New York: Harper and Row Publishers, 1979), 294.

18 Quoted in Thomas M. DeFrank, *Write It When I'm Gone* (New York: G. P. Putnam and Sons, 2007), 114.

19 See Michael K. Deaver, *A Different Drummer: My Thirty Years with Ronald Reagan* (New York: HarperCollins, 2001), 113.

20 Quoted in William A. Henry III, *Visions for America: How We Saw the 1984 Election* (Boston: Atlantic Monthly Press, 1985), 9.

21 Ronald Reagan, "A Time for Choosing," Los Angeles, California, October 27, 1964.

22 Quoted in John Kenneth White, *Still Seeing Red: How the Cold War Shapes the New American Politics* (Boulder: Westview Press, 1997), 181.

23 Ibid.

24 Ibid., 182.

25 Ibid.

26 Hamilton Jordan, *Crisis: The Last Year of the Carter Presidency* (New York: Berkley Books, 1983), 284.

27 Richard B. Wirthlin, *Reagan for President: Campaign Action Plan*, June 29, 1980, 164, 12. Unpublished confidential campaign document given to the author.

28 Cited in John Kenneth White, *The New Politics of Old Values* (Hanover, New Hampshire: University Press of New England, 1990), 50.

29 Ronald Reagan, Acceptance Speech, Republican National Convention, Detroit, July 17, 1980.

30 "Face-Off: A Conversation with the Presidents' Pollsters, Patrick Caddell and Richard Wirthlin," *Public Opinion* (December/January 1980), 2.

31 Jimmy Carter, Address to the Nation, Washington, D.C., July 15, 1980. Carter never used the term "malaise." It was a moniker placed on the speech first by Edward Kennedy and later by Reagan.

32 Ronald Reagan, Announcement Speech, Los Angeles, November 13, 1979.

33 Wirthlin, *Reagan for President*, 21.

34 Wirthlin, with Hall, *The Greatest Communicator*, 70.

35 See Jon Thurber, "Witty Reagan Aide and Gun Control Advocate, James S. Brady," *Washington Post*, August 5, 2014, A-1. Brady had famously run through the Reagan campaign plane yelling, "Killer trees, killer trees."

36 Deaver, *A Different Drummer*, 74.

37 Jordan, *Crisis*, 318–319.

38 Wirthlin, with Hall, *The Greatest Communicator*, 69.

39 Cited in Paul Kengor, "The Great Forgotten Debate," *National Review Online*, May 22, 2007.

40 Jordan, *Crisis*, 284.

41 Quoted in Wirthlin, with Hall, 76.

42 Independent candidate John Anderson received 6.61 percent of the vote and won no states.

43 Wirthlin, *Reagan for President*, 25. Nineteen percent called themselves independents.

44 CBS News/*New York Times*, exit poll, November 4, 1980.

45 Gallup poll, December 27–29, 1988. Text of question: "Apart from whether you approve or disapprove of the way Reagan is handling his job as president, what do you think of Reagan as a person? Would you say you approve or disapprove of him?" Approve, 79 percent; disapprove, 13 percent; no opinion, 8 percent.

46 Thomas P. O'Neill with William Novak, *Man of the House: The Life and Political Memoirs of Speaker Tip O'Neill* (New York: Random House, 1987), 357.

47 *Washington Post*, poll, June 15–19, 1988. Text of question: "Which of the following statements comes closest to your own views: A. I like Reagan personally, and approve of most of his policies. B. I like Reagan personally, but I disapprove of most of his policies. C. I don't like Reagan personally, but I approve of most of his policies. D. I don't like Reagan personally, and I disapprove of most of his policies. Statement A, 38 percent; Statement B, 29 percent; Statement C, 10 percent; Statement D, 21 percent; don't know/no opinion, 1 percent; no answer/refused, 1 percent.

48 After Reagan's 1980 win, Republicans held 53 Senate seats and 192 House seats. By 1988, Republican ranks had shrunk to 46 and 175, respectively. In 1980, the GOP won twenty-three governorships; eight years later the number of Republican governors diminished by one. Republicans controlled 2,922 state legislative seats in 1988, seventy fewer than in 1980.

49 Everett Carll Ladd, *Where Have All the Voters Gone? The Fracturing of America's Political Parties* (New York: W. W. Norton, 1982), 74–109.

50 Laurence I. Barrett, *Gambling with History: Reagan in the White House* (Garden City, New York: Doubleday and Company, 1983), 164.

51 See Theodore J. Lowi, *The Personal President: Power Invested, Promise Unfulfilled* (Ithaca, New York: Cornell University Press, 1985), especially 97–133.

52 For more on this see James MacGregor Burns, *Running Alone: Presidential Leadership JFK to Bush II* (New York: Basic Books, 2006), especially 21–42.

53 Quoted in Joe Scarborough, *The Right Path: From Ike to Reagan, How Republicans Once Mastered Politics—and Can Again* (New York: Random House, 2013), 93.
54 See White, *Still Seeing Red*, 148.
55 Committee on Political Parties, *Toward a More Responsible Two-Party System* (New York: Rinehart, 1950), 94.
56 Hugh Sidey, "A Conversation with Reagan," *Time*, September 3, 1984.
57 Quoted in White, *The New Politics of Old Values*, 53.
58 James F. Clarity and Warren Weaver, Jr., "Briefing: Conversion Rites," *New York Times*, October 21, 1985, A-16.
59 Deaver, *A Different Drummer*, passim.
60 Richard M. Scammon and Ben J. Wattenberg, *The Real Majority* (New York: Coward-McCann, Inc., 1970), especially 45–71.
61 Ronald Reagan 1984 campaign, "It's Morning in America," transcript of television advertisement.
62 James Q. Wilson, "Reagan and the Republican Revival," *Commentary*, October 1980, 26.
63 See Wirthlin, *Reagan for President*, 35–36.
64 James Q. Wilson, "A Guide to Reagan Country: The Political Culture of Southern California," *Commentary*, May 1, 1967.
65 Daniel Patrick Moynihan, "Of 'Sons' and Their 'Grandsons,'" *New York Times*, July 7, 1980, 15.
66 Ibid.
67 *Merv Griffin Show*. See https://www.youtube.com/watch?v=pNk6d2hauw4. Accessed July 8, 2014.
68 Moynihan, "Of 'Sons' and Their 'Grandsons.'"
69 Barack Obama, *The Audacity of Hope: Thoughts on Reclaiming the American Dream* (New York: Crown Publishers, 2006), 31.
70 Quoted in Helene von Damm, *Sincerely, Ronald Reagan* (Ottawa, Illinois: Green Hill Publishers, 1976), 84.
71 Ronald Reagan, Acceptance Speech, Republican National Convention, Detroit, July 17, 1980.
72 1980 Republican National Platform (Washington, D.C.: Republican National Committee, 1980).
73 Ronald Reagan, State of the Union Address, Washington, D.C., January 26, 1982.
74 Ronald Reagan, Radio Address to the Nation on the Observance of Mother's Day, Washington, D.C., May 7, 1983.
75 Ronald Reagan, Remarks on arrival at West Lafayette, Indiana, West Lafayette, Indiana, April 9, 1987.
76 Quoted in Michael Rogin, *Ronald Reagan, the Movie and Other Episodes in Political Demonology* (Berkeley: University of California Press, 1987), 7.
77 Richard B. Wirthlin, "Final Report of the Initial Actions Project," January 29, 1981, 12.
78 Decision/Making/Information, post-election survey for the Republican National Committee, November 7–10, 1984.
79 Wirthlin, "Final Report of the Initial Actions Project," 1.
80 Decision/Making/Information, post-election survey for the Republican National Committee, November 7–10, 1984.
81 Wirthlin, *Reagan for President*, 56.
82 See ABC News, exit poll, November 6, 1984, and Decision/Making/Information, post-election survey for the Republican National Committee, November 7–10, 1984.

83 CBS News, exit poll, November 6, 1984.

84 Decision/Making/Information, merged data from studies done for the Republican National Committee, November 5, 1986–January 29, 1987.

85 Morrow, "Yankee Doodle Magic," 12.

86 Patrick Caddell, "What Is Needed Is an Indirect Approach," memo reproduced in Peter Goldman and Tony Fuller, *The Quest for the Presidency, 1984* (New York: Bantam Books, 1985), 426.

87 Tom Wicker, "A Party of Access?" *New York Times*, November 25, 1984, E-17.

88 Cited in "Moving Right Along? Campaign '84's Lessons for 1988: An Interview with Peter Hart and Richard Wirthlin," *Public Opinion* (December/January 1985), 62.

89 See Wayne King, "Republican Inroads Put Texas on Edge," *New York Times*, February 21, 1985, A-10.

90 Quoted in "State Political Parties Are Playing a New Role," *New York Times*, June 16, 1985, E-20.

91 William Schneider, "Half a Realignment," *The New Republic*, December 3, 1984, 19.

92 Cited in Goldman and Fuller, *The Quest for the Presidency, 1984*, 451.

93 Peter Jennings, "The Presidential Election: Smoke and Mirrors," in ABC News, *The '84 Vote* (New York: American Broadcasting Company, 1985), xxxix.

94 CBS News/*New York Times*, poll, November 8–14, 1984.

95 Decision/Making/Information, post-election survey for the Republican National Committee, November 1986.

96 Decision/Making/Information, post-election survey for the Republican National Committee, November 7–10, 1984.

97 Quoted in William Schneider, "The Democrats in '88," *Atlantic Monthly*, April 1987, 54.

98 Quoted in Jack W. Germond and Jules Witcover, "GOP Gains of Five Governors Possible in 1986," *National Journal*, December 14, 1985, 2873.

99 Ronald Reagan, "Remarks to Members of the Republican National Committee and the Reagan-Bush Campaign Staff," Dallas, Texas, August 24, 1984.

100 See Theodore C. Sorensen, *Kennedy* (New York: Harper & Row, 1965), 392.

101 From Richard Nixon's address to the nation announcing the incursion of U.S. troops into Cambodia, April 9, 1970. Quoted in Stephen E. Ambrose, *Nixon: The Triumph of a Politician, 1962–1972* (New York: Simon and Schuster, 1989), 345.

102 John Kenneth White, interview with Richard B. Wirthlin, Washington, D.C., November 22, 1988.

103 Quoted in Emmet John Hughes, *The Living Presidency* (New York: Coward McCann and Geohegan, 1973), 89.

104 Quoted in Bernard Weinraub, "The Reagan Legacy," *New York Times Magazine*, June 22, 1986, 13.

105 The Jennings-Koppel Report, "Ronald Reagan: Memo to the Future," ABC News broadcast, April 23, 1987.

106 Quinnipiac University, poll, June 24–30, 2014. Text of question: "Thinking about the United States Presidents we have had since World War Two: Harry Truman, Dwight Eisenhower, John Kennedy, Lyndon Johnson, Richard Nixon, Gerald Ford, Jimmy Carter, Ronald Reagan, George Bush Senior, Bill Clinton, George W. Bush, and Barack Obama, which one would you consider the best president?" Among Republicans only: Harry Truman, 4 percent; Dwight Eisenhower, 4 percent; John Kennedy, 6 percent; Lyndon Johnson, 0 percent; Richard Nixon, 2 percent; Gerald Ford, 1 percent; Jimmy Carter, 0 percent; Ronald

Reagan, 66 percent; George Bush Senior, 6 percent; Bill Clinton, 3 percent; George W. Bush, 1 percent; Barack Obama, 4 percent; don't know/no answer, 2 percent.

107 See Lydia Saad, "Best President? Lincoln on Par with Reagan, Kennedy," Gallup press release, February 11, 2009.

108 Morrow, "Yankee Doodle Magic," 12.

109 Quoted in Chuck McCutcheon, "Ronald Reagan Remains a GOP Icon," *CQ Researcher*, October 24, 2014, 902.

110 Quoted in Michael Gerson, "The Reagan Time Warp," *Washington Post*, November 4, 2014, A-15.

Chapter 2

Outmaneuvered and Angry

Bill Clinton and the Republicans

"This is *not* the party of Reagan."
Chris McDaniel, Mississippi Republican state senator

June 9, 1981. A defeated Democratic governor caught in the maelstrom of the Reagan landslide traveled to North Carolina to ruminate on his party's losses. Expressing admiration for the new president, the Democratic pol pointed to a weakness that would ultimately undermine the political colossus Ronald Reagan was assembling. Speaking before the Mecklenburg County Democratic Men's Club in Charlotte, the ex-governor told listeners that while Reagan had accomplished a good deal in a few months, both he and the Republican Party were courting eventual trouble:

> Reagan is pandering to the people who want to tell the rest of us how to live. The Republican party is trying to tell the rest of us whether we are moral or not. We will never make heaven on Earth; that is what heaven's for.[1]

Bill Clinton's analysis was, as usual, spot on. As Clinton watched Reagan dominate the landscape, the Arkansas governor was biding his time and waiting for the chance to run for president. In 1991, Clinton declared his candidacy—a long-shot bet given that George H. W. Bush had high job approval ratings. Many believed that the forthcoming election, while constitutionally mandated, was unnecessary since a Bush victory was all but assured following the success of the Persian Gulf War. In addition to his high poll standings, Bush's prior outing on the presidential hustings garnered an astounding 426 electoral votes. In this last of landslides, Bush carried states now considered solidly Democratic: California, Connecticut, Illinois, Maine, Maryland, Michigan, New Jersey, Pennsylvania, and Vermont. In 1988, Bush had done what no vice president since Martin Van Buren had accomplished: win a de facto third term for his boss. But Bush's triumph turned out to be a "last hurrah." None of the states listed above have voted

Republican since, and no GOP presidential candidate after George H. W. Bush has exceeded 300 electoral votes, never mind 400. — The Donald.

Embarking on his come-from-behind bid for the White House, Bill Clinton noticed a weakness in George H. W. Bush—something he could exploit for his own purposes. In 1988, Bush was repeatedly asked to describe his vision for what America could be at the end of his presidency. Responding to the many queries, Bush spoke of wanting to be "the education president" and "the environmental president." His aspirations, while lofty, were bound to disappoint. After all, being the "education president" surely meant that children were achieving scholarly goals in idealized classrooms. Or being the "environmental president" would ensure an end to pollution and a restoration of clean air and pure water. Both wannabe Presidents Bush were encased in panaceas that were bound to disappoint once reality intruded.[2] In the end, Bush gave up trying to paint a vision of the future, and derisively referred to reporters' questions about it as "the vision thing."[3]

In a sense, Bush's tongue-tied responses didn't matter. The country was prosperous and happy, with 53 percent saying the nation was "on the right track."[4] Addressing delegates at the 1988 Republican convention, Ronald Reagan took note of the "liberal elites'" desire for change and declared, "We are the change"—a reference to his reversal of the economic malaise that gripped the Carter years.[5] George Bush also agreed that a fundamental change was out of order:

> In 1940, when I was barely more than a boy, Franklin Roosevelt said we shouldn't change horses in midstream. My friends, these days the world moves even more quickly, and now, after two great terms, a switch will be made. But when you have to change horses in midstream, doesn't it make sense to switch to the one who's going the same way?[6]

In a candid moment, Bush policy adviser Deborah Steelman said that if her candidate were to fully answer "the vision thing," "We'd have less of a chance to win than we do."[7]

In many respects, George H. W. Bush was the polar opposite of Ronald Reagan. Reagan was not particularly well versed in governmental affairs, as attested to by the people closest to him. Office of Management and Budget director David Stockman wrote, "Reagan's body of knowledge is primarily impressionistic: he registers anecdotes rather than concepts."[8] Treasury secretary and later White House chief of staff Donald T. Regan drew an equally uncomplimentary picture:

> [I]t was a rare meeting in which he made a decision or issued orders. Reagan's personality and infectious likability [sic] are founded on a natural diffidence. He hesitates to ask questions or confess a lack of knowledge in the presence of strangers—and thanks to the way his staff

operated, nearly everyone was a stranger to this shy President except the membership of his innermost circle.[9]

Unlike Reagan, George H.W. Bush mastered the details of government with a first-class resume that included U.S. congressman, Republican national chair, envoy to China, CIA director, UN ambassador, and vice president. If Reagan was "hands-off," Bush would be "hands-on," "Ready on Day One" (as his gauzy commercials promised) to manage the affairs of government.

There is much to be lauded about Bush's mastery of detail, especially when it came to running U.S. foreign policy at a time when the Berlin Wall collapsed and the Soviet Union imploded. At the 1992 Republican Convention, a large slab of the Berlin Wall was on display outside the Houston Astrodome, and Bush made his case for reelection, saying: "I hope every Mother and Dad out there says, 'Hey, we ought to give this president a little credit out there for the fact that our little kids don't worry so much about nuclear war.' Isn't that important?"[10] It was important, but by 1992 a restless public had turned its attention to a faltering economy at home. Bush was a Cold War president without a Cold War to fight.

George H.W. Bush didn't lack vision so much as he lacked Ronald Reagan's imagination. Reagan's ability to connect with voters rested on his ability to conjure vivid scenes that listeners found fulfilled in their imaginations. One illustration: as noted in the previous chapter, Reagan presided over one of the most powerful Fourth of July celebrations ever telecast. He re-created the scene for his Saturday radio listeners: "We had an exciting 4th of July, celebrating that beautiful lady, who for a hundred years now had stood watch over New York Harbor and this blessed land of ours."[11] But Reagan's words were uttered *the day before* he mounted the deck of the USS *John F. Kennedy*, as he taped the radio address prior to departing for New York Harbor. Reagan's ability to draw vivid portraits was honed during his career as a baseball broadcaster for Iowa radio station WHO back in 1933. In those days, plays were relayed by coded telegraph messages. On one memorable occasion, the telegraph went dead. Faced with the choice admitting the truth and playing transcribed music, or holding the attention of his audience until the telegraph was repaired, Reagan chose the latter. He had batter Billy Jurges foul a ball from pitcher Dizzy Dean. (A foul ball is the only play not recorded in the record books; thus, Reagan could not be caught in a lie.) After one foul ball, Reagan eagerly looked to the control booth, but the technician shook his head, indicating that the wire was still dead. Reagan had Jurges put another of Dean's pitches in play, and described a fight between two kids trying to retrieve the ball. Next, Reagan had the batter foul another pitch, one that just missed being a home run. Finally, the wire resumed its hum, and its first message caused Reagan to burst out laughing: Jurges had popped out on the first ball pitched.[12] As Mario Cuomo famously said, "You campaign in poetry, but you govern in prose." Thanks to his long resume George H. W. Bush had mastered the prose, but none of Ronald Reagan's poetry. Bill Clinton would not make the same mistake.

The Gipper and the Comeback Kid

On July 24, 1963, at precisely 9:45 a.m., John F. Kennedy, accompanied by members of the Joint Chiefs of Staff, stepped out of the Oval Office and walked a few short steps onto the White House colonnade. There waiting to greet the president and the military officers was a delegation from the American Legion's Boys Nation, which was meeting in Washington, D.C. The summer day was already warm, and the boys standing in neat rows in front of the president were brimming with excitement. Speaking to the young men, Kennedy lauded their "initiative" in rejecting a states' rights provision proposed by the group's southern representatives. Knowing that some of the young men were attracted to conservative Republican and prospective presidential candidate Barry Goldwater, Kennedy proudly declared that under his administration the United States stands for freedom "all the way from Berlin to Saigon."[13] Standing in the front row was sixteen-year-old Bill Clinton. The six-foot, three-inch teenager, weighing two hundred pounds, had elbowed his way to the front row hoping Kennedy would greet the boys upon concluding his remarks.[14] Indeed, the president did so, and as Kennedy approached the wavy-haired Arkansan, Clinton made a slight bow and grasped the president's hand. An iconic photograph recorded the event.

Returning home, Clinton's mother, Virginia, noticed a change in her son. He was brimming with a desire to enter public service and was determined to learn everything he could about politics. This ambition exhibited itself a few months later when Clinton began speaking before small hometown groups about being one of the last persons in Hot Springs to see the living JFK. Clinton's biographer, David Maraniss, wrote, "The handshake on that July morning in 1963 had begun its transformation—from personal exploit to community myth."[15]

Bill Clinton's desire to be president was evident to everyone who encountered him. At Georgetown University, Denise Hyland, a fellow student, told anyone who would listen, "Remember this name—Bill Clinton—because someday he will be president."[16] Years later, at the Mecklenburg County Democratic Men's Club meeting, one observer described Clinton as "the most impressive 34-year-old I had ever met," and predicted a bright future for the ex-governor: "Although he was out of office and his path toward a comeback was by no means clear, I felt by the end of the evening that I had met a future president of the United States."[17] David Maraniss observed that Clinton's desire to sit in the Oval Office "was always there, not a matter of predestination but of expectation and will, and it had built up year by year, decade by decade."[18]

But desire and fulfillment are two separate things. To enter the White House, Bill Clinton would have to accommodate himself to existing realities. And those realities were not friendly to Clinton's Democratic Party. By the time Clinton thought himself ready to seek the presidency, the Democratic Party was in deep trouble. Ronald Reagan and George Bush had beaten the Democrats badly in three straight elections, and Bush's job approval rating stood at a then record high of 89 percent following the successful Persian Gulf War.[19] The Reagan-Bush years not only kept Democrats out of the White House, but put them out of touch with ordinary Americans. Pollster Stanley B. Greenberg advised candidate Clinton that his path to the presidency would be difficult: "Democrats were seen not to understand the values that were important to mainstream, middle-class families."[20]

By being so long excluded from the presidency, Democrats were not only losing hope, they were losing their own history. The fond memories Democrats had of John F. Kennedy, which Clinton shared in abundance, were fading. By 1992, Kennedy had been dead for twenty-nine years and an entire generation had grown up knowing only Republicans as their presidents. Democratic strategist Robert Shrum warned: "The Democratic party has lived off the legacy of John F. Kennedy [since his assassination]. The torch will go out unless it finally passes to a new generation. We need to invent a new legacy."[21] To invent that legacy, Democrats would need a successful president. (Jimmy Carter had fallen short, and redeemed his reputation only in his post-White House years.) Many Democrats, including Shrum, despaired of their party's chances. In June 1992, as he was about to capture his party's nomination, Clinton told the *New York Times* that since Hubert H. Humphrey's defeat in 1968, "the Democrats have had a lot of trouble," adding:

> What I have tried to do during this campaign, and before that during my work with the Democratic Leadership Council, is to articulate a new approach for the Democrats that goes beyond where both parties have been, one that emphasizes a commitment to strong economic growth and opportunity, one that assumes more responsibility in certain critical areas, moving from welfare to work, strong child-care enforcement, changes in the nature of the American workplace and the nature of American schools. Changes in the behavior of our corporate executives, up and down the line. And one that was unabashedly pro-growth and for rebuilding in America a sense of American strength based on mainstream values.[22]

To speak to mainstream values, Clinton would have to learn, in the words of his speechwriter David Kusnet, to "speak American."[23] While Clinton was an ardent admirer of JFK, in order to "speak American" he became a close observer of Ronald Reagan. Clinton had no better teacher than the fortieth president. To take one small example: once, in an endeavor to improve his presidential salute, Clinton watched old television outtakes of Reagan saluting awaiting soldiers while departing Marine One.[24] Indeed, Clinton admired how Reagan fulfilled the presidential role—something Reagan attributed to his strong acting skills: "There have been times in this office when I've wondered how you can do this job if you hadn't been an actor."[25]

By the time Clinton ran, the lessons Reagan imparted were evident in Clinton's communication skills. When asked why Democrats had been spectacularly unsuccessful in seeking the presidency, Clinton answered:

> I'll tell you why: because too many of the people who used to vote for us, the very burdened middle class that we are talking about, have not trusted us in national elections to defend our national interests abroad, to put their values into our social policy at home, or to take their tax money and spend it with discipline.[26]

Clinton then uttered a formulation he termed the "New Covenant"—a cleverly designed religious formulation consisting of the words "opportunity, community, and responsibility":

> Our burden is to give the people a new choice, rooted in old values, a new choice that is simple, that offers *opportunity*, demands *responsibility*, gives citizens more say, provides them with responsive government—all because we recognize that we are a *community*. We are all in this together, and we are going up and down together.[27]

Something else Bill Clinton learned from Ronald Reagan was placing himself in the shoes of ordinary voters. On the eve of the 1980 election, Reagan was asked by a reporter what he thought people saw in him. His response was revealing: "Would you laugh if I told you that I think, maybe, they see themselves and that I'm one of them?"[28] Clinton absorbed this lesson well, becoming infamous for feeling people's pain. One such moment occurred during the 1992 town hall debate. An African-American woman asked the candidates this awkward question, "How has the national debt personally affected each of your lives. And if it hasn't how can you honestly find a cure for the economic problems of the common people if you have no experience in what's ailing them?" George H. W. Bush clumsily asked the lady to "help me with the question," and gave this rambling answer:

> Well, you ought to be in the White House for a day and hear what I hear, and see what I see, and read the mail I read, and touch the people that I touch from time to time. I was in the Lomax A.M.E. Church. It's a black church just outside of Washington, D.C. And I read in the bulletin about teen-age pregnancies, about the difficulty that families are

having to make ends meet. I talk to parents. I mean, you've got to care. Everybody cares if people aren't doing well. But I don't think it's fair to say, "You haven't had cancer, therefore you don't know what it's like."[29]

Bill Clinton needed no such help. Rising from his stool, Clinton took a few steps toward the distraught woman, and while allaying her concerns he eviscerated Bush:

> Well, I've been governor of a small state for 12 years. I'll tell you how it's affected me. Every year, Congress and the President sign laws that makes us do more things, and gives us less money to do it with. I see people in my state, middle-class people, their taxes have gone up in Washington, and their services have gone down while the wealthy have gotten tax cuts. I have seen what's happened in this last four years when in my state, when people lose their jobs, there's a good chance I'll know them by their names. When a factory closes I know the people who ran it. When the businesses go bankrupt, I know them. And I've been out here for 13 months meeting in meetings just like this ever since October with people like you all over America, people that have lost their jobs, lost their livelihood, lost their health insurance.[30]

In that moment, Clinton won the presidency.

Clinton understood that the secret to Reagan's success lay not only in empathy but also in using a powerful script. In the Reagan years, those scripts were his speeches, especially the State of the Union addresses given before a joint session of Congress. Each year, the House of Representatives was transformed into a theater in which Reagan eschewed drab legislative proposals and told personal stories about heroic citizens with the central characters sitting in the First Lady's box. In his 1982 speech, for example, the Great Communicator hailed Lenny Skutnik, who saw a woman lose her grip on a helicopter line after an airplane crashed into the Potomac River and dove into the icy waters to rescue her.[31] Two years later he lauded Sergeant Stephen Trujillo, an Army medic who risked his life saving his wounded comrades in Grenada.[32] In 1985, Reagan praised Jean Nguyen, a Vietnamese refugee who had graduated from West Point, and Mother Hale, a Harlem resident who cared for drug-addicted infants.[33] The following year he hailed Tyrone Ford, a twelve-year-old music prodigy; Shelby Butler, a thirteen-year-old school crossing guard who rescued a classmate from an errant school bus; and Trevor Ferrell, a thirteen-year-old who helped the homeless.[34] To Reagan, these stories were parables with a common theme: "For us, faith, work, family, neighborhood, freedom, and peace are not just words; they're expressions of what America means, definitions of what makes us a good and loving people."[35]

Bill Clinton understood. Like Reagan, Clinton used his State of the Union addresses to tell heroic tales. In his 1995 speech, Clinton told not one story, but *six*. There was Lynn Woolsey, a single mother from California who found her way off welfare to become a member of Congress. Then came Cindy Perry, a mother of four who passed her high school equivalency exam and taught second-graders in rural Kentucky. Next was Steven Bishop, the police chief of Kansas City, Missouri, an AmeriCorps volunteer, and an innovator in community policing. Then, Corporal Gregory Depestre, a Haitian-American who was part of the U.S. force that landed in Haiti, was asked to stand. His commander in chief took note: "We must be the only country in the world that could have gone to Haiti and taken Haitian Americans there who could speak the language and talk to the people, and he was one of them, and we're proud of him." Clinton praised the Reverends John and Diana Cherry, whose church had grown to 17,000 members and expanded into the high-crime and drug-infested neighborhoods of Washington, D.C. Finally, Clinton recognized Jack Lucas, a World War Two veteran from Hattiesburg, Mississippi. Lucas was badly wounded at Iwo Jima after he threw himself on two grenades and saved the lives of three of his fellow soldiers. Only seventeen at the time, Lucas miraculously survived and became the youngest citizen to win the Congressional Medal of Honor. For Clinton, the moral lesson contained in each of these stories was clear:

> We all gain when we give and we reap what we sow. That's at the heart of this New Covenant: responsibility, opportunity, and citizenship. More than stale chapters in some remote civics book they are still the virtues by which we can fulfill ourselves and reach our God-given potential and be like them, and also to fulfill the eternal promise of this country, the enduring dream from that first and most sacred covenant. I believe every person in this country still believes that we are created equal, and given by our Creator the right to life, liberty, and the pursuit of happiness. This is a very great country and our best days are still to come.[36]

Like Reagan, Clinton's State of the Union addresses were a tour de force. Late into his second term, as he continued to invoke his New Covenant mantra, Clinton's poll ratings skyrocketed. After leaving the stage of his 1998 State of the Union address (just as the Monica Lewinsky affair was breaking), 79 percent liked what Clinton said; two-thirds said he held their attention; and an equal number approved of the way Clinton was handling his job—figures that matched Ronald Reagan at his zenith.[37] Listening to one of Clinton's hour-long State of the Union speeches, House Speaker Newt Gingrich thought to himself: "We're dead. There's no way we're going to beat this guy."[38] *Newsweek*'s Jonathan Alter wrote that "when the history of the latter part of this century is written, these two authentic actors

[Ronald Reagan and Bill Clinton] will be the only ones living large in the theater of our public imagination."[39]

GOP Agonistes

In 1992, Reagan advisor Richard Wirthlin was envious, noting that Clinton had "cleaned our clocks" on values issues.[40] Clinton's appropriation of Reagan-like rhetoric proved the Comeback Kid had learned valuable lessons from the Great Communicator. Ending his campaign that year, Clinton did his best Reagan-like impression:

> I believe America is a nation of boundless hopes and endless dreams. And the only limit to what we can do is what our leaders ask of us, and what we are willing to ask of ourselves. I believe in America. . . . Together we can do it.[41]

Shortly after claiming victory, Clinton met with Reagan, who grudgingly offered the president-elect a large jar of his favorite brand of jelly beans—a container Clinton kept in the Oval Office, untouched, until his last day. Wanting to learn more lessons from the Great Communicator, the Comeback Kid left the meeting disappointed. Like so many others who encountered Reagan, Clinton found him remote:

> Reagan was something of a mystery to me, at once friendly and distant. I was never sure how much he knew about the human consequences of his harshest policies, or whether he was using the hard-core right or was being used by them; the books don't give a definitive answer, and because he developed Alzheimer's disease, we'll probably never know. Regardless, his own life is both more interesting and more mysterious than the movies he made.[42]

The arrival of the Clintons at 1600 Pennsylvania Avenue—replete with Reagan's jelly bean jar gift in hand—was an enormous irritant to Republicans. To them, Bill and Hillary Clinton represented the worst of the excesses of the 1960s. As the first Baby Boomer to secure a major party nomination for president, Clinton was subjected to a series of questions that created doubts about his capacity to serve. In an interview with *60 Minutes*, Clinton tacitly admitted that he had not always been faithful to his wife, after Hillary Clinton emphatically declared that she was not "some little woman standing by my man like Tammy Wynette." Later, Clinton acknowledged experimenting "a time or two" with marijuana, although he "didn't inhale." The press discovered that Clinton avoided military service during the Vietnam War by winning a student deferment, and that he had undertaken a number of contorted efforts to obtain it. At the 1992 Republican

National Convention, Patrick J. Buchanan excoriated both Bill and Hillary Clinton, comparing them to an overzealous law firm:

> The agenda Clinton & Clinton would impose on America—abortion on demand, a litmus test for the Supreme Court, homosexual rights, discrimination against religious schools, women in combat—that's change, all right. But it is not the change America wants. It is not the kind of change America needs. And it is not the kind of change we can tolerate in a nation that we still call God's country. . . . There is a religious war going on in our country for the soul of America. It is a cultural war, as critical to the kind of nation we will one day be as was the Cold War itself. And in that struggle for the soul of America, Clinton & Clinton are on the other side, and George Bush is on our side.[43]

Bill Clinton's 1992 victory disrupted the Republicans' sense of entitlement that the presidency belonged to them. Not only had a Democrat evicted them from the White House, it was someone whose moral character they despised. Looking back, Clinton recalled:

> They figured there'd never be another Democratic president. I really think a lot of them thought they could hold the White House until a third party came along to basically offer a competing vision. So they just never saw me as a legitimate person.[44]

These feelings became exacerbated during the Monica Lewinsky scandal. Former two-time GOP presidential candidate Lamar Alexander said of Clinton: "If he were the head of a large company, he'd be fired. If he were a Cabinet officer, he'd be indicted. If he were a military commander, he'd be court-martialed."[45] Former vice president Dan Quayle quipped: "My friends, I'm proud to announce that I have a very tough anti-crime proposal for our party. And here's the centerpiece of our anti-crime plan: Three interns and you're out!"[46] White House press secretary Mike McCurry poignantly noted that the only way Republicans could win was to "totally destroy [Clinton] as a human being."[47]

Even so, voters rallied to Clinton's defense: two-thirds wanted him to remain at the helm, and 62 percent expressed confidence he was up to the job.[48] In the 1998 midterm elections, Democrats *gained* five House seats—the first time a party had gained in its sixth year of power since Thomas Jefferson's Democratic-Republican Party added House seats in the midterm election of 1822. The better Clinton did, the more infuriated and envious Republicans became. As the impeachment saga concluded, Republican pollster Frank Luntz offered Clinton grudging praise: "Reagan was likeable. People don't like Bill Clinton, and yet they follow him."[49]

One reason voters were willing to follow Clinton was because he was lucky in who his enemies were. Collectively, the Newt Gingriches, Rush Limbaughs, Pat Robertsons, and other assorted Clinton-haters constituted the most unappealing opposition since the obdurate Landonites who railed against Franklin D. Roosevelt's New Deal. One particular Clinton-hater, special prosecutor Kenneth Starr, was singled out by voters for condemnation: 52 percent believed that Starr should immediately cease and desist prosecuting Clinton, and 64 percent said he inappropriately called Monica Lewinsky's mother before the grand jury to testify against her daughter.[50] As Starr continued undeterred, Republican rhetoric became even more strident. Dan Burton, chairman of the House Government Reform and Oversight Committee, called Clinton a "scumbag," adding, "That's why I'm out to get him."[51] Mark Corallo, a senior aide to House Speaker-designate Bob Livingston, urged the Republican leadership to remain vigilant, telling Livingston, "Boss, we have a *rapist* in the White House."[52] Clinton strategist James Carville delighted in such name-calling, saying of Starr: "How could you have a better guy there? You've got a guy investigating you that two-thirds of the country hates."[53] But none of this stopped House Republicans from impeaching Clinton—an embarrassment he wore as a badge of honor while denouncing "the politics of personal destruction."[54] Once more, Clinton had defied the conventional rules of politics: 82 percent "disagreed strongly" with the Republican-led vote to impeach Clinton, and 61 percent described the vote as "partisan politics."[55]

Whether by design or inadvertently, Bill Clinton led Republicans to pursue a values strategy that was the polar opposite of Ronald Reagan's. Throughout his career, Reagan extolled his middle-class suburban (and mostly white) audiences—believing that if only someone who shared their values was elected, seemingly intractable problems would give way to commonsense solutions. Bill Clinton absorbed the same lesson, having an uncanny ability to read his audiences. Artfully tacking here and there, Clinton made sure never to leave a room without finding some area of agreement, even from people who swore they would never vote for him. This infuriated Republicans, who inverted Reagan's values strategy from complimenting the audience into one that denounced their opponents who, they claimed, did not share their values.

The first time this happened was in 1988, when George H. W. Bush tarred and feathered Massachusetts governor Michael Dukakis as being un-American. That year, the Bush campaign invited two dozen residents of Paramus, New Jersey, to a local hotel to talk about the candidates, paying each twenty-five dollars and dividing them into two groups. Most were blue-collar workers and Roman Catholics, many of whom had voted for Ronald Reagan. When asked how they planned to vote, a majority answered, "Dukakis," even though most were only dimly aware of his background. Because these were representative target voters whom Bush had to win over, the moderator began probing for issues that would separate them from Dukakis. Each thrust was parried until the moderator asked, "What if I told you that Dukakis vetoed a bill requiring schoolchildren to say the Pledge of Allegiance? Or that he was against the death penalty? Or that he gave weekend furloughs to first-degree murderers?" One exclaimed, "He's a liberal!" Another retorted, "If those are really his positions, I'd have a hard time supporting him." Forty percent in one group and 60 percent in another switched their votes on the spot.[56] The Bush campaign had its strategy, and it was able to turn a summertime 17-point deficit into an 8-point win on Election Day.[57] After the election, Dukakis strategist John Sasso reflected on the lessons learned:

> [I]t is potentially dangerous to take for granted that voters will automatically assume the Democratic candidate holds dear the country's basic values: God, patriotism, family, and freedom. In some historically perverse way, Democrats must—at least for now—work hard to somehow prove they are as politically wholesome and decent as Republicans.[58]

By 1994, Republicans had perfected their strategy. Newt Gingrich accused Bill Clinton of advocating a "multi-cultural nihilistic hedonism that is inherently destructive of a healthy society."[59] Gingrich advised his fellow GOP congressional candidates to use "contrast words" such as "decay," "failure," "shallow," "traitors," "pathetic," "self-serving," "criminal rights," "incompetent," and "sick" to label their Democratic opponents.[60] Republicans took Gingrich's advice with gusto and ramped up the culture wars using a simplistic slogan: "God, Guns, and Gays." In a single stroke, Clinton was depicted as anti-religious; his support of the Brady Bill made him anti-gun; and his military induction "don't ask, don't tell" policy made him pro-gay. Clinton immediately saw that the core of Gingrich's strategy

> was not just that his ideas were better than ours; he said his *values* were better than ours, because Democrats were weak on family, work, welfare, crime, and defense, and because being crippled by the self-indulgent sixties, we couldn't draw distinctions between right and wrong.[61]

As if to make Clinton's point, Gingrich told a meeting of interest group lobbyists that the Clinton administration was the "enemy of normal Americans"—meaning the un-young, un-poor, and un-black.[62]

"This Is Not Reagan's Party"

This inverted values strategy backfired on the Republican Party. In 1996, Clinton won 31 states (and the District of Columbia) and 379 electoral votes—thereby becoming the first Democrat to secure a second term since

Franklin D. Roosevelt. His opponent, Bob Dole, sensed a lack of appreciation for his long party service, and promised his fellow Republicans, "If that's what you want, I'll be another Ronald Reagan."[63] To that end, Dole reversed his long-standing opposition to federal deficits and supported an across-the-board 15 percent tax cut. But Dole was no Reagan. For one thing, the seventy-three-year-old Dole looked and acted his age—an unflattering image when juxtaposed against the youthful, vigorous Clinton. In an era when the Internet was becoming an important political tool, Dole actually gave the wrong website address for his campaign during one of the televised debates. Simon Rosenberg of the centrist New Democrat Network observed, "For a newer, younger America, Bob Dole was always a black and white movie in a color age."[64] Don Sipple, a media strategist fired by Dole, told *Newsweek*:

> This is a very good, very decent man. Noble. But my inescapable conclusion is that his clock stopped in the late 1950s or early 1960s. He is not a man of this time. . . . He thought the presidency was a reward system and he was next in line for the ring.[65]

After the election, Republicans comforted themselves with the knowledge that Bill Clinton was a minority president—capturing just 43 percent and 49 percent of the vote respectively in 1992 and 1996. But, in reality, the double losses of George H. W. Bush and Bob Dole signaled an important *Republican Party* problem when it came to winning the presidency. By any measure, George Bush's 37 percent in 1992 and Bob Dole's 41 percent in 1996 were dismal showings. Many chose to explain away the poor numbers by arguing that third-party candidate Ross Perot had lured away Republican-minded voters, even though there was no empirical evidence to support this hypothesis. George W. Bush fared only a bit better: winning 48 percent of the popular vote in 2000, and 51 percent in 2004—the latter at a time when Bush was a war president following the September 11, 2001, terrorist attacks. After the second Bush, presidential politics reverted to normal, with John McCain winning 46 percent of the popular vote, and Mitt Romney scoring 47 percent.

Shortly after the 1996 balloting, former New Hampshire governor Steve Merrill declared: "It is time for reflection in our party. The losses we've suffered at the presidential level should cause us to reflect that we really have not explained our vision of the future as well as we should have."[66] Yet such reflection was not forthcoming. And any future ruminations were deferred by the disputatious election of 2000. Looking back, it took the Supreme Court to put George W. Bush into the White House. That year, Bush lost the popular vote and barely won in the electoral college (by one vote)—and this happened only after the Supreme Court placed the disputed electoral votes from Florida into the Republican column. Meanwhile, like Democrats in the

1980s, Republicans contented themselves by retaining their House majorities. MSNBC host and former congressman Joe Scarborough noted that by 1994 "a new Republican congressional majority would soon arise . . . but this new Republican Party would trade the power of the presidency for the speaker's gavel. . . . " Scarborough concluded: "That exchange seems about as balanced as the one that gave Dutch traders possession of Manhattan in 1626 for beads worth twenty-four dollars. The only question now is when Republicans will realize that they have been scammed."[67]

In many ways, it's a question that still haunts the GOP. A dozen years after leaving the White House, Republican anger at Bill Clinton still lingers. Kentucky senator and likely 2016 GOP presidential candidate Rand Paul has accused Clinton of "predatory behavior." Missouri Republican Todd Akin—whose use of the term "legitimate rape" led to his defeat in 2012—recently reminded Fox News viewers of Clinton's "long history of sexual abuse and indecency."[68] For his part, Clinton continues to castigate Republicans for their intolerance. On the hustings in 2013 for Democrat Terry McAuliffe (who was campaigning to be Virginia governor against GOP conservative culture warrior Ken Cuccinelli), Clinton told voters:

> If we become ideological, then we're blind to evidence. We can only hear people who already agree with us. We think we know everything right now, we've got nothing to learn from anybody, and the most important thing we can do is impose our views on everybody else. And you can choose that course here. But I'm telling you it doesn't work. . . . The only thing that works is cooperation.[69]

But the longer Republicans remain excluded from the presidency, the greater difficulty they have refraining from inflammatory rhetoric aimed at Democrats *and Republicans*. In 2014, 57 percent of Republicans agreed with former GOP vice presidential candidate Sarah Palin that Barack Obama deserved impeachment.[70] Believing that impeachment was too drastic a step, House Speaker John Boehner opted to sue Obama over the delayed implementation of the employer mandate in the Affordable Care Act—a move that drew widespread public denunciation: 51 percent believed the lawsuit to be a "political stunt"; 46 percent said it made them less likely to support the GOP; 58 percent said it would not improve their lives; and 63 percent wanted Congress to focus on creating jobs.[71] In the meantime, both parties are fund-raising from their respective bases, which are either angry with Obama (Republicans) or outraged at the intransigence of the GOP (Democrats).

GOP anger at Barack Obama was exacerbated by Obama's decision to sign an executive order that would allow up to five million undocumented immigrants to remain in the United States without any threat of prosecution. Republican congressional leaders warned Obama not to take action, and they promised retribution, with newly minted Senate Majority Leader

Mitch McConnell warning that Obama's actions were akin to "waving a red flag in front of a bull."[72] Even as GOP leaders promised action, they tried to contain their rhetoric, knowing that Mitt Romney's "self-deportation" comment gave Obama and the Democrats a weapon with which to skewer him in the 2012 general election. The problem, however, is that the GOP base is unwilling to give Obama any ground on this issue. Polls conducted by Stanley Greenberg and James Carville find that 76 percent of Tea Party supporters and 67 percent of evangelicals are "very cool" to the presence of undocumented immigrants in the United States. They conclude, "Hostility to undocumented immigrants and immigration reform are big hurdles at the heart of the Republican party."[73]

The Republican antipathy toward Obama—that includes calls for his impeachment and lawsuits against the president—are the latest illustrations of a GOP anger that has only grown more fierce since the Clinton years. Many Republicans now refer to Obama as an "emperor," arguing that his use of executive authority exceeds the limits imposed on the president by the U.S. Constitution. Thus, Republicans turn to the judiciary (still dominated at the Supreme Court level by Republican presidential appointees) in the hopes of resolving their differences.

But unlike the Clinton years, Republicans are also aiming their anger against fellow Republicans. A recent example occurred in the 2014 Mississippi Republican U.S. senatorial primary. State senator Chris McDaniel argued that long-time incumbent Thad Cochran had become too cozy with the Washington, D.C. establishment, and that his legislative logrolling on behalf of his poor state was anathema to conservative ideals. Cochran bested McDaniel in a primary runoff—thanks to support from crossover Democrats, most of them African-American—but the Tea Party challenger refused to endorse Cochran, lamenting that something more had been lost than his political ambitions:

> For too long, conservatives have needed a voice; someone to stand for them; someone to fight for them. . . . The party that I was born with, the party that I joined when I was thirteen years old, was the party of a man, a former actor from California, named Ronald Reagan. One afternoon my father called me into the room and said, "You've got to watch this. You've got to see what this man is saying." And there on the TV was this former actor from California, and he looked right at me, he looked right at my father . . . and he said things to us that intuitively made sense. He talked about liberty and freedom. He talked about balanced budgets. He talked about traditional values and personal responsibility. And my father looked at me and said, "Son, we must be Republicans." And indeed we were, and are.
>
> That's the party I joined. That's the party I've always been a part of. It was the party of principle at one point. A party of courage at one point.

It was Reagan who said we will be a party of bold colors, not pastels.

And yet, there are millions of people who feel like strangers in their own party. . . . There is nothing dangerous or extreme about wanting to balance the budget. There was nothing dangerous or extreme about defending the Constitution and the civil liberties therein. And there is nothing strange at all about standing as a people of faith for a country that we built, that we believe in.

But there is something a bit strange, there is something a bit unusual, about a Republican primary that is decided by liberal Democrats. So much for bold colors. So much for principle. I guess they can take some consolation in the fact that they did something tonight by once again compromising, by once again reaching across the aisle, by once again abandoning the conservative moment. I would like to know which part of that strategy today our Republican friends endorsed. I would like to know which part of that strategy today our statewide officials endorsed. This is *not* the party of Reagan.[74]

As Republicans denounce their Democratic rivals (and even other Republicans), their anger at Clinton has been muted by a grudging admiration—along with a hope that a Clinton-like figure can rescue the GOP from its present difficulties. Remembering Clinton, conservative commentator Kate O'Beirne believes there is a lesson for her party, "A talented politician can turn things around pretty handily, right?"[75] Alas, for the GOP there is no Clinton in sight. Clinton strategist Paul Begala once said of his old boss, "He was the best that ever was."[76] Although Clinton's successors, George W. Bush and Barack Obama, were adroit, they were hardly his equal. In an aptly titled book, *The Natural*, Joe Klein wrote of Clinton: "He was, without question, the most talented politician of his generation. At close range, his skills could be breathtaking: He was always the center of attention; he filled any room he entered."[77]

Bill Clinton's legacy does not lie in the scandals that beset his administration. Decades later, the Monica Lewinsky episode seems to be all-but-forgotten in the wake of a Great Recession, two wars, and an ongoing terrorist threat. Republican pollster Kellyanne Conway says the words "Monica" and "liberal" rarely come up in her polls about Clinton. Instead, the words "global" and "philanthropic" are the words most frequently mentioned.[78] Looking back, Americans remember Clinton fondly: 74 percent approve of the way he handled his job as president; 64 percent have a favorable impression of him; 55 percent believe he was an "outstanding" or "above average" president; and 42 percent name him as the most admired president of the past twenty-five years, far ahead of Barack Obama (18 percent) and George W. Bush (17 percent).[79] When the first line of Clinton's obituary is written, it is less likely to contain the words, "First president to be impeached since Andrew Johnson," and more likely to say, "He rescued the Democratic

Party and began a new era in American politics." Clinton often liked to say that his administration was "a bridge to the twenty-first century."[80] But his bridge building not only involved reshaping the U.S. economy for a global era, it meant constructing a new Democratic majority based upon a changing demography. Looking back, Clinton was instrumental in relegating Reagan Country to the history books, and he helped create a presidential fortress that twenty-first century Republicans would find difficult to scale.

Notes

1 Quoted in David S. Broder, "A Prescient Assessment of Reagan," *Washington Post*, December 9, 1992, A-23.
2 This was eerily similar to Lyndon B. Johnson's 1964 grandiose pledge to create a "Great Society." Like Bush, the Johnson presidency was already set on a trajectory to disappointment.
3 "An Interview with Bush," *Newsweek*, January 30, 1988, 32.
4 Market Opinion Research, poll, December 10–13, 1988. Text of question: "Do you feel things are moving in the right direction or do you feel things are pretty seriously off on the wrong track?" Right direction, 53 percent; wrong track, 37 percent; don't know/refused, 9 percent.
5 Ronald Reagan, Remarks at the Republican National Convention, New Orleans, August 15, 1988.
6 George H. W. Bush, Acceptance Speech, Republican National Convention, New Orleans, August 18, 1988.
7 Fred Barnes, "Campaign '88: Bush's Mandate," *New Republic*, November 14, 1988, 12.
8 David A. Stockman, *The Triumph of Politics: Why the Reagan Revolution Failed* (New York: Harper & Row, 1986), 90.
9 Donald T. Regan, *For the Record: From Wall Street to Washington* (San Diego: Harcourt Brace Jovanovich, 1988), 188.
10 George H. W. Bush, CNN interview, June 15, 1992.
11 See Bernard Weintraub, "Notebook: Reagan Amid 'All the Hoopla,' " *New York Times*, July 6, 1986, 16.
12 See John Kenneth White, *The New Politics of Old Values* (Hanover, New Hampshire: University Press of New England, 1988), 13–14.
13 John F. Kennedy, "Remarks to Delegates to the 18th Annual American Legion 'Boys Nation,' " Washington, D.C., July 24, 1963.
14 David Maraniss, *First in His Class: The Biography of Bill Clinton* (New York: Simon and Schuster, 1995), 12.
15 Ibid., 44.
16 Ibid., 68.
17 Quoted in Broder, "A Prescient Assessment of Reagan."
18 Maraniss, *First in His Class*, 437.
19 Gallup poll, March 1, 1991. Text of question: "Do you approve or disapprove of the way George Bush is handling his job as President?" Approve, 89 percent; disapprove, 8 percent; don't know, 3 percent.
20 Quoted in Dan Balz, "Picking Up Votes in a Maze of Ideals," *Washington Post*, October 5, 1998, A-1.
21 Quoted in Wilson Carey McWilliams, *Beyond the Politics of Disappointment? American Elections, 1980–1998* (New York: Chatham House Publishers, 2000), 49.

22 "Excerpts from Interview with Clinton on Goals for Presidency," *New York Times*, June 28, 1992, 17.

23 David Kusnet, *Speaking American: How the Democrats Can Win in the Nineties* (New York: Thunder's Mouth Press, 1992).

24 Michael Deaver once asked Reagan how he perfected his salute. Reagan replied, "You bring it up like honey and shake it off like shit." See Michael K. Deaver, *A Different Drummer: My Thirty Years with Ronald Reagan* (New York: Harper-Collins, 2001), 88.

25 "Ronald Reagan and David Brinkley: A Farewell Interview," ABC News, December 22, 1988.

26 Quoted in Joe Klein, *The Natural: The Misunderstood Presidency of Bill Clinton* (New York: Doubleday, 2002), 38–39.

27 Ibid., 39.

28 Quoted in Lou Cannon, "Why the Band Has Stopped Playing for Ronald Reagan," *Washington Post*, December 21, 1986, D-1.

29 "The 1992 Campaign; Transcript of 2nd TV Debate Between Bush, Clinton, and Perot," *New York Times*, October 16, 1992.

30 Ibid.

31 Ronald Reagan, State of the Union Address, Washington, D.C., January 26, 1982.

32 Ronald Reagan, State of the Union Address, Washington, D.C., January 25, 1984.

33 Ronald Reagan, State of the Union Address, Washington, D.C., February 6, 1985.

34 Ronald Reagan, State of the Union Address, Washington, D.C., February 4, 1986.

35 Reagan, State of the Union Address, January 25, 1984.

36 Bill Clinton, State of the Union Address, Washington, D.C., January 24, 1995.

37 ABC News, poll, January 27, 1998. Text of question: "Would you say you approve or disapprove of most of what Bill Clinton said in his State of the Union speech?" Approve, 79 percent; disapprove 15, percent; no opinion, 7 percent. Gallup poll, January 28, 1998. Text of question: "Do you approve or disapprove of the way Bill Clinton is handling his job as president?" Approve, 67 percent; disapprove, 28 percent; no opinion, 5 percent.

38 Quoted in Klein, *The Natural*, 14.

39 Jonathan Alter, "Playing the Gipper Card," *Newsweek*, February 1, 1999.

40 Richard B. Wirthlin, lecture, Catholic University of America, Washington, D.C., September 29, 1992.

41 Bill Clinton, Election Eve Address, NBC broadcast, November 2, 1992.

42 Bill Clinton, *My Life* (New York: Alfred A. Knopf, 2004), 345–346.

43 Patrick J. Buchanan, Speech to the Republican National Convention, Houston, Texas, August 17, 1992.

44 Quoted in Klein, *The Natural*, 86.

45 Quoted in Richard L. Berke, "Republicans End Silence on Troubles of President," *New York Times*, March 1, 1998, 20.

46 Ibid.

47 Quoted in Lars-Erik Nelson, "The Republicans' War," *New York Review of Books*, February 4, 1999, 6.

48 Gallup/CNN/*USA Today*, poll, January 25–26, 1998. Sixty-eight percent said it would be better for the country if Clinton remained in office; 26 percent wanted Clinton to leave. Sixty-two percent expressed confidence in Clinton's ability to carry out his duties; 37 percent were not confident.

49 Quoted in Evan Thomas, Karen Breslau, Debra Rosenberg, Leslie Kaufman, and Andrew Murr, *Back from the Dead: How Clinton Survived the Republican Revolution* (New York: Atlantic Monthly Press, 1997), 209.

50 Gallup/CNN/*USA Today*, poll, February 13–15, 1998. Text of questions: "Do you think Kenneth Starr should continue his investigation into the allegations

surrounding Clinton and Monica Lewinsky or should he stop the investigation now?" Continue, 44 percent; stop it now, 52 percent; no opinion, 4 percent. "Regardless of your opinion of Ken Starr or the Lewinsky controversy, do you think it is appropriate or inappropriate that Monica Lewinsky's mother was called as a witness to testify about matters relating to her daughter?" Appropriate, 31 percent; inappropriate, 64 percent; no opinion, 5 percent.

51 "Burton Draws Fire for Clinton 'Scumbag' Remark," CNN/AllPolitics, homepage, April 22, 1998.

52 A reference to a charge that Clinton had raped a woman in Arkansas two decades before. See Peter Baker, *The Breach: Inside the Impeachment and Trial of William Jefferson Clinton* (New York: Scribner, 2000), 16.

53 Quoted in Bob Woodward and Peter Baker, "Behind Calm Air, President Hides Rage Over Starr," *Washington Post*, March 1, 1998, A-1.

54 Bill Clinton, Remarks Following the House of Representatives Vote on Impeachment, Washington, D.C., December 19, 1998.

55 CBS News/*New York Times*, poll, December 19–20, 1998. Text of question: "Yesterday, the U.S. House of Representatives voted to impeach President Clinton and send articles of impeachment to the Senate for a trial. Do you approve or disapprove of the House voting to impeach President Clinton? (If disapprove, ask:) Do you disapprove strongly or only somewhat?" Disapprove strongly, 82 percent; disapprove somewhat, 16 percent; don't know/no answer, 2 percent. ABC News/*Washington Post*, poll, December 19–20, 1998. Text of question: "Do you think the House voted to impeach Clinton on the basis of the facts of the case, or on the basis of partisan politics?" Facts of case, 36 percent; partisan politics, 61 percent; no opinion, 3 percent.

56 Accounts of this session are taken from Donald Morrison, *The Winning of the White House, 1988* (New York: Time, 1988), 219; and "How Bush Won: The Inside Story of Campaign '88," *Newsweek*, November 21, 1988, 100.

57 Gallup poll, July 22–24, 1988. Text of question: "Suppose the presidential election were being held today. If George Bush were the Republican candidate and Michael Dukakis were the Democratic candidate, which would you like to see win?" Dukakis, 54 percent; Bush, 37 percent; undecided, 9 percent.

58 John Sasso, World Trade Center Club Speech, Boston, Massachusetts, January 19, 1989.

59 Quoted in Norman Mailer, "By Heaven Inspired," *New Republic*, October 12, 1992, 30.

60 Quoted in Clyde Wilcox, *The Latest American Revolution? The 1994 Elections and Their Implications for Governance* (New York: St. Martin's Press, 1995), 46.

61 Clinton, *My Life*, 635.

62 Quoted in John Kenneth White, "Reviving the Political Parties: What Must Be Done?" in John Kenneth White and John C. Green, eds., *The Politics of Ideas* (Lanham, Maryland: Rowman and Littlefield, 1995), 21.

63 Samuel G. Freedman, "Why Bob Dole Can't Be Reagan," *New York Times*, October 27, 1996, E-4.

64 Quoted in Evan Thomas, "The Small Deal," *Newsweek*, November 18, 1996.

65 Quoted in Jonathan Alter, "A Man Not of His Time," *Newsweek*, November 4, 1996, 30.

66 Quoted in David S. Broder, "Factions, Competing Ideologies Challenge Coalition Builders," *Washington Post*, November 7, 1996.

67 Joe Scarborough, *The Right Path: From Ike to Reagan, How Republicans Once Mastered Politics—and Can Again* (New York: Random House, 2013), 138.

68 Maureen Dowd, "A Popular President," *New York Times*, July 19, 2014.

69 See http://www.theatlantic.com/politics/archive/2013/10/the-redemption-of-clintonism/280933.

70 Sarah Palin, "It's Time to Impeach Obama," *Breitbart News*, July 8, 2014. See http://www.breitbart.com/Big-Government/2014/07/08/Exclusive-Sarah-Palin-Time-to-Impeach-President-Obama. CNN/Opinion Research Corporation, poll, July 18–20, 2014. Text of question: "Based on what you have read or heard, do you believe that President Obama should be impeached and removed from office, or don't you feel that way?" Republicans: Should be impeached, 57 percent; don't feel that way, 42 percent; no opinion, 1 percent.

71 Justin Sink, "Poll: Boehner Lawsuit a 'Political Stunt,'" *The Hill*, July 14, 2014. See http://thehill.com/blogs/blog-briefing-room/news/212243-poll-boehner-lawsuit-v-obama-a-political-stunt

72 See Brendan Bordelon, "McConnell Warns Obama on Amnesty: 'Like Waving a Red Flag in Front of a Bull,'" *National Review Online*, November 5, 2014.

73 Stanley Greenberg and James Carville, "Why the GOP Really Hates the Immigration Executive Order," Democracy Corps memo, November 21, 2014.

74 Chris McDaniel, Concession Speech, Hattiesburg, Mississippi, June 24, 2014.

75 Quoted in John Harwood, "Shut Out of White House, G.O.P. Looks to Democrats of 1992," *New York Times*, July 4, 2014.

76 Quoted in Klein, *The Natural*, 42.

77 Ibid., 3.

78 Quoted in Dowd, "A Popular President."

79 CNN/Opinion Research Corporation, poll, November 18–20, 2013. Text of question: "From what you have heard, read, or remember about some of our past presidents, please tell me if you approve or disapprove of the way each of the following handled their job as president? . . . Bill Clinton." Approve, 74 percent; disapprove, 26 percent; no opinion, 1 percent. Gallup poll, June 5–8, 2014. Text of question: "Next we'd like to get your overall opinion of some people in the news. As I read each name, please say if you have a favorable or unfavorable opinion of these people—or if you have never heard of them. How about . . . Bill Clinton?" Favorable, 64 percent; unfavorable, 34 percent; no opinion, 2 percent. Gallup poll, November 7–10, 2013. Text of question: "How do you think each of the following presidents will go down in history—as an outstanding president, above average, average, below average, or poor? . . . Bill Clinton." Outstanding, 11 percent; above average, 44 percent; average, 29 percent; below average, 9 percent; poor, 6 percent; no opinion, 1 percent. See also Janet Hook, "Poll: Bill Clinton Most Admired President of Past Twenty-Five Years," *Washington Wire*, June 15, 2014.

80 See especially Bill Clinton, Acceptance Speech, Democratic National Convention, Chicago, August 29, 1996.

Chapter 3

Outmanned

Barack Obama and a New Politics of Demography

"We rely too hard on white guys for votes."
Ken Mehlman, former chair, Republican National Committee

June 13, 1998. Bill Clinton was escaping the dreadful present of a nation's capital obsessed with the Monica Lewinsky affair to focus on a more hopeful future. Traveling cross-country aboard Air Force One to give a commencement address at Portland State University, Clinton was already looking ahead to the next century and the kind of country the United States would be in it. That nation was going to be very different from the one both Clinton and his Baby Boomer contemporaries had known. Speaking before the mostly white graduates in a crowded university gymnasium, Clinton hailed the coming of a "third great revolution"—one as powerful as the American Revolution, which gave birth to the democratic ideas of the eighteenth and nineteenth centuries, and as formidable as the civil rights and women's rights revolutions that broadened the definition of personal liberties in the late twentieth. According to Clinton, this gathering revolution was being manned by an army of immigrants:

> Each year, nearly a million people come legally to America. Today, nearly one in ten people in America was born in another country; one in five schoolchildren are from immigrant families. Today, largely because of immigration, there is no majority race in Hawaii, or Houston, or New York City. Within five years, there will be no majority race in our largest state, California. In a little more than fifty years, there will be no majority race in the United States.[1]

For Clinton and his contemporaries, a rising tide of immigrants posed serious questions, the answers to which, he declared, "can either strengthen and unite us, or they can weaken and divide us."[2] For his part, Clinton gave an unequivocal response:

> I believe new immigrants are good for America. They are revitalizing our cities. They are building our new economy. They are strengthening

our ties to the global economy, just as earlier waves of immigrants settled the new frontier and powered the Industrial Revolution. They are
energizing our culture and broadening our vision of the world. They are
renewing our most basic values and reminding us all of what it truly
means to be an American.[3]

Clinton's plea that Americans should welcome new immigrants was not
widely shared at the time: 50 percent believed having so many foreign-
ers "weakens the American character";[4] 55 percent said controlling and
reducing illegal immigration should be a "very important" foreign policy
goal;[5] and 59 percent gave Clinton either "fair" or "poor" marks on handling the immigration issue.[6] Two years later, presidential candidate Patrick J. Buchanan was approached by many voters who collectively said,
"Pat, we're losing the country we grew up in."[7] One place where those
feelings were especially prevalent was in Gainesville, Georgia. Described as
the "Poultry Capital of the World," longtime resident Joe Merck observed
that his city was being "overrun" with Hispanics, adding: "We need to send
'em back home."[8] Despite such hostile receptions, waves of migrants continued to pour across U.S. borders during the Clinton years. But even as the
short-term immigration debate was heating up, a changing demography was
inexorably altering our long-term politics.

Future Faces: From White to Café au Lait

When Bill Clinton told the Portland University students that immigrants
would alter the country they knew, he spoke an important truth. The face of
the typical, mostly white American was being recast into a twenty-first century shade of bronze.[9] With each passing year, this transformation is becoming increasingly evident in the presidential electorate. Back when Ronald
Reagan was chosen in 1980, a whopping 89 percent of voters self-identified
as white; only 11 percent were African-American; and Hispanics accounted
for less than 1 percent.[10] By the time Barack Obama was first elected
twenty-eight years later, the number of white voters had fallen to 74 percent
while non-whites stood at 26 percent.[11] In 2012, the white vote fell once
more to 72 percent while non-whites rose to a record 28 percent.[12] The keys
to Obama's twin victories lay in these changing statistics. Put another way,
if the composition of both the 2008 and 2012 electorates had been as it
was when Reagan was chosen, Presidents John McCain and Mitt Romney
would be residing in the White House, and Barack Obama would still be a
backbencher U.S. senator from Illinois.

Hispanic migration to the United States began its steady march in 1965
when Lyndon B. Johnson signed an immigration reform bill into law. That
measure lifted the punitive quotas established in 1924, which had been
endorsed by a Republican-controlled Congress and president. The 1924
law was designed to curb a rise in immigration from eastern, central, and

southern Europe that had been underway for three decades and was viewed by many Republicans as potentially benefitting the Democratic Party—just as the earlier Irish migration that began in the 1840s eventually added to the Democrats' numbers.[13] In addition, the 1924 law severely restricted Hispanics, Asians, and Africans from gaining entrance to the United States. After Calvin Coolidge signed the legislation, just three countries (Germany, Britain, and Ireland) supplied 70 percent of all U.S. immigrants. In 1963, John F. Kennedy called the 1924 quotas "arbitrary" and "without basis in either logic or reason."[14] Assuming the presidency after Kennedy's assassination, Lyndon B. Johnson vowed to get Kennedy's desire for immigration reform translated into law, and he made good on his promise. Signing the bill at the feet of the Statue of Liberty (with New York U.S. senator Robert F. Kennedy in attendance), Johnson boasted that the new law

> corrects a cruel and enduring wrong in the conduct of the American nation. . . . No longer will an arbitrary quota system divide children from their parents, and separate brother from brother. No longer will the people of one nation be less welcome here than the people of another nation.[15]

Seeking to reassure those who worried about lifting the quotas, Johnson maintained that the new statute was not "revolutionary," adding: "It does not affect the lives of millions. It will not reshape the structure of our daily lives, or really add importantly to either our wealth or our power."[16]

Johnson was wrong. Beginning in 1965, a march of immigrants larger than any other in history crossed into U.S. borders. When Johnson's successor, Richard M. Nixon, took the oath of office in 1969, there were approximately 9.6 million foreign-born residing in the United States. By the time Barack Obama raised his hand to take the presidential oath forty-three years later, that number had risen to nearly 42 million.[17] Viewed from another perspective, a decade after Johnson signed the Hart-Cellar Act into law there were 400,000 persons entering the United States annually; by the 1980s, that figure rose to 800,000; and when Bill Clinton spoke to the graduates at Portland State University, the annual number of migrants exceeded 1,000,000.[18] Today, there are more foreign-born living in California (10.2 million) than there are people residing in all of New Jersey (8.8 million), and there are nearly as many foreign-born in New York State (4.2 million) as there are people in all of South Carolina (4.6 million).[19] Estimates are that by midcentury 162 million Americans (37 percent of the population) will be of "immigrant stock"—i.e., immigrants themselves or their U.S.-born children, the highest figure in U.S. history.[20]

Today, the Pew Hispanic Research Center estimates that there are 41.7 million immigrants residing in the United States. Of these, 11.7 million are *illegal*, 1.7 million are *temporary legal residents*, and 28.3 million are *legal residents*.[21] This proliferation of immigrants extends to all corners of the United States, and even into the U.S. military, where 69,300 soldiers are foreign-born—including 35,000 non-U.S. citizens who remain on active duty.[22] Their presence is found in the names of the war dead from Iraq and Afghanistan: Falaniko, Valdez, Perez, Ramos, and Le. In 2002, George W. Bush signed an executive order giving noncitizens an expedited path to citizenship if they served in the military. Since then, more than 37,000 soldiers have become citizens and naturalization ceremonies have been held around the world—including in the war zones of Iraq and Afghanistan.[23]

Many of these new arrivals are Hispanic. Since 1965, half of all new arrivals have been from Latin America.[24] In 2011, the U.S. Census Bureau reported that Latinos outnumbered blacks for the first time (52 million to 43.9 million) to become the nation's leading minority group.[25] Should present trends continue, it is estimated that Hispanics will approach 29 percent of the total population in 2050, and could even reach 33 percent by 2100.[26] And in another sign of the times, 60.6 million Americans speak a language other than English at home, with 37.5 million conversing in Spanish.[27] In New York City, half of all residents over five years old speak a language other than English at home (3.8 million people), and English-as-Second-Language classes offered in the city's libraries are filled to overflowing.[28]

Hispanics are not alone in coming to America. Asians have also substantially increased their presence—including Chinese, Japanese, Koreans, and Vietnamese (the latter beginning their journey after Johnson's failed war in Vietnam). Today, there are 17.3 million Asians residing in the United States, with 10.5 million of these being immigrants.[29] Prior to Johnson's 1965 law, prospective Asian immigrants were routinely discriminated against. According to the Pew Research Center's Paul Taylor,

> In the late nineteenth century, all immigration from China was explicitly prohibited by act of Congress; in the early twentieth century Indian-Americans had their official race designation changed from Asian to white and then back again; during World War Two, 120,000 law-aiding Japanese-Americans were rounded up and sent off to internment camps; and it was not until 1952 that Asian-American immigrants were permitted to apply for U.S. citizenship.[30]

Thanks to Johnson's reform, Asians have more than quintupled their numbers, rising from 5 percent in 1960 to 28 percent in 2009.[31] Even more significantly, recent census figures show Asians have surpassed Hispanics as the largest group of new immigrants to the United States.[32]

Bigger numbers mean that Asian migrants are making their presence felt politically. In Virginia, for example, Koreans demanded that school textbooks inform children that the Sea of Japan is also known as the East Sea. Koreans wanted the reference inserted to protest Japanese imperialism in the twentieth century. In 2014, Democratic governor Terry McAuliffe kept his promise to the Korean community and signed a law mandating such references.[33] That same year, first-time Republican congressional candidate Barbara Comstock told the local Korean Chamber of Commerce and the Organization of Korean Women, "You always have a seat at the table with the Republican party."[34] Local Republican strategist Chris LaCivita states the obvious: "To not have a minority outreach strategy is not to have a campaign."[35] Comstock won easily, beating her Democratic rival 57 percent to 40 percent.

Indian migrants are also a growing minority, with 1.9 million Indians living in the United States.[36] According to one estimate, 300,000 Indians work in California's Silicon Valley, earning a median income of $200,000 per year; another figure estimates that Indians own 30 percent of the nation's hotels and motels.[37] Commenting on the fact that Indian-Americans are the fastest-growing minority in his adopted home state of Delaware, Vice President Joseph Biden once observed, "You cannot go into a 7–11 or a Dunkin' Donuts unless you have a slight Indian accent."[38] In her victorious 2014 congressional campaign, Republican Barbara Comstock regularly visited ethnic events such as the Punjabi Mela Festival, a celebration of Indian and Pakistani culture.[39] Another sign of the increased Indian presence occurred when a daughter of Indian immigrants was crowned Miss America 2013.[40]

Other data provide several shards of evidence that the United States is rapidly becoming a multiracial, multiethnic society. In 2008, the Census Bureau issued a bulletin stating that by 2042 (eight years earlier than anticipated), whites will be the nation's *new minority*.[41] Four years later the Census Bureau announced that a majority of the nation's births (50.1 percent) were non-white—a first.[42] Moreover, survey research shows 80 percent of Americans say they have close friends from a different race; 75 percent would marry someone from a different race; and 52 percent have dated someone of a different race (with 65 percent of those eighteen to twenty-nine years old answering in the affirmative).[43]

The presence of so many new migrants is transforming the southern and western border states. California, for example, has seen its Anglo population fall to record lows thanks to waves of Hispanic immigrants. Today, only 46.7 percent of Californians are white; 32.4 percent are Hispanic.[44] Author Dale Maharidge writes that many white Californians are afraid to live in their new majority-minority state:

> They fear the change that seems to be transforming their state into something different from the rest of the United States. They fear losing not only their jobs but also their culture. Some feel that California will become a version of South Africa, in which whites will lose power when minorities are the majority.[45]

The changes happening in today's California will inevitably spread eastward: estimates are that by 2060, just 43 percent of the *entire* U.S. population will be white.[46]

Los Angeles is a microcosm of the demographic and political transformations that are rocking California and the rest of the nation. In its schools, 71.9 percent of the students are Hispanic; only 9.4 percent are white.[47] Some years earlier, writer Joan Didion observed that for many of Los Angeles's Anglos, Spanish had become "part of the ambient noise, the language spoken by the people who worked in the car wash and came to trim the trees and cleared the tables in restaurants."[48] Today, that "ambient noise" has reached a crescendo, as Hispanics grow in numbers and acquire both cultural and political power. In 2005, Antonio Villaraigosa became the first Latino mayor of Los Angeles since Cristol Aguilar left that office in 1872.[49] Striding to the microphone on election night, the new mayor thrilled the crowd by shouting, "Si, se puede!" ["Yes, we can!"][50]

Suburbs—places where second- and third-generation immigrants went to after living in major cities awhile—are now on the front lines of today's immigration wave. *New York Times* columnist David Brooks writes that when he once opened a local newspaper in Loudoun County, Virginia, the National Scholar Award winners included Kawi Cheung, Anastasia Cisneros Fraust, Dantam Do, Hugo Dubovy, and Maryanthe Malliaris.[51] From 2000–2010, the Hispanic population in this suburban Virginia county nearly *tripled*.[52] Nearby Fairfax County also saw its Hispanic population rise by 57 percent during the same period.[53] Prince William County followed a similar pattern, as the number of Hispanics in this suburb grew from 27,319 in 2000 to 81,460 in 2010.[54]

Even rural areas have witnessed a profound demographic transformation. In Marshalltown, Iowa (population 27,552), migrants from Villachuato, Mexico (population 15,000) hold 900 of the 1,600 jobs in the JBS Swift and Company meat-packing plant, the town's largest employer.[55] Bilingual signs proliferate in area groceries and banks; there is a Hispanic soccer league; a Hispanic festival; and Spanish Catholic masses are routine. But these changes have created tensions. On December 12, 2006, federal agents arrested ninety illegal JBS Swift and Company workers and transferred them to Camp Dodge in Johnston, Iowa. From there, the detained workers were either deported or moved to out-of-state detention centers.[56] In addition, four hundred other meatpacking workers (many of them Hispanic) either quit or were terminated, and JBS Swift and Company reported losses of $45 to $50 million (as five other Swift plants were raided on the same day).[57] Local businesses also suffered; homes were foreclosed; and new home sales plummeted. After the raid, one Latino declared: "Now I live in fear. I don't feel secure in my own house . . . and even when I just see a policeman, he arouses fear in me."[58] A white Anglo media person noted the rise in racial animosities:

People crawled out of the woodwork like you wouldn't believe. We ran a special section [in the paper] a year after the raids, and the number of comments—we actually had to disable comments on our website because of the problems we had with people complaining: "All you people do is write about the sad, sad story. Have you forgotten what the word 'illegal' means?"[59]

Still, the future continues to advance. One area is the increase in interracial marriage. In 1960, only 2.4 percent of all marriages were interracial; by 2011, that figure rose to 8.6 percent.[60] Moreover, just among the marriages performed in 2011, a record 15.5 percent of them were either interracial or interethnic.[61] Among the recent examples are newly minted medical school graduate Priscilla Chan, who married Facebook founder Mark Zuckerberg in 2012.[62] The children these marriages will inevitably produce further blurs racial self-identification and takes the United States further away from the nineteenth century concept of a white-black world. Ellis Cose, author of *Color Blind: Seeing Beyond Race in a Race-Obsessed World*, writes that race has become a "slippery slope," adding:

> Tomorrow's multi-racial people could just as easily become the next decade's something else. A name, in the end, is just a name. The problem is that we want those names to mean so much—even if the only result is a perpetuation of an ever-more refined kind of racial madness.[63]

Henry Pachon, president of the Tomas Rivera Policy Institute at the University of Southern California, says the combination of immigration and interracial marriage means " 'white' is going to get darker over the coming decade. People will legitimately call themselves white, but they may be a shade darker, a café au lait sort of look."[64] Pachon's observation is borne out in the U.S. census data. In 2010, 9 million respondents marked more than one racial category on their forms (selecting from a choice of fifteen different racial categories), up from 6.8 million in 2000 (the first time more than one choice was permitted).[65]

In many ways, Barack Obama personifies the demographic transformations from the twentieth into the twenty-first century. Obama is the offspring of a Kansas-born white woman and a Kenyan father. When his parents married in 1961, the best estimates are that only one marriage in one thousand was between a white and black person.[66] In addition, miscegenation laws prohibiting interracial marriage were still enforced in sixteen states.[67] As Obama remembered:

> In many parts of the South, my father could have been strung up from a tree for merely looking at my mother the wrong way; in the most sophisticated of northern cities, the hostile stares, the whispers, might have driven a woman in my mother's predicament into a back-alley abortion—or at the very least to a distant convent that could arrange for adoption. Their very image together would have been considered

lurid and perverse, a handy retort to the handful of softheaded liberals who supported a civil rights agenda.[68]

Today, Obama is much more than the offspring of a white woman and black man who self-identifies as black. Indeed, his family relations are extremely complicated, given his mother's subsequent marriage to an Indonesian man. As Obama once put it:

I have got a sister who is half-Indonesian, who is married to a Chinese Canadian. I have got a niece who looks like, you know, she's all mixed up. . . . I have got family members that look like Margaret Thatcher. I have got family members that look like Bernie Mac.[69]

In 2008, Obama told voters,

I think that if you can tell people, 'We have a president in the White House who still has a grandmother living in a hut on the shores of Lake Victoria and has a sister who's half-Indonesian, married to a Chinese-Canadian,' then they're going to think that he may have a better sense of what's going on in our lives and in our country. And they'd be right.[70]

Obama's racial heritage is hardly unusual. Indeed, a group of A-list celebrities lays claim to a mixed (or multi-) race heritage, including Halle Berry, Beyoncé, Keanu Reeves, Selma Hayek, Derek Jeter, Mariah Carey, Norah Jones, and Tiger Woods.[71] These are the faces of the future.

As whites decline in population—thanks to what Ben J. Wattenberg describes as a "birth dearth"—there is an increasing fear among Tea Party Republicans about living in a majority-minority country.[72] According to one survey, nearly two-thirds of Tea Party Republicans want to eliminate birthright citizenship, which is guaranteed under the U.S. Constitution, and 82 percent report feeling "anxious or fearful" about undocumented immigrants. The result is a kind of self-imposed isolation that is reinforced by the congressional maps. In 2014, only 13 of 234 Republican-held congressional districts were majority-minority (5 percent). By contrast, 49 percent of Democratic districts were majority-minority. Even more telling, two-thirds of the Republican-held seats had populations that were more than 70 percent white. By contrast, fewer than three in ten Democratic seats were 70 percent white.[73] Put another way, Republican districts more closely resembled Ronald Reagan's America while Democratic districts lay in Barack Obama's America. This type of demographic gerrymandering that is designed to permit Republican candidates to compete and win in Reagan's America means that there is little incentive for Republican lawmakers to tackle immigration reform. When it comes to race, congressional Republicans and Democrats target their appeals to entirely different audiences.

The Modern Family

In 2005, pollster Stanley Greenberg asked respondents to define the term "family." It was a challenging exercise, as the answers received were as numerous as America's families have become. Only 34 percent defined a family as consisting of a "mother, father, and children," or "a husband, wife, and children," or "parents and children."[74] The remaining responses consisted of varied descriptions, though all centered on love as a founding concept. In 2010, a similar study conducted by the Pew Research Center asked respondents whether certain living arrangements constituted a "family." The affirmative results were as follows:

- A married couple with children, 99 percent.
- A married couple without children, 88 percent.
- A single parent with children, 86 percent.
- An unmarried couple with children, 80 percent.
- A same-sex couple with children, 63 percent.
- A same-sex couple without children, 45 percent.[75]

The transformation of the family away from its 1950s-era nuclear model of a mom, dad, and kids is a profound and relatively recent development. Back in the 1980s when Ronald Reagan inhabited the Oval Office, televised depictions of the family included popular programs such as *Family Ties* and *The Cosby Show*. (*Family Ties* also reflected Reagan's political strengths, as the show's principal character, Alex P. Keaton, routinely defended Reagan and castigated government—much to the annoyance of his sitcom parents who recalled the 1960s fondly.) Today, television shows consisting of a married mom, dad, and kids are often relegated to TV Land and other nostalgic cable programming channels because they bear so little resemblance to contemporary families. Only 28.6 percent of today's married couples have children under the age of eighteen living with them.[76] Thus, it is not surprising that one survey of eighteen to twenty-four year olds found only 30 percent saying their own families reminded them of the Huxtables from *The Cosby Show*—i.e., a close-knit family with two working parents and loving children living at home.[77] Paul Taylor writes:

> [I]t has been a long time since a happily married nuclear television family grabbed and held the primetime zeitgeist. Instead television has served up a steady diet of relationship shows, buddy shows, and parenthood shows—*Friends, Seinfeld, Sex and the City, Desperate Housewives, The Good Wife, Two and a Half Men, Parenthood*. When marriage appears at all on the small screen, it's usually a bridge too far, a cautionary tale, or a full-on calamity.[78]

Today, the types of families that were dominant in the Reagan years have been torn apart and reassembled into several different forms. The following data points illustrate how dramatic the revolution in living arrangements has become:

- In 1980, 60.8 percent of households were headed by married couples; today, 48.7 percent.[79]
- In 1980, 22.6 percent of households consisted of people living alone; today, 27.5 percent. More than half of those living alone were single women (55 percent).[80]
- In 1980, nearly one in five children were born to an unmarried mother; today, more than four in ten.[81]

Political scientist Alan Wolfe writes that these choices represent a newfound "moral freedom" that characterizes family life in the twenty-first century: "Never have so many people been so free of moral constraint as contemporary Americans."[82] With so many once-forbidden taboos falling by the wayside, it is not surprising that intimate relationships are so incredibly diverse. The varieties include married couples, cohabitating couples (straight or gay), singles, blended families, "friendships with privileges" (meaning sex with no enduring commitment), civil unions (though this term is rapidly becoming antiquated), and gay marriages. Today, only 19.6 percent of U.S. households have a "traditional" family structure consisting of a mother, father, and children—a sharp decline from the 30.9 percent in 1980.[83] Moreover, only 20 percent of all adults aged eighteen to twenty-nine are married—a sharp contrast with the 59 percent recorded in 1960.[84]

In 1955, former (and soon-to-be-again) Democratic presidential nominee Adlai E. Stevenson told the female graduates of Smith College that "most of you" are going to assume "the humble role of housewife," adding, "Whether you like the idea or not just now, later on you'll like it."[85] Today, no aspiring politician would make such a pronouncement. From an era where women (and men) had few moral choices, we have been transported into an age where innumerable moral choices cause many to delay marriage (or even abandon it altogether). In 2006, a milestone was reached when a *minority* of all U.S. households (49.7 percent) consisted of married couples.[86] In the twenty-first century, most Americans will spend more of their adulthood outside of marriage than in it. Sociologist Stephanie Coontz writes that there are many reasons for the "disestablishment" of once-stable conjugal unions:

Marriage is no longer the institution where people are initiated into sex. It no longer determines the work men and women do on the job or at home, regulates who has children and who doesn't, or coordinates care-giving for the ill or aged. For better or worse, marriage has been displaced from its pivotal position in personal and social life, and will not regain it short of a Taliban-like counterrevolution.[87]

Survey research data confirm the point. According to a 2010 Pew Research poll, nearly four in ten Americans (and 44 percent of millennials) agree that marriage is becoming obsolete.[88]

If marriage is on the decline, what is replacing it? For one thing, more Americans are choosing to stay single. In 2011, nearly 32 million Americans were living alone, the highest number in U.S. history.[89] Another option is cohabitation without marriage: between 1960 and 2010, the number of unmarried couples grew from 439,000 to more than 7.8 million.[90] As sociologists Barbara Dafoe Whitehead and David Popenoe write, "When blushing brides walk down the aisle at the beginning of the new millennium, well over half have already lived together with a boyfriend."[91] Another option is to have children without being married. In 2011, a record 41 percent of babies were born outside of marriage, up from 18 percent in 1980.[92] Six in ten single mothers have live-in boyfriends when they give birth, and while more than eight in ten unmarried mothers say they hope to marry the father of their child, fewer than one in seven actually do so.[93] Today, 29 percent of births to white women are to unwed mothers; Hispanics, 53 percent; and African-Americans, 72 percent.[94] Stephanie Coontz believes so many out-of-wedlock children portends the end of heterosexual marriage itself:

It took more than one-hundred-fifty years to establish the love-based, male breadwinner marriage as the dominant model in North America and Western Europe. It took less than twenty-five years to dismantle it. No sooner had family experts concluded that the perfect balance had been reached between the personal freedoms promised by the love match and the constraints required for social stability, than people began to behave in ways that fulfilled conservatives' direst predictions.[95]

The other major revolution in American life involves increased acceptance of homosexuality and the idea that families can be built upon same-sex couples. In 2003, Massachusetts became the first state to legalize gay marriage thanks to a decision by that state's supreme court. In the ruling, Justice John M. Greaney noted that same-sex couples are "our neighbors, our friends who volunteer in the schools and worship beside us in our religious houses."[96] But not everyone was enthusiastic. Then-Massachusetts governor Mitt Romney ordered the state attorney general to enforce a 1913 statute that forbade the issuance of marriage licenses to nonresidents whose unions would be void in their home states. At the time this law was enacted, it was intended to prevent miscegenation. (The Massachusetts legislature repealed the law in 2008.[97]) George W. Bush also greeted the decision with disdain, telling Congress in his 2004 State of the Union Address: "If judges insist on forcing their arbitrary will upon the people, the only alternative left to the people would be the constitutional process. Our nation must defend the sanctity of marriage."[98] Fifty-eight percent opposed gay marriage that year, and the Bush campaign designed a strategy to place anti-gay marriage initiatives on the ballot in eleven states.[99] In each instance the anti-gay, pro-Bush forces prevailed, with votes ranging from 56.6 percent against in Oregon to 86.0 percent in Mississippi.[100] In 2015 the world changed when the U.S. Supreme Court made gay marriage legal in all fifty states. Writing for the Court, Justice Anthony Kennedy declared: "Far from seeking to devalue marriage, the petitioners seek it for themselves because of their respect—and need—for its privileges and responsibilities. And their immutable nature dictates that same-sex marriage is their only real path to this profound commitment. . . . Their hope is not to be condemned to live in loneliness, excluded from one of civilization's oldest institutions. They ask for equal dignity in the eyes of the law. The Constitution grants them that right."[101]

One reason for the legal and legislative shifts is the willingness of so many gays to step out of the closet and acknowledge their sexuality. Former Massachusetts congressman Barney Frank, himself gay and married, says:

The key is that so many people have acknowledged being gay and lesbian to their families. You're not just beating up on gays and lesbian kids, you're beating up on all their relatives. That's why there has been a real change of opinion.[102]

Frank's observation is born out in the 2010 census data, which reported 593,324 same-sex households. In addition, 115,064 of these couples reported having children living with them.[103]

The transformation of public attitudes toward homosexuality is nothing short of astonishing. In 1950, the American Psychiatric Association listed homosexuality as a "mental disorder."[104] Three years later Dwight D. Eisenhower signed an executive order automatically denying security clearances to gays, saying,

many loyal Americans by reason of instability, alcoholism, homosexuality, or previous tendencies to associate with Communist-front groups are unintentional security risks. In some instances, because of moral lapses, they become subjected to the threat of blackmail by enemy agents.[105]

Ronald Reagan's 1968 presidential campaign was marred by press reports that the California governor's office contained a "homosexual ring."[106] In 1965, 70 percent believed homosexuals were harmful to the American way of life; a dozen years later, an overwhelming 77 percent opposed allowing homosexuals to adopt children—attitudes typical for their times.[107]

Today, public attitudes have undergone a dramatic transformation, as the following data points demonstrate:

- 68 percent would vote for a "generally qualified" homosexual for the presidency. This number increases to 76 percent among those aged eighteen to twenty-nine, but drops to just 56 percent among Republicans. Eighty-two percent of Democrats and 69 percent of independents answer in the affirmative.[108]

- 54 percent believe homosexual relations between consenting adults is *not* wrong. Republicans are split on this issue: 47 percent, not wrong; 43 percent, wrong. Sixty percent of Democrats and 57 percent independents do not believe consenting homosexual relations are wrong.[109]

- Prior to the Supreme Court's historic decision, 60 percent approved of legalizing gay marriage.[110]

- Nearly nine in ten Americans say they know someone who is gay or lesbian, and 80 percent know a gay couple that is in a long-term, committed relationship.[111]

- 61 percent favor allowing gay or lesbian couples to adopt a child.[112]

- More than nine in ten lesbian, gay, bisexual, and transgender (LGBT) adults believe social acceptance of their community has grown in the past decade.[113]

These numbers mean that supporting gay rights does not come with a high political cost as it once did. In his first term, Barack Obama ended the "don't ask, don't tell" policy instituted by Bill Clinton in 1993. Campaigning for reelection, Obama became the first major-party presidential nominee to endorse gay marriage—a position first staked out by Obama's voluble vice president, Joe Biden.

The popular culture also reflects these altered public attitudes. Today, 62 percent of *Fortune 500* companies offer healthcare benefits to domestic partners (whether they be of the same sex or opposite sex).[114] One of these is Boeing, where Joyce E. Tucker, a vice president of global diversity and employee rights, observed:

> I think the corporations are recognizing that in order to be as innovative as we have to be and as competitive as we have to be, we have to avail ourselves of all the talent out there. Everyone has something to contribute. Wherever the talent is coming from, we want that.[115]

A year later another cultural milestone was achieved when the Walt Disney theme parks decided to permit gay-themed weddings at its resorts. For the starting price of $4,000, gay couples could exchange vows; have Disney characters in costume at their reception; and ride in a horse-drawn, glass-enclosed carriage. Disney spokesman Donn Walker defended the change: "We believe this change is consistent with Disney's longstanding policy of welcoming guests in an inclusive environment."[116]

Changing social mores have upset many older Americans, conservatives, and evangelical Republicans. In 1992, Vice President Dan Quayle won plaudits from the Religious Right when he criticized television's *Murphy Brown* for having an out-of-wedlock baby, saying Brown mocked "the importance of fathers by bearing a child alone, and calling it just another 'lifestyle choice.'"[117] Quayle believed the program's subtext reflected a "poverty of values" among cultural elites whom, he declared, "sneer at the simple but hard virtues—modesty, fidelity, integrity."[118] Former 2012 Republican presidential candidate Rick Santorum agrees, writing that family decay is the result of misguided social policies propagated by a "liberal elite" that has resulted in

> an epidemic of promiscuity and sexually transmitted diseases among the young; . . . extreme violence and offensive sexual content on everything from video games to the Internet; 3,500 healthy expectant mothers carrying healthy children exercising a "choice" to end the lives of their children every day; . . . [and] the foundational institution of every civilization known to man—marriage—under siege.[119]

Despite these criticisms, the breaking apart and reassembling of the "traditional" family continues. Today, 66 percent view premarital sex as being "morally acceptable";[120] 58 percent say divorce is preferable to maintaining an unhappy marriage; 67 percent agree that children are better off when unhappy parents get divorced;[121] and 52 percent believe the decision of an unmarried woman to have children is either only "sometimes wrong" or "not wrong at all" (with 67 percent of those aged eighteen to twenty-nine in agreement).[122] When asked whether "one parent can bring up a child as well as two parents together," respondents are evenly split: 51 percent, yes; 48 percent, no.[123] And when it comes to cohabitation, attitudes have radically changed: 55 percent approve of having an unmarried man and woman live together if they want to.[124] Among the younger age cohort, the onus once associated with the term "living in sin" has evaporated. According to surveys of high school seniors, 66 percent endorse cohabitation before marriage—up from 37 percent in 1980.[125]

Even some Republicans are willing to acknowledge the change. Sixteen years after Dan Quayle excoriated the mythical Murphy Brown, John McCain nominated Sarah Palin to be his vice president knowing that her teenage daughter, Bristol, was pregnant and not married to the father of her child. The news hardly caused a ripple and even *endeared* Palin to the party's conservative wing, since her daughter did not have an abortion. Former George W. Bush press secretary Ari Fleischer recently declared that the GOP must stop "scaring" young voters away on cultural issues, especially gay rights: "People simply won't vote for you if they think you don't like them. The GOP needs to modernize its appeal or too many young voters will roll their eyes when they see a Republican presidential candidate coming."[126] Conservative columnist David Frum agrees that Republicans can no longer afford to show their animosity at the outcome of the culture wars, writing, "Those who seem to despise half of America will never be trusted to govern any of it."[127] *New York Times* columnist Ross Douthat concurs: "The conservative argument still has serious exponents, but it's now chuckled at in courtrooms, dismissed by intellectuals, mocked in the media and (in a sudden recent rush) abandoned by politicians."[128]

A Rising American Electorate

At 11:12 p.m. eastern time, NBC News became the first network to call the 2012 election for Barack Obama.[129] It wasn't even close: Obama won 332 electoral votes and 51 percent of the popular vote, abruptly ending what many Republicans believed would be a long election night and possible recount to follow. After NBC News made the announcement, Obama confidante Valerie Jarrett turned to the president and exclaimed, "You won!" to which Obama replied, "I'll believe it when Fox calls it."[130] Four and a half minutes later, Fox News did just that.

Disbelief was profound in the GOP ranks. On Election Day, Republican pollster Neil Newhouse sent an email to Romney supporters with the headline, "IN EVERY SINGLE STATE WE HAVE A SIGNIFICANT MOMENTUM LEAD."[131] Newhouse projected the 2012 turnout would include more whites than in 2008 (similar to the turnouts of 2004 and 2010), making that year an exception, not the rule.[132] Under that model, Newhouse projected Romney would carry every one of the contentious states in an electoral college landslide. (In fact, Romney carried just one, North Carolina.) Conservative columnist George Will joined the chorus, predicting Romney would amass more than 300 electoral votes and win Minnesota (which had voted Democratic in every election since 1976).[133] Obama beat Romney in Minnesota by 7 points. The second half of the Republican ticket, Paul Ryan, was told by Romney headquarters on election morning that victory was certain and he should prepare to assume the vice presidency. Later, Ryan shared his recollections with New Jersey governor Chris Christie, who harrumphed, "Well, that just shows how shitty they were."[134]

At Fox News, the election night drama took an unexpected turn when Karl Rove questioned the call that Ohio (and thus the election) had gone into the Obama column. Rove went into overdrive claiming that the projection was inaccurate. After several minutes of contentious back-and-forth on-air discussion, television history was made when anchor Megyn Kelly took her cameras backstage to the Fox News Decision Desk and had its analysts confront Rove. More minutes went by, and eventually Rove conceded the obvious when political historian Michael Barone came on the set and concluded (rightly) that there were not enough outstanding Romney votes in Ohio for a win.

Disbelief also gripped the Boston hotel headquarters of Mitt Romney and his confidants. Romney began the day convinced that he would easily beat Obama. Months earlier, confident of victory, Romney assembled a transition team led by former Utah governor Mike Leavitt. The group began collecting resumes of potential job seekers and had begun the task of preparing cabinet recommendations for Romney, who, they were certain, would be the president-elect once the night was over.[135] Romney himself was so certain of victory that he failed to draft a concession speech (a rarity in modern presidential annals). One aide described the Republican nominee as being "shell-shocked,"[136] while his wife, Ann, sat nearby crying, asking, "How did this happen?"[137] At once, some Republicans cried foul. Donald Trump tweeted that the election returns were "a travesty, a total sham, a disgusting injustice."[138] A few days later in a conference call with top donors, Romney offered his own analysis: "What the president's campaign did was focus on certain members of his base coalition, give them extraordinary financial gifts from the government, and then work very aggressively to turn them out to vote."[139] Former Republican National Committee chair Ed Gillespie had a similar take. In his view, Obama won by advancing a series of "rifle-shot policies" aimed at key constituencies: free contraceptives for women, the DREAM Act for Latinos, and cuts in student-loan interest rates. Said Gillespie: "They played small ball, but they went small in a big way."[140] In many ways, these remarks echoed Romney's gaffe earlier in the campaign that 47 percent of the electorate were "takers" and thus unreachable from a GOP perspective.

Early the following morning, Newt Gingrich went on CBS television and admitted he and other analysts (including Rove) were wrong in their prior assurances that Romney was the next president. Said Gingrich, "We, frankly, misunderstood what was happening in the country."[141] Indeed, they had. For they not only misunderstood the temper of the voting public, but its composition. Prior to the election, former Howard Dean campaign manager and Fox News political analyst Joe Trippi warned that projections of an easy Romney win were a fantasy, telling colleagues: "You guys think Barack Obama created all the change. He's the *result* of the change."[142] Addressing himself to Rove, Trippi said, "The Republicans are the party of old white guys, and old white guys die."[143] Such warnings were hardly new. In 2006, Republican National Chair Ken Mehlman warned: "America is every day less of a white country. We rely too hard on white guys for votes."[144] Mehlman's RNC predecessor, Edward Gillespie, agreed: "Our majority already rests too heavily on white voters, given that current demographic voting percentages will not allow us to hold our majority in the future."[145]

By 2012, the retreat of white voters and the ascendancy of new minority voters was clear: whites constituted 72 percent of the electorate (the lowest percentage ever recorded) while minorities (black, Hispanic, Asian) comprised a record 28 percent. While Romney won 59 percent of the white vote (better than Ronald Reagan's 56 percent in 1980), this did not translate into what heretofore would have been GOP popular vote and electoral college landslides. Obama's dismal showing among whites (39 percent) was more than offset by his overwhelming victories among non-whites: African-Americans, 93 percent; Asians, 73 percent; Hispanics, 71 percent. Announcing for the presidency in 2008, Obama semi-joked that he did not look like any of his predecessors pictured on the dollar bills. But his twin victories have assured him a prominent place in the parade of white-faced presidents.[146] In short, Obama's race was not a liability in either 2008 or 2012—*it was an asset*. This was a startling change from a 1959 Gallup poll that asked respondents if they would support "a generally well-qualified man for president and he happened to be a Negro": 49 percent answered yes; 46 percent said no.[147] The world had most certainly changed, but Republican assumptions about the composition of the electorate and the nature of twenty-first century politics had not.

In many ways, the 2012 election pitted Barack Obama's America with that which supported Ronald Reagan and his heir, Mitt Romney. As Tables 3.1 and 3.2 demonstrate, Romney did extraordinarily well with Reagan's America (those constituencies that gave Reagan overwhelming backing), whereas Obama's America gave him strong support despite a 7.9 percent unemployment rate on Election Day—the highest number ever recorded for a reelected president since World War Two. While issues and a faltering economy had some effect on the outcome, where voters placed themselves in a changing demography was much more determinative. As one Democratic strategist so smartly put it in 2012: "We're not having an election. We're having a census."[148]

All signs point toward future electorates with more minorities and fewer whites. If in 2016 Democrats replicate the number of minority votes they received in 2012, they will be at 24 percent of the popular vote—nearly half of what a winning presidential candidate might need to win. Under this scenario, a Republican presidential nominee would have to get 64 percent of the white vote—a record number that not even Ronald Reagan could achieve.[149]

Table 3.1 Mitt Romney's/Ronald Reagan's America

Demographic	Romney's Percentage
65+ years old	56
White	59
White men	62
Married	56
Married with children	54
Attend religious services weekly	59
White born-again Christian	78
Support Tea Party Movement	87
Republicans	93

Source: Edison Research, exit poll, November 6, 2012.

Table 3.2 Barack Obama's America, 2012

Demographic	Obama's Percentage
18–29 year olds	60
African-American	93
Latino	71
Asian	73
Unmarried	62
Unmarried women	67
Gay	76
Oppose Tea Party Movement	89
Democrats	92
Never attend religious services	62
Not born-again	60

Source: Edison Research, exit poll, November 6, 2012.

Time and the GOP

After his 2012 win, Barack Obama expressed the hope that Republicans would discontinue their scorched earth opposition to his administration. In an interview with *Rolling Stone*, Obama was optimistic that the partisan gridlock was about to end:

> My hope is that if the American people send a message to [Republicans], there's going to be some self-reflection going on—that it might break the fever. They might say to themselves, "You know what, we've lost our way here. We need to refocus on trying to get things done for the American people."[150]

The election outcome, Obama reasoned, would force the minority party to do what minority parties have historically done: adapt or die.

It didn't happen. Instead, Republican opposition to Obama became even more fierce. House Republicans nearly brought the United States to default in 2013, and the federal government was shutdown for more than two weeks. In 2014, House Speaker John Boehner decided to sue Obama for failing to enforce a provision of the Affordable Care Act, which Boehner vehemently opposed. Democrats retorted that the lawsuit was one step away from impeachment and fired up their base to donate huge sums of cash to thwart any impending impeachment. Immigration reform, though it passed the Senate in 2013, was never put to a vote in the House, and Congress adjourned without passage of a measure Republicans previously stated was a top party priority—leaving Obama to sign a series of executive orders allowing certain classes of undocumented aliens to remain in the United States free of prosecution, a measure Republicans denounced as "executive amnesty."

In addition, the 113th Congress made history by passing the fewest number of bills ever recorded (making Harry Truman's "Do-Nothing" 80th Congress look like a "Do-Plenty" Congress). Meanwhile, Republicans lost the most precious commodity one can have in politics: time. In the first two years of Obama's second term, time was lost refocusing the Republican brand and rethinking what conservatism meant in a post-Reagan world. Time was also lost making explicit appeals to minorities where Republicans need improved numbers to win the presidency. Indeed, Republicans took several steps back in this regard. South Carolina's Lindsey Graham, a sponsor of the Senate immigration measure that failed, posed this challenge to his fellow Republicans: "Shame on us as Republicans for having a body [the House of Representatives] that cannot generate a solution to an issue that's national security, that's cultural, that's economic. Are we still the party of self-deportation?"[151] Finally, time was lost (and money spent) on internal GOP debates over which of the 2014 Republican congressional candidates was the most conservative. Though the party establishment won nearly every contested primary and avoided nominating unelectable candidates (unlike 2010 and 2012), it could be said that Tea Party Republicans lost a few battles (especially in Mississippi) but won the war—as the Republican Party moved ever further to the right and more distant from the mainstream of the American electorate.

Most significantly, what Republicans failed to do in Obama's second term was to give themselves room to disagree amongst themselves and allow their leaders a certain degree of latitude in order to set themselves apart from some of the party's hard-line conservative positions. This was quite unlike the Democrats who, after three consecutive presidential defeats in the 1980s, saw the rise of the Democratic Leadership Council and the Progressive Policy Institute. These organizations—with their emphasis on a "Third Way" and their willingness to eschew traditional, big government, New Deal-like solutions to the country's problems—made it possible for Bill Clinton to pursue a different path without having to worry about a backlash from liberal Democrats. Why the Republicans have had such difficulty giving some degree of ideological latitude to their leaders is the subject of the next chapter.

Notes

1 Bill Clinton, Commencement Address, Portland State University, Portland, Oregon, June 13, 1998.
2 Ibid.
3 Ibid.
4 NBC News/*Wall Street Journal*, poll, February 26–March 1, 1998. Text of question: "When it comes to immigration, which statement most closely represents your feelings? Statement A: Immigration strengthens the American character, as new arrivals increase our diversity and bring ambition and new approaches to the country. Statement B: Immigration weakens the American character, as new arrivals do not adopt our language and culture, and put a strain on public services. Statement A, 36 percent; Statement B, 50 percent; both (volunteered), 8 percent; neither, 3 percent; not sure, 3 percent.
5 Gallup poll, October 15–November 10, 1998. Text of question: "I'm going to read a list of possible foreign policy goals that the United States might have. For each one, please say whether you think that it should be a very important foreign policy goal of the United States, a somewhat important foreign policy goal, or not an important goal at all. How important a foreign policy goal should controlling and reducing illegal immigration be?" Very important, 55 percent; somewhat important, 34 percent; not important, 6 percent; don't know, 5 percent.
6 Gallup poll, October 15–November 10, 1998. Text of question: "How do you rate the Clinton administration's handling of immigration policy?" Excellent, 6 percent; good, 22 percent; fair, 30 percent; poor, 29 percent; not sure, 13 percent.
7 See Patrick J. Buchanan, *The Death of the West: How Dying Populations and Immigrant Invasions Imperil Our Country and Civilization* (New York: St. Martin's Press, 2002), 1.
8 Quoted in Peter Slevin, "Town's Eye View of Immigration Debate," *Washington Post*, April 3, 2006, A-1.
9 Of course, race has always been complicated in U.S. history. Rachel Swarns points out that Michelle Obama, whom most would consider to be African-American, is part American Indian and has several white relatives. See Rachel Swarns, *American Tapestry: The Story of the Black, White, and Multiracial Ancestors of Michelle Obama* (New York: Harper Collins, 2012).
10 ABC News, exit poll, November 4, 1980.
11 Edison Media Research and Mitofsky International, exit polls, November 4, 2008.
12 Edison Media Research and Mitofsky International, exit poll, November 2, 2010.
13 See Daniel Chauncey Brewer, *The Conquest of New England by the Immigrant* (New York: G. P. Putnam and Sons, 1926).
14 John F. Kennedy, *A Nation of Immigrants* (New York: Harper and Row Publishers, 1964), 103.

15 See Lyndon B. Johnson, Remarks at the Signing of the Immigration Bill, Liberty Island, October 3, 1965, and Lyndon B. Johnson, Remarks to the American Committee on Italian Migration on the Occasion of the Termination of the National Origins Quota System, Washington, D.C., July 1, 1968.

16 Johnson, Remarks at the Signing of the Immigration Bill.

17 See Kim M. Williams, *Mark One or More: Civil Rights in Multiracial America* (Ann Arbor: University of Michigan Press, 2006), 33, and Nathan P. Walters and Edward N. Trevelyan, "The Newly-Arrived Foreign-Born Population of the United States, 2010," U.S. Census Bureau, American Community Survey Reports, November 2011, 1.

18 See Samuel P. Huntington, *Who Are We? The Challenges to America's National Identity* (New York: Simon and Schuster, 2004), 196.

19 See Walters and Trevelyan, "The Newly-Arrived Foreign-Born Population of the United States, 2010," 4.

20 Paul Taylor, *The Next America: Boomers, Millennials, and the Looming Generational Showdown* (New York: Public Affairs, 2014), 70.

21 Jeffrey S. Passel, D'Vera Cohn, and Ana Gonzalez-Barrera, "Population Decline of Unauthorized Immigrants Stalls, May Have Reversed," Pew Research Center Hispanic Trends Project, press release, September 23, 2013.

22 See Anita U. Hattiangadi, Aline O. Quester, Gary Lee, Diana S. Lien, and Ian MacLeod with David L. Reese and Robert Shuford, "Non-Citizens in Today's Military Research Brief," Center for Naval Analyses. See more at http://www.cna.org/centers/marine-corps/selected-studies/non-citizens-brief#sthash.phOWfFv0.dpuf. Accessed July 26, 2014.

23 Jeanne Batalova, "Immigrants in the Armed Forces," Migration Information Service, May 15, 2008.

24 See Taylor, *The Next America*, 71.

25 U.S. Census Bureau, "Most Children Younger than Age One Are Minorities, Census Bureau Reports," press release, May 17, 2012.

26 See Jeffrey S. Passel and D'Vera Cohn, *U.S. Population Projections: 2005–2050*, Pew Research Center report, February 11, 2008, 1, and Amitai Etzioni, *The Monochrome Society* (Princeton: Princeton University Press, 2001), 31.

27 See Camille Ryan, "Language Use in the United States, 2011," U.S. Census Bureau, American Community Survey Reports, August 2013, 3.

28 See Winnie Hu, "New York City Libraries Struggle to Meet Demand for English-Language Classes," *New York Times*, August 7, 2014, A-19.

29 See "Most Children Younger than Age One Are Minorities," and Elizabeth M. Hoeffel, Sonya Rastogi, Myoung Oak Kim, and Hasan Shahid, "The Asian Population, 2010," U.S. Census Bureau, Washington, D.C., March 2012, 4.

30 Taylor, *The Next America*, 76.

31 Jeanne Batalova, "Asian Immigrants in the United States," Migration Information Service, May 24, 2011.

32 U.S. Census Bureau, "Most Children Younger than Age One Are Minorities," and Taylor, *The Next America*, 77.

33 Laura Vozzella, "McAuliffe Signs East Sea Bill That Pitted Korean Americans Against Japan," *Washington Post*, April 2, 2014.

34 Quoted in Paul Schwartzman, "In Virginia's 10th Congressional District, GOP Struggles to Woo Minority Voters," *Washington Post*, July 20, 2014.

35 Ibid.

36 See Monica Whatley and Jeanne Batalova, "Indian Immigrants in the United States," Migration Policy Institute, press release, August 21, 2013.

37 See Ronald Fernandez, *None of the Above: Immigrants, Fusions, and the Radical Reconfiguration of American Culture* (Ann Arbor: University of Michigan Press, 2007), 148.

38 Quoted in "Perspectives," *Newsweek*, July 17, 2006, 21.

39 See Schwartzman, "In Virginia's 10th Congressional District, GOP Struggles to Woo Minority Voters."

40 Taylor, *The Next America*, 96.

41 See Passel and Cohn, *U.S. Populations Projections: 2005–2050*, 9, and Sam Roberts, "A Generation Away, Minorities May Become the Majority in U.S.," *New York Times*, August 14, 2008.

42 U.S. Census Bureau, "Most Children Younger than Age One Are Minorities."

43 Henry J. Kaiser Family Foundation/*Washington Post*, poll, October 6–November 2, 2011. Text of first question: "How many of your close friends are a different race than you—all of them, most of them, some of them, hardly any of them, or none of them?" All, 5 percent; most, 19 percent; some, 56 percent; hardly any, 14 percent; none, 5 percent; no opinion, 1 percent. Text of second question: "Would you be willing to marry someone of another race, or not?" Yes, 75 percent; no, 21 percent; no opinion, 5 percent. Text of third question: "Have you ever dated someone who was of a different race, or not?" Yes, 52 percent; no, 48 percent. By age the affirmative answers were 18–29, 65 percent; 30–49, 61 percent; 50–64, 45 percent; 65 and over, 29 percent.

44 See Michael Barone and Richard E. Cohen, *The Almanac of American Politics, 2004* (Washington, D.C.: National Journal, 2003), 154.

45 Quoted in Etzioni, *The Monochrome Society*, 4–5.

46 See Taylor, *The Next America*, 71.

47 Huntington, *Who Are We?*, 227.

48 Ibid., 253.

49 See Michael Finnegan and Mark Z. Barabak, "Villaraigosa Landslide: Voter Discontent Helps Propel Challenger to a Historic Victory," *Los Angeles Times*, May 18, 2005, A-1.

50 Quoted in John M. Broder, "Latino Defeats Incumbent in L.A. Mayor's Race," *New York Times*, May 18, 2005, A-1.

51 David Brooks, *On Paradise Drive: How We Live Now (And Always Have) in the Future Tense* (New York: Simon and Schuster, 2004), 35.

52 See http://censusviewer.com/county/VA/Loudoun. Accessed July 27, 2014.

53 See http://censusviewer.com/county/VA/Fairfax. Accessed July 27, 2014.

54 See http://censusviewer.com/county/VA/Prince%20William. Accessed July 27, 2014.

55 Huntington, *Who Are We?*, 207.

56 Jan L. Flora, Claudia M. Prado-Meza, and Hannah Lewis, "After the Raid Is Over: Marshalltown, Iowa, and the Consequences of Worksite Enforcement Raids," Immigration Policy Center Report, January 2011, 4.

57 Ibid., 9, 5.

58 Ibid., 17.

59 Ibid., 16.

60 See Taylor, *The Next America*, 91.

61 Ibid.

62 Ibid., 77.

63 Ellis Cose, *Color-Blind: Seeing Beyond Race in a Race-Obsessed World* (New York: HarperCollins, 1997), 25.

64 Quoted in D'Vera Cohn, "Area Soon to Be Mostly Minority," *Washington Post*, March 25, 2006, A-1.

65 See Nicholas A. Jones and Jungmiwha Bullock, "The Two or More Races Population, 2010," U.S. Census Bureau Briefs, September 2012, 1.

66 Taylor, *The Next America*, 89.

67 Ibid. In 1967, the Supreme Court invalidated these remaining laws in the case of *Loving v. Virginia*.

68 Barack Obama, *Dreams from My Father: A Story of Race and Inheritance* (New York: Times Books, 1995), 11.

69 Chris Matthews, *Hardball*, MSNBC, April 2, 2008.

70 Quoted in James Traub, "Is (His) Biography (Our) Destiny?," *New York Times Magazine*, November 4, 2007, 50.

71 See Taylor, *The Next America*, 96.

72 Ben J. Wattenberg, *The Birth Dearth* (New York: Pharos Books, 1987).

73 Christopher Ingraham, "Whites Uneasy at Idea of Mostly Minority U.S.," *Washington Post*, August 13, 2014.

74 Greenberg Quinlan Rosner Research, poll, July 25–August 7, 2005. Text of question: "When I say the word 'family,' people may think of different things. Some may think of a mother, father, and children, whereas others may think of being with a long-term partner or just a parent alone with a child. How about for you? How do you define a 'family'?" Mother, father, children, 27 percent; children, 8 percent; husband, wife, and children, 6 percent; one parent and child, 4 percent; married couple with kids, 1 percent; parent/parents, 9 percent; immediate family, 7 percent; man and woman, 2 percent; related by marriage or blood, 1 percent; husband and wife, 1 percent; brother, sister, siblings, 1 percent; the whole family/entire family/extended family, 8 percent; relatives, 2 percent; people who care for each other, 3 percent; close group of people/anyone close to you, 2 percent; people working towards common goals and needs, 1 percent; people you put trust in, 1 percent; loving relationships, 1 percent; loving people/loved ones/anyone who loves you, 1 percent; people who live together and care for each other, 2 percent; whoever lives with you/anyone you live with, 1 percent; caring/loving/nurturing environment, 1 percent; caring, 1 percent; love, 1 percent; togetherness, 1 percent; union, 1 percent; unity and love of relations, 2 percent; related people who care about each other, 1 percent; partnership/partner/long-term partner, 4 percent; everyone, 2 percent; friends, 1 percent; support, 1 percent; support for each other financially and emotionally, 1 percent; family is what you make it, 1 percent; don't know, 3 percent.

75 Taylor, *The Next America*, 121.

76 See Jonathan Vespa, Jamie M. Lewis, and Rose M. Kreider, "America's Families and Living Arrangements: 2012," U.S. Census Bureau, report, August 2013, 12.

77 "Coming of Age in America, Part II," Greenberg Quinlan Rosner, press release, September 2005.

78 Taylor, *The Next America*, 110.

79 Derived from Vespa, Lewis, and Kreider, "America's Families and Living Arrangements: 2012," 5.

80 Ibid., 5, 6.

81 See "Births to Unmarried Women," Child Trends Data Bank. http://www.childtrends.org/?indicators=births-to-unmarried-women.   Accessed August 3, 2014.

82 Alan Wolfe, *Moral Freedom: The Impossible Idea That Defines the Way We Live Now* (New York: W. W. Norton, 2001), 199.

83 See Vespa, Lewis, and Kreider, "America's Families and Living Arrangements: 2012," 5.

84 See Taylor, *The Next America*, 107.

85 Quoted in Stephanie Coontz, *Marriage, a History: From Obedience to Intimacy or How Love Conquered Marriage* (New York: Viking, 2005), 236–237. See also Adlai E. Stevenson, "A Purpose for Modern Woman," Commencement Address, Smith College, Northampton, Massachusetts, June 6, 1955.
86 See Sam Roberts, "It's Official: To Be Married Means to Be Outnumbered," *New York Times*, October 15, 2006, 14.
87 Stephanie Coontz, "For Better, For Worse; Marriage Means Something Different Now," *Washington Post*, May 1, 2005, B-1, and Coontz, *Marriage, a History*, 278.
88 Taylor, *The Next America*, 108.
89 See Vespa, Lewis, and Kreider, "America's Families and Living Arrangements: 2012," 4.
90 See David Popenoe, *The Future of Marriage in America* (New Brunswick, New Jersey: Rutgers University National Marriage Project, 2007), 20, and Vespa, Lewis, and Kreider, "America's Families and Living Arrangements: 2012," 20.
91 David Popenoe and Barbara Dafoe Whitehead, *Should We Live Together?: What Young Adults Need to Know about Cohabitation before Marriage* (Rutgers, New Jersey: The National Marriage Project, 2002), 1.
92 Taylor, *The Next America*, 114, 115.
93 Ibid., 114. Also see Eduardo Porter and Michelle O'Donnell, "Facing Middle Age with No Degree, and No Wife," *New York Times*, August 6, 2006, A-1.
94 Taylor, *The Next America*, 227.
95 Coontz, *Marriage, a History*, 247.
96 Quoted in Kathleen Burge, "Gays Have Right to Marry Supreme Judicial Court Says in Historic Ruling," *Boston Globe*, November 19, 2003, A-1.
97 Group News Blog, "Massachusetts Repeals 1913 Law Intended to Ban Interracial and Now Same-Sex Marriages," July 30, 2008. See http://www.groupnewsblog.net/2008/07/massachusetts-repeals-1913-law-intended.html. Accessed May 30, 2015.
98 George W. Bush, State of the Union Address, Washington, D.C., January 20, 2004.
99 Winston Group, poll, June 23–24, 2004. Text of question: "Do you favor or oppose gay marriage?" Favor, 27 percent; oppose, 58 percent; don't know/refused, 15 percent.
100 See Rhodes Cook, "Gay Marriage Ban and the Bush Vote in 2004," in *The Rhodes Cook Letter*, May 2005, 8.
101 *Obergefell v. Hodges* 576 U.S. 2015, 9, 33.
102 John Kenneth White, interview with Barney Frank, Washington, D.C., December 20, 2000.
103 See Daphne Lofquist, "Same-Sex Couple Households," U.S. Census Bureau report, September 2011, 3.
104 "Gays on the March," *Time*, September 8, 1975, 36. This position was reversed in 1973.
105 Dwight D. Eisenhower, *Mandate for Change: 1953–1956* (Garden City, New York: Doubleday and Company, 1963), 309.
106 See Patrick J. Buchanan, *The Greatest Comeback: How Richard Nixon Rose from Defeat to Create the New Majority* (New York: Crown Forum, 2014), 144, 225.
107 Louis Harris and Associates, poll, September 1965. Text of question: "America has many different types of people in it. But we would like to know whether you think each of these different types of people is more helpful or harmful to American life, or don't they help or harm things one way or the other? . . . Homosexuals." More harmful, 70 percent; more helpful, 1 percent; doesn't

matter, 29 percent. Gallup poll, June 17–20, 1977. Text of question: "Do you think homosexuals should or should not be allowed to adopt children?" Should, 14 percent; should not, 77 percent; no opinion, 9 percent.

108 Gallup poll, June 7–10, 2012. Text of question: "If your party nominated a generally well-qualified person for president who happened to be gay or lesbian, would you vote for that person?" Yes, would, 68 percent; no, would not, 30 percent; no opinion, 2 percent. Eighteen to twenty-nine years old: Yes, would, 76 percent; no, would not, 24 percent. Republicans: yes, would, 56 percent; no, would not, 43 percent; don't know, 1 percent. Democrats: yes, would, 82 percent; no, would not, 17 percent; don't know, 1 percent. Independents: yes, would, 69 percent; no, would not, 29 percent; don't know, 2 percent.

109 CBS News, poll, March 20–24, 2013. Text of question: "Do you think homosexual relations between consenting adults is wrong, or not?" Yes, 37 percent; no, 54 percent; don't know/no answer, 9 percent. Republicans: yes, 43 percent; no, 47 percent; don't know/no answer, 10 percent. Democrats: yes, 34 percent; no, 60 percent; don't know/no answer, 6 percent. Independents: yes, 35 percent; no, 57 percent; don't know/no answer, 9 percent.

110 Gallup poll, May 6–10, 2015. Text of question: "Do you think marriages between same-sex couples should or should not be recognized by the law as valid, with the same rights as traditional marriages?" Should be valid, 60 percent; should not be valid, 37 percent; no opinion, 3 percent.

111 See Taylor, *The Next America*, 119, and NBC News/*Wall Street Journal*, poll, April 5–8, 2013. Text of question: "Do you personally know a gay or lesbian couple who are in a long-term committed relationship, civil union, or marriage?" Yes, committed relationship, 51 percent; yes, civil union, 14 percent; yes, marriage, 15 percent; no, 30 percent; not sure, 3 percent. Adds to more than 100 percent due to multiple responses.

112 ABC News/*Washington Post*, poll, February 27–March 2, 2014. Text of question: "Do you favor or oppose allowing gay or lesbian couples to adopt a child?" Favor, 61 percent; oppose, 34 percent; no opinion, 5 percent.

113 Taylor, *The Next America*, 119.

114 "LGBT Equality at the Fortune 500," Human Rights Campaign. See http://www.hrc.org/resources/entry/lgbt-equality-at-the-fortune-500.   Accessed August 15, 2014.

115 Quoted in Amy Joyce, "For Gays, Some Doors Open Wider," *Washington Post*, September 24, 2006, F-1.

116 Quoted in Frank Ahrens, "Disney's Theme Weddings Come True for Gay Couples," *Washington Post*, April 7, 2007, A-1.

117 Dan Quayle, Address to the Commonwealth Club of California, San Francisco, May 19, 1992.

118 Dan Quayle, *Standing Firm: A Vice Presidential Memoir* (New York: HarperCollins, 1994), 318, 326.

119 Rick Santorum, *It Takes a Family: Conservatism and the Common Good* (Wilmington, Delaware: ISI Books, 2005), 5.

120 Gallup poll, May 8–11, 2014. Text of question: "Next, I'm going to read you a list of issues. Regardless of whether or not you think it should be legal, for each one, please tell me whether you personally believe that in general it is morally acceptable or morally wrong. How about sex between an unmarried man and woman?" Morally acceptable, 66 percent; morally wrong, 31 percent; depends on situation (volunteered), 1 percent; not a moral issue (volunteered), 1 percent; no opinion, 1 percent.

121 See Taylor, *The Next America*, 117.

122 Princeton Survey Research Associates International, poll, February 16–March 14, 2007. Text of question: "How about unmarried women having children? Do you think this is always wrong, almost always wrong, wrong only sometimes, or not wrong at all?" Always wrong, 26 percent; almost always wrong, 18 percent; wrong only sometimes, 33 percent; not wrong at all, 19 percent; don't know/refused, 4 percent. Aged eighteen to twenty-nine years old: Always wrong, 16 percent; almost always wrong, 14 percent; wrong only sometimes, 40 percent; not wrong at all, 27 percent; don't know/refused, 3 percent.

123 Princeton Survey Research Associates International, poll, April 4–15, 2012. Text of question: "Here is another series of statements on some different topics. One parent can bring up a child as well as two parents together. Do you completely agree, mostly agree, mostly disagree, or completely disagree?" Completely agree, 27 percent; mostly agree, 24 percent; mostly disagree, 27 percent; completely disagree, 21 percent; don't know/refused, 2 percent.

124 Gallup/*USA Today*, poll, September 7–8, 2007.

125 See Robert G. Wood, Sarah Avellar, and Brian Goesling, "Pathways to Adulthood and Marriage: Teenagers' Attitudes, Expectations, and Relationship Patterns," report to U.S. Department of Health and Human Services, October 2008, 27.

126 Ari Fleischer, "What the GOP Must Do to Win in 2016," *Washington Post*, November 5, 2014.

127 David Frum, *Why Romney Lost and What the GOP Can Do about It* (Newsweek ebook, published online, 2012).

128 Quoted in Taylor, *The Next America*, 119

129 See Jonathan Alter, *The Center Holds: Obama and His Enemies* (New York: Simon and Schuster, 2013), 355.

130 Ibid.

131 Ibid., 352.

132 Ibid., 358.

133 Ibid., 357.

134 Quoted in Mark Halperin and John Heilemann, *Double Down: Game Change 2012* (New York: Penguin Press, 2013), 466.

135 See Alter, *The Center Holds*, 355.

136 Ibid., 359.

137 Quoted in Halperin and Heilemann, *Double Down*, 465.

138 See Alter, *The Center Holds*, 357.

139 Quoted in Halperin and Heilemann, *Double Down*, 469.

140 Ibid.

141 See https://www.youtube.com/watch?v=txvIEU2mmlw. Accessed August 15, 2014.

142 Quoted in Alter, *The Center Holds*, 357.

143 Ibid.

144 Quoted in Mark Silva, "GOP Chairman: 'Message Received,'" *Washington Post*, November 9, 2006, A-1.

145 Edward Gillespie, "Populists Beware: The GOP Must Not Become an Anti-Immigrant Party," *Wall Street Journal*, April 2, 2006, A-6.

146 A 2014 measure passed in California requires history and social science students be taught that Obama's 2008 election was historic. According to the bill's Democratic sponsor, Chris Holden, "We want to make sure that future generations understand that the election of our nation's first African-American president was a historic step in the effort towards equality and that previous elections involved

intimidation and violence that prevented millions of African-Americans from voting." See Hunter Schwarz, "Obama Presidency Is One for the Textbooks," *Washington Post*, August 27, 2014, A-13.

147 Gallup poll, December 10–15, 1959. Text of question: "Between now and the time of the conventions in 1960, there will be much discussion about the qualifications of presidential candidates—their education, age, religion, race, and the like. If your party nominated a generally well-qualified man for president and he happened to be a Negro, would you vote for him?" Yes, 49 percent; no, 46 percent; no opinion, 5 percent.

148 Quoted in Jeb Bush and Clint Bolick, *Immigration Wars: Forging an American Solution* (New York: Threshold Editions, Simon and Schuster, 2013), 200.

149 See Glen Bolger and Neil Newhouse, "Congrats, GOP! Now Here's a Reality Check," *Washington Post*, November 2, 2014, B-1.

150 Quoted in Halperin and Heilemann, *Double Down*, 471.

151 Quoted in Rebecca Shabad, "'Shame on Us' for Not Passing Immigration Reform, Graham Says," *The Hill*, November 23, 2014.

Chapter 4

A Conservative Imprisonment

"Each party has true believers and true believers alone can't build majorities."

Richard B. Wirthlin, pollster to Ronald Reagan

A few days after Republicans lost control of both houses of Congress in the 1954 midterm elections, Dwight D. Eisenhower wrote an impassioned letter to his brother, Edgar, warning his fellow partisans to avoid any lingering adherence to a moss-backed conservatism that aimed to dismantle Franklin D. Roosevelt's New Deal:

> Should any political party attempt to abolish social security, unemployment insurance, and eliminate labor laws and farm programs, you would not hear of that party again in our political history. There is a tiny splinter group, of course, that believes you can do these things. Among them are H.L. Hunt (you possibly know his background), a few other Texas oil millionaires, and an occasional politician or business man from other areas. Their number is negligible and they are stupid.[1]

Ike's admonition was premised on his own run-ins with his fellow conservatives. Two years earlier he wrestled the presidential nomination away from "Mr. Conservative" himself, Robert A. Taft, in a bitter floor fight at the Republican National Convention. Eisenhower believed Taft was a sure loser in 1952 (a belief shared by many Democrats). One reason was Taft's lambasting of the New Deal, and his desire to return to a 1920s-era of limited government. Said Taft:

> The measures undertaken by the Democratic administration [of Franklin D. Roosevelt] are alarming. Whatever may be said for them as emergency measures, their permanent incorporation into our system would practically abandon the whole theory of American government, and inaugurate in fact socialism.[2]

After Taft's loss to Eisenhower, Robert Welch, founder of the John Birch Society, maintained that the Republicans' "betrayal" of Taft was "the dirtiest deal in American political history, participated in if not entirely engineered by Richard Nixon in order to make himself vice president (and to put Earl Warren on the Supreme Court as part of that deal)."[3] Two years into his presidency, Eisenhower told his press secretary, James Haggerty, "[B]efore I end up, either this Republican Party will reflect progressivism, or I won't be with them anymore."[4] Eisenhower vowed to oppose Taft and his fellow conservatives should they try to nominate their own candidate for the presidency two years hence: "I'll go up and down this country, campaigning against them. I'll fight them right down the line."[5]

Dwight Eisenhower's ambition was to move the Republican Party away from its harsh, anti-FDR rhetoric and reposition it into the mainstream of political life. In his 1953 State of the Union address, Eisenhower announced his intention to govern by consensus:

> There is, in our affairs at home, a middle way between untrammeled freedom of the individual and the demands for the welfare of the whole nation. This way must avoid government by bureaucracy as carefully as it avoids neglect of the helpless.[6]

Political scientist Fred I. Greenstein perceptively noted that Eisenhower's leadership style included a hefty dose of moderation:

> [B]y enunciating "broad and liberal objectives," advancing moderate improvements in social programs, and establishing a reputation (and above all a record) for fostering a thriving economy, [Eisenhower] could (if he could preserve an untroubled international environment) reconstitute the electoral base of his party. "Twentieth Century Republicanism," he hoped, would deprive the Democrats of their corner on "the common man," especially if his own "broad and liberal" Republican programs (and his personal appeal) helped bring young, attractive leaders into the party—leaders who would modernize the party's organizational procedures as well as its policy stance.[7]

By 1956, Eisenhower could claim a victory that was based on more than his charismatic persona. Accepting renomination, a triumphant Ike told the GOP delegates:

> The Republican party is again the rallying point of Americans of all callings, ages, races, and incomes. They see in its broad, forward-moving, straight-down-the-road, fighting program the best promise for their own steady progress toward a bright future. Some opponents have tried to call this a "one-interest party." Indeed it is a one-interest party,

and that one interest is the interest of every man, woman, and child in America! And most surely, as long as the Republican party continues to be the kind of one-interest party—a one-universal interest party—it will continue to be the Party of the Future.[8]

Helping Eisenhower refashion the Republican Party was his undersecretary of labor and a former Rhodes scholar, Arthur Larson. Author of the book *A Republican Looks at His Party*, Larson maintained that Eisenhower had forged a "New Republicanism" by occupying the "Authentic American Center" that spoke for the common good.[9] Rather than being the naysayers of the 1930s, Republicans under Eisenhower became a party that stuck up for U.S. interests abroad (particularly in the Cold War with the Soviet Union), while promoting a moderate progressivism at home that included a broad use of federal powers. Thus, early in his administration Eisenhower approved the creation of the Department of Health, Education, and Welfare—the first addition to a president's cabinet in forty years. Later, he secured passage of two landmark laws—the National Defense Education Act and the Federal Highway Act—by using the cloak of national security to create a groundswell of public approval. Approved by large bipartisan majorities in both houses of Congress, these measures changed the nation as much as the New Deal ever did. The $1 billion contained in the 1957 National Defense Education Act provided for a fivefold increase in funds for the National Science Foundation; created 5,500 graduate fellowships; established a system of matching grants to allow colleges to expand their graduate programs in the sciences; and allocated federal dollars to the states to employ additional science and math teachers, purchase laboratory equipment, improve testing and guidance programs, and expand foreign language programs.[10] At the signing ceremony, Eisenhower noted the National Defense Education Act would do much "to strengthen our American system of education so it can meet the broad and increasing demands of national security."[11] The Federal Highway Act, approved in 1956, created a vast network of interconnected highways running from Long Island, New York, to Long Beach, California. Once again, Eisenhower presented his proposal as being in the national security interest: "Motorists by the millions would read a primary purpose [of this project] in the signs that would sprout up alongside the pavement: 'In the event of an enemy attack, this road will be closed.' "[12] In other words, the new highway system would facilitate military and tank movements as well as provide for civilian evacuations in the event of a national emergency.

By occupying a defense-oriented "Authentic American Center" that would preserve the New Deal—even as it expanded government in areas vital for both economic and military strength—Eisenhower believed the Republican Party would be unbeatable. Winning a landslide reelection victory in 1956, he declared: "I think that Modern Republicanism has now proved itself and America has approved of Modern Republicanism."[13] Arthur Larson agreed:

> Now we have as much government activity as is necessary, but not enough to stifle the normal motivations of private enterprise. And we have a higher degree of government concern for the needs of people than ever before in our history, while at the same time pursuing a policy of maximum restoration of responsibility to individuals and private groups. This balance, together with a gradual restoration of a better balance between federal and state governments, is allowing all these elements in society to make their maximum contribution to the common good.[14]

Richard Nixon adopted a similar position during his presidency. Indeed, Nixon was not shy about using the powers of the federal government to advance his own political interests. Thus, he instituted wage and price controls in 1971 in order to try to control runaway inflation. He declared a "war on cancer" and promised to use the resources of the federal government to tame this dreaded disease. In addition, he proposed (but could not get adopted) a Family Assistance Plan that guaranteed a $1,600 annual income to a family of four. Advocated by Daniel Patrick Moynihan, a domestic adviser to Nixon who had previously served in the Johnson administration, the program drew fire from liberals who felt it did not go far enough and conservatives who were appalled at Nixon's daring. The *Suburban List* in Essex Junction, Vermont, declared: "Hubert [Humphrey] has been out-Humphried and Richard Milhous Nixon did it. We could hardly believe our ears!"[15] The *Detroit Free Press* called it "more radical than virtually anything done by the Johnson administration."[16] Perceptively, *New York Times* columnist James Reston noted that Nixon's proposal "has cloaked a remarkably progressive welfare policy in conservative language."[17] Eulogizing Nixon many years later at his 1994 funeral, Bill Clinton remembered that he had "signed bills establishing the Environmental Protection Agency, the Legal Services Corporation, and the Occupational Safety and Health Administration, and had supported affirmative action."[18] These measures—anathema to conservatives—made Nixon the last New Deal president. As Clinton concluded years later, "Compared with the Republicans who took over the party in the 1980s and 1990s, President Nixon was a wild-eyed liberal."[19]

Aiding both Eisenhower and Nixon in their desire to occupy an "Authentic American Center" was Democratic control of Congress. When Dwight Eisenhower was returned to the White House in 1957, he became the first president since Grover Cleveland in 1885 to inherit a Congress controlled by the opposition party.[20] Richard Nixon faced similar circumstances in his two successful runs for the presidency. While Democratic congressional leaders expressed their willingness to work with these Republican presidents, they sought to temper their mandates by claiming a share of them. In 1956, for example, then-Senate Majority Leader Lyndon B. Johnson maintained that Eisenhower won a "qualified mandate":

> A political party at a national convention draws up a program to present to the voters. The voters can either accept it by giving the party full power, reject it by taking the party completely out of power, or give it qualified approval by giving one party the Congress and the other party the Presidency. And when we in the Congress have been given a qualified mandate, as we were in 1956, it means that we have a solemn responsibility to cooperate with the President and produce a program that is neither his blueprint nor our blueprint but a combination of the two. It is the politician's task to pass legislation, not to sit around saying principled things.[21]

Conservative frustration was tempered by sustained Republican presidential victories. As Nixon put it in 1968, "Winning's a lot more fun."[22] Governing in a divided nation meant placing a premium on compromise, which, in the view of many GOP purists, signaled the emergence of a "me-too" Republicanism. Barry Goldwater, for one, accused Eisenhower of "running a dime store New Deal," a criticism Eisenhower brushed off from a disgruntled, immature minority that Goldwater himself advised to "grow up" after Nixon won the 1960 GOP nomination.[23] If "me-tooism" and occupying the "Authentic American Center" were requirements for winning, the Republican establishment was content to expunge the word "conservative" from the party's vocabulary, as Arthur Larson explained:

> [If], as seems unlikely, the Republicans were some day to nominate a candidate for the presidency who was identified with an extreme conservative position, and if, as seems equally unlikely, the Democrats were to seize that moment to choose a nominee who took over the formula of the great middle way, the Democratic candidate would most certainly win, and thereafter it would be difficult indeed for the Republicans to get back in.[24]

Even Ronald Reagan bowed to extant political realities. In 1980, as he successfully sought the presidency, those savvy political analysts Richard Scammon and Ben Wattenberg colorfully wrote:

> The Republican party having brought its traditional conservatives to the moderate mainstream of economics and politics—a mainstream with deep, cool water and good fishing—can risk the whole catch by herding off into the shallow, rocky swirling eddies of right wing social issues.

> Emphasis on prayer-in-the-school, anti-E.R.A., anti-abortion amendments and anti-evolution is a one-way ticket to the Swamp of No Return.[25]

Long thought by conservatives as being "one of them," party purists were disappointed when President Reagan raised taxes and increased government spending. Conservative columnist George F. Will complained in 1988 that Reagan's "almost complete acceptance of the welfare state that evolved at a remarkably steady pace under his predecessors of both parties for half a century" meant that while Republicans were "free to talk like Jeffersonians, celebrating that government which governs least . . . they live in, and want to be the dominant party in, Hamilton's America."[26]

As the disappointments mounted, a conservative rallying cry took hold: "Let Reagan be Reagan." But while Reagan threw conservatives a bone every so often—e.g., his denunciation of the Soviet Union as the "evil empire"—he refused to be wedded to a dour ideology that emphasized American decline and spoke only to a committed group of true believers. By keeping the conservative pessimists at bay, Reagan pollster Richard Wirthlin maintained that the GOP had a much more realistic chance to build a new majority: "Each party has true believers and true believers alone can't build majorities."[27]

Analyzing Mitt Romney's defeat in 2012, David Frum advised Republicans to harken back to the winning strategies of Eisenhower, Nixon, and Reagan:

> Winning presidential candidates have always spoken to the entire country and promised to represent all Americans. "I ask you to trust that American spirit which knows no ethnic, regional, or economic boundaries; the spirit that burned with zeal in the hearts of millions of immigrants from every corner of the earth who came here in search of freedom." That's Ronald Reagan, accepting the Republican nomination in 1980. The tragedy of the modern Republican party is that it remembers Ronald Reagan's lyrics—the specific policies he recommended for his time—but has lost the music.[28]

Part of that music involved a reenergized conservative movement that was brimming with optimism back when Reagan was elected president. Daniel Patrick Moynihan was among the first to see it coming. In 1980, he perceptively wrote, "Of a sudden, the GOP has become a party of ideas."[29] One set of ideas involved reinvigorating "mediating institutions"—among them religious groups, unions, community and professional organizations, and volunteer groups such as neighborhood fire departments and crime prevention patrols. For too long, Ronald Reagan declared, these voluntary organizations had been supplanted by the "puzzle palaces on the Potomac."[30]

Around the same time, Representative Jack Kemp and Senator William Roth proposed a 30 percent federal income tax cut that they believed would be both a stimulus to the economy and a means to increase federal revenues. In addition, Kemp proposed creating "enterprise zones" in areas of urban blight. Such tax-free zones, Kemp thought, would do more for cities than Lyndon B. Johnson's Great Society.

Conservative politicians were hardly operating in a vacuum. Intellectual think tanks gave a new effervescence to conservative ideas. The American Enterprise Institute became a place of intellectual thought with its publications *Public Opinion* and *The American Enterprise*. The Heritage Foundation, founded in 1973, prepared a vast document outlining a governing strategy for the new Reagan administration and proposing men and women who could staff it. The Cato Institute saw its libertarian philosophy modified to promote new solutions to vexing problems—one of the most important being healthcare, with its 1990s proposal to require every American to purchase health insurance. Two billionaire brothers, Charles and David Koch, used their vast fortune to fund 150 programs at colleges and universities to promote their libertarian ideas.[31] The Federalist Society, with its impressive list of law school alumni, began to move the judiciary in a conservative direction. Even the Republican National Committee pursued its own form of intellectual engagement by publishing *Commonsense*. Modeled after academic journals, *Commonsense* included articles by Democratic and Republican thinkers (including the late Jeane Kirkpatrick) that helped create, in Moynihan's words, "an intellectual class."[32] Adding to the intellectual class were Irving Kristol, who with Daniel Bell and Nathan Glazer founded *The Public Interest*, along with Norman Podhoretz, who established *Commentary*. In the midst of this conservative ferment, liberal Democrats floundered as they tried to devise a new intellectual underpinning that was different from outdated New Deal-era thinking.

In addition, Republicans were busy building, in the words of journalist Thomas B. Edsall, "red America." Beginning in the mid-1960s, Edsall wrote,

[T]he Republican party and the conservative movement have together created a juggernaut—a loosely connected but highly coordinated network of individuals and organizations—with a shared stake in a strong, centralized political machine. This machine includes the national party itself, a collection of campaign contributors large and small, a majority of the country's business and trade associations, the bulk of the corporate lobbying community, and an interlocking alliance of muscular conservative "values" organizations and churches (The Family Research Council, the Coalition for Traditional Values, Focus on the Family, the Southern Baptist Convention, thriving Pentecostal, evangelical, and right-leaning Catholic communities, and so forth). It includes a powerful array of conservative foundations with focused social and economic agendas (Scaife, Bradley, Olin, Koch, Smith Richardson, Carthage, Earhart, etc.), as well as prosperous right-of-center think tanks such as the American Enterprise Institute, the Cato Institute, the Free Congress Foundation, the Heritage Foundation, and the Manhattan Institute.

In Edsall's view, these organizations had "proven deft at redefining key American concepts of social justice, at marketing conservative ideologies in both domestic and international affairs, and at successfully integrating these redefined ideals—in the eyes of many voters—with goals of economic efficiency."[33]

"The Paranoid Style"

But underneath the successes of these organizations lay a fundamental fear of the future. In 1985, Daniel Patrick Moynihan saw an emerging mutation of conservatism that would pose problems in the years ahead. According to Moynihan, "there have been few voices heard from the political ranks" to quash what he called an emerging "paranoid style on the Right." "Frankly," Moynihan wrote, the reason for the paucity of voices was because "I smell fear."[34] Fear among the Republican establishment of a conservatism that saw liberal conspiracies everywhere had been previously heightened by the nomination of Barry Goldwater in 1964. Writing in the October issue of *Harper's* that year, Columbia University political scientist Richard Hofstadter described an emerging "paranoid style" in U.S. politics:

> As a member of the avant-garde who is capable of perceiving the conspiracy before it is fully obvious to an as yet unaroused public, the paranoid is a militant leader. He does not see social conflict as something to be mediated and compromised, in the manner of the working politician. Since what is at stake is always a conflict between absolute good and absolute evil, what is necessary is not compromise but the will to fight things out to a finish. Since the enemy is thought of as being totally evil and totally unappeasable, he must be totally eliminated—if not from the world, at least from the theatre of operations to which the paranoid directs his attention. This demand for total triumph leads to the formulation of hopelessly unrealistic goals, and since these goals are not even remotely attainable, failure constantly heightens the paranoid's sense of frustration. Even partial success leaves him with the same feeling of powerlessness with which he began, and this in turn only strengthens his awareness of the vast and terrifying quality of the enemy he opposes.[35]

For many, the Goldwater nomination signaled the emergence of a new and different conservatism that would brook no compromise with the Democrats.

Interviewing delegates to the 1964 Republican convention, political scientist Aaron B. Wildavsky found them committed to Goldwater because he was a purist: "He is straightforward." "He does not compromise." "He doesn't pander to the public; he's against expediency." "He is frank." "He has courage." "He stands up for what he believes." "He won't play footsie with the people." "He votes his convictions when he knows he's right." "He doesn't go along with the crowd." "He meets issues head-on." "Goldwater speaks about things others avoid. Most politicians like to avoid issues." "He keeps promises." "He doesn't change his mind." "He is not confused." As one memorably concluded, "I would rather be one against 20,000, and believe I was right."[36] Richard Hofstadter noted that this "paranoid style" saw politics as a "confrontation of opposed interests which are (or are felt to be) totally irreconcilable and thus by nature not susceptible to the normal political processes of bargain and compromise."[37]

Thus, when Goldwater uttered his memorable lines in his acceptance speech—"Extremism in the defense of liberty is no vice. Moderation in the pursuit of justice is no virtue"—his supporters were ecstatic, while the GOP establishment writhed in agony.[38] Goldwater's last-ditch rival, Pennsylvania governor William Scranton, issued a broadside that claimed, "*Goldwaterism has come to stand for a whole crazy-quilt collection of absurd and dangerous positions that would be soundly repudiated by the American people in November*" [emphasis in original].[39] Even seasoned analysts were amazed that Goldwater (unlike Eisenhower and Nixon before him) refused to temper his conservatism in order to appeal to the center. Theodore H. White remembered one reporter who, "halfway through Goldwater's speech, slowly became aware of the politics of no compromise, then turned and remarked, 'My God, he's going to run as Barry Goldwater.' "[40]

A. James Reichley, then a member of Scranton's staff, noted that Goldwater's convention triumph ended a reign of GOP pragmatism that began with Eisenhower.[41] While Ronald Reagan would later belie Reichley's observation, it had merit in the emergence of a hard-line conservatism that, in the post-Reagan years, would create its own form of intellectual and political imprisonment. Even the much-vaunted conservative think tanks were not immune. The Heritage Foundation—once an innovator of conservative thought—was taken over in 2013 by Jim DeMint, who left the Senate to assume the presidency of Heritage saying he could be more powerful there than as one of a hundred senators. At Heritage, DeMint established the Senate Conservatives Fund, which targeted DeMint's fellow Republicans who, in his view, were not conservative enough. Utah senator Orrin Hatch was dismayed at Heritage's transformation:

Right now, I think it's in danger of losing its clout and its power around Washington, D.C. There's a real question in the minds of many Republicans now, and I'm not just speaking for myself, for a lot of people that [question is]: is Heritage going to go so political that it really doesn't amount to anything anymore.[42]

Other organizations followed a similar path. The Club for Growth aimed its ire at "me-too" Republicans and elected one of their own, Pat Toomey, to the U.S. Senate in 2010. The Cato Institute became embroiled in a legal dispute following the death of its chairman emeritus, William Niskanen, between the Koch brothers and Cato stalwarts charging that the Kochs were trying to turn Cato into "some sort of auxiliary of the GOP."[43] Even the American Enterprise Institute has become more polemical under its current president, Arthur C. Brooks. In his book, *The Battle: How the Fight Between Free Enterprise and Big Government Will Shape America*, Brooks declared that Obama's presidency created a

> new culture war . . . [that is] a struggle between two competing visions of America's future. In one, America will continue to be a unique and exceptional nation organized around the principles of free enterprise. In the other, America will move toward European-style statism grounded in expanding bureaucracies, increasing income redistribution, and government-controlled corporations.[44]

(As an indication of the intellectual sloppiness behind Brooks's work, the book's index lists Obama's first name as "Barak," not Barack.)

Rather than promote new conservative ideas, an intellectual stultification ensued. In 2012, it was expected that any would-be GOP presidential nominee must tow the party line rather than enunciate new ideas. After Texas governor Rick Perry asked Republicans to have a "heart" by supporting public education for illegal immigrant minors, former Pennsylvania senator Rick Santorum pounced, saying Perry's stance was "soft."[45] At another GOP debate, Mitt Romney uttered his devastating line that immigrants should "self-deport"—a comment that Republican National Chairman Reince Priebus later called "horrific."[46] A gay soldier who asked about ending "the don't ask, don't tell policy" was booed.[47] Even moderates like Jon Huntsman raised his hand when asked if he would "walk away" from a deal that raised taxes by one dollar for every ten dollars in spending cuts.[48] Thomas B. Edsall explains why compromise has become a dirty word in GOP circles:

> By its very nature, the Republican agenda precludes a political strategy of consensus or moderation. First and foremost, the conservative agenda is not moderate. It is an attempt to dismantle the welfare state, a structure build up over the last two-thirds of the twentieth century. Second, the conservative agenda does not have the decisive support of the people. In a two-party democracy such as the United States, the achievement of a

radical change in the direction of government without the support of a clear majority of voters has required the strategic division of the electorate into two separate camps, a commitment to aggressively capitalize on all Republican victories, and purposeful polarization to force the electorate to pick between extremes. When Republicans have won—even without a majority of the popular vote—they have claimed that their election sanctioned the adoption of policies more extreme than voters favor when they have more ideologically varied choices.[49]

The result is a false kind of political choice that voters themselves find either stultifying or irrelevant. By being stuck in a kind of political time warp that cannot escape the Reagan era, Republicans are unable to rewrite their platforms largely because its conservative base refuses to allow the party to do so. Former George W. Bush administration staffers Michael Gerson and Peter Wehner believe Republican policies have become "stale," adding, "[T]hey are very nearly identical to those offered up by the party more than thirty years ago."[50] Even the Republican National Committee noticed. After Mitt Romney's loss, the authors of the "Growth and Opportunity Project," an autopsy of what went wrong in 2012, concluded:

The Republican party needs to stop talking to itself. We have become expert in how to provide ideological reinforcement to like-minded people, but devastatingly we have lost the ability to be persuasive with, or welcoming to, those who do not agree with us on every issue.[51]

MSNBC commentator and former Republican congressman Joe Scarborough agrees, "Everybody's afraid to talk," adding, "The national conversation is more constricted, with radio stars, websites and magazines functioning as unofficial arbiters and limiters of domestic and foreign policy debate."[52] David Frum concurs:

For a generation a certain brand of political commentator has urged conservatives to think of politics as a form of warfare, and to regard their opponents as enemies. This way of thinking does its severest harm to conservatives themselves. It embitters them, isolates them, alienates them, and perverts the judgment of people and things. It causes them to disparage their most effective leaders and instead elevate those who offer confrontation in place of results.[53]

Frum adds that among serious conservative scholars "the price of influence... remains circumspection."[54] Frum should know, having been asked to leave the American Enterprise Institute in 2010.

A political arena filled with invective results in name-calling without serious thinking. This imprisons the GOP in a kind of intellectual time warp whereby the party remains locked into the policies of the Reagan era without Reagan himself to explain them. As Gerson and Wehner conclude, "For Republicans to design an agenda that applies to the conditions of 1980 is as if Ronald Reagan designed his agenda for conditions that existed in the Truman years."[55]

The most powerful echo chamber within today's Republican Party is Fox News. In its own way, Fox serves to amplify the Republican message while at the same time excoriating those who deviate from it. A focus group of Tea Party Republicans conducted by Democratic pollster Stanley B. Greenberg and former Bill Clinton strategist James Carville shows their devotion to the news channel:

> "I absolutely love Bill O'Reilly." (Tea Party woman, Roanoke)
> "I wish there was more Fox News." (Tea Party woman, Roanoke)
> "It's the only news channel I watch." (Tea Party man, Raleigh)
> "I like it. I'm missing two hours of it." (Tea Party man, Raleigh)[56]

Like most political information-gathering today, both Republicans and Democrats often resort to news sources that aim to ratify preexisting views rather than seek new information. Such behavior helps to foster the current polarization that views politics as a form of asymmetrical warfare.[57] In 2010, Barack Obama cited a letter from a kindergartner asking why people weren't being "nice." His answer was instructive:

> Well, if you turn on the news today or yesterday—or a week ago, or a month ago—particularly one of the cable channels—you can see why a kindergartner would ask this question. We've got politicians calling each other all sorts of unflattering names. Pundits and talking heads shout at each other. The media tends to play up every hint of conflict because it makes for a sexier story—which means anyone interested in getting coverage feels compelled to make their arguments as outrageous and as incendiary as possible.[58]

Obama called for a "new civility" in public discourse, urging that his fellow citizens seek out alternative sources of information—including those with which they disagree:

> [I]f you're somebody who only reads the editorial page of *The New York Times*, try glancing at the page of *The Wall Street Journal* once in a while. If you're a fan of Glenn Beck or Rush Limbaugh, try reading a few columns on *The Huffington Post* website. It may make your blood boil; your mind may not be changed. But the practice of listening to opposing views is essential for effective citizenship.[59]

Obama's pleas have fallen on deaf ears. On both the right and the left, the desire to motivate listeners to action forms the heart of today's information-disseminating entities. In 2010, Fox News host Steve Doocey asked viewers, "Should the 47 percent who pay no taxes even be allowed to vote?"[60] Other examples include conservative commentator Dinesh D'Souza, who published a 2010 book titled *The Roots of Obama's Rage*, which became the basis for a movie titled *2016: Obama's America*. In both, D'Souza claimed Obama's worldview was rooted in "Kenyan anti-colonial behavior."[61] While such incendiary remarks may prompt the occasional apology, they are designed to emote anger and inspire political action. *New York Times* columnist David Brooks notes that the inflammatory language used by many conservatives is

about the Palinization of parts of the GOP. This is not about passing legislation, not about, well, we're in a party. We should pay attention to our leaders. We should craft some compromise. We should compromise with the other side. This is about making a statement that will sound good on Fox. . . . Who is going to stand up for Republican values, but believe in governing? And, so far, that person has not emerged.[62]

David Frum agrees:

The alternative information system built by conservative elites imprisons them as much as it does the movement's rank and file. Exactly at the moment when realism and restraint are most needed, those qualities are spurned by a political movement that has furnished its collective mind with pseudo-facts and pretend information.[63]

Nowhere is this more evident than in the emergence of the Tea Party.

The Rise of the Tea Party

On February 19, 2009, CNBC television reporter Rick Santelli delivered an on-air tirade against the Obama administration's plan to rescue homeowners from defaulting on their mortgages. Speaking from the floor of the Chicago Mercantile Exchange, Santelli emoted:

The government is promoting bad behavior! Because we certainly don't want to put stimulus pork and give people a whopping eight or ten dollars in their check and think they ought to save it. . . . I tell you what. I have an idea. The new administration is big on computers and technology. How about this—president [of the] new administration? Why don't you put up a website to ask people to vote on the Internet as a referendum to see if we really want to subsidize the losers' mortgages? Or would we, at least, like to buy cars and buy houses in foreclosure and give 'em to people who might have a chance to prosper down the road, and reward people that carry the water instead of drink the water? [Applause] . . . This is America! How many of you people want to pay for your neighbor's mortgage that has an extra bathroom and can't pay their bills? Raise your hand [Boos]. President Obama, are you listening? . . . Cuba used to have mansions and a relatively decent economy. They moved from the individual to the collective. Now they're driving '54 Chevys—maybe the last great car to come out of Detroit. . . . We're thinking of having a Chicago Tea Party in July. All you capitalists who want to show up at Lake Michigan, I'm going to start organizing [applause]. . . . If you read our Founding Fathers, people like Benjamin Franklin and [Thomas] Jefferson, what we're doing in this country now is making them roll over in their graves.[64]

Santelli's outburst struck a chord, going viral on the Internet. It headlined the *Drudge Report* and resulted in a rebuke from then-White House Press Secretary Robert Gibbs, who charged that Santelli did not know what was in the plan, and that its participants would not be exempt from mortgage payments. Gibbs joked that he would be "happy to buy him a cup of coffee—decaf."[65] From Santelli's rant, the Tea Party was born and its anti-tax rallies, scheduled for April 15, 2009, were promoted and covered extensively by Fox News.

The Tea Party is motivated by a "back-to-basics" argument. In its founding documents, the Tea Party states:

We hold that the United States is a republic conceived by its architects as a nation whose people were granted "unalienable rights" by our Creator. Chief among these are the rights to "life, liberty, and the pursuit of happiness." The Tea Party Patriots stand with our Founders as heirs to the Republic, to claim our rights and duties which preserve their legacy as our own. We hold, as did the Founders, that there exists an inherent benefit to our country when private property and prosperity are secured by natural law and the rights of the individual.[66]

Simply stated, the Tea Party sees the federal government providing handouts to people who don't deserve them, and it is deeply disturbed by Obamacare, which, in its view, is more of the "something-for-nothing" Democratic philosophy at work. In 2010, Tea Party senatorial candidate Rand Paul won consistent applause when he pledged not to vote for any legislation that was not authorized in the U.S. Constitution.[67] Stella Fisher of Surprise, Arizona, explains why she and her husband, Larry, gravitated to the Tea Party: "We think the federal government is overstepping their authority. Take health care, take the education. All those things. . . . The EPA, they've shut down I forget how many timber plants in Arizona because of the spotted owl."[68] Bonnie Sims of southeastern Virginia is another who, along with her husband, was moved to action:

> It's so sad the way the country is now. We worked for everything we got. . . . [We never] lived a day in our life off welfare. We had to earn our rights. [But such] values are not taught anymore. . . . [The] young generation [is all] Obama, Obama, Obama. I am not a racist [but Obama] is a socialist [who] got a lot of it from his father.[69]

Another Tea Party supporter liked the fact that she and her peers were "standing up": "People are saying hey, this isn't what's in our Constitution, and it's not what's in our schools. And I think people are taking a stand now, and we need to, before it's too late."[70]

Further motivating Tea Party support is a sullen anger at the GOP establishment. Many agree with a Colorado Springs woman who declared Republican leaders "cave all the time."[71] The emergence of the Tea Party served Republican purposes in the 2010 midterm elections when it was a fresh arrival on the political scene. Exit polls that year found 41 percent approved of the Tea Party, with 92 percent of Republicans saying they "strongly supported" it.[72] In effect, the Tea Party became a stand-in for a discredited Republican Party that was still suffering from the aftereffects of the George W. Bush presidency.[73]

Four years later, things changed dramatically. Following the Tea Party-inspired government shutdown of 2013, favorable ratings for the Republican Party and its Tea Party adherents hit new lows. In October 2013, NBC News and the *Wall Street Journal* reported that GOP approval stood at 22 percent.[74] The Tea Party saw its unfavorable scores exceed its favorable ones: 47 percent to 21 percent.[75] Exit polls from the 2014 midterm elections showed only 13 percent of voters "strongly supported" the Tea Party, while 26 percent were "strongly opposed." Even as Republicans gained control of both houses of Congress, GOP congressional leaders were negatively rated by 60 percent of the Republican-leaning midterm electorate.[76]

The Tea Party presents the Republican Party with a dilemma. As its adherents have grown and become more vocal, their influence in intraparty affairs has increased. Studies conducted by Stanley B. Greenberg and James Carville find that Tea Partiers constitute one-fourth of Republican voters. When evangelicals are added to the mix, the figure rises to 54 percent.[77] They are united in their opposition to Barack Obama, and their racial uniformity is also striking: 90 percent are white.[78] Yet their unwillingness to compromise, along with their desire to adhere to their own kind of ideological purity, has led to several unfortunate candidate selections that have resulted in the forfeiture of five U.S. senatorial seats to the Democrats. In 2010, Tea Party-backed candidates Christine O'Donnell, Sharron Angle, and Ken Buck proved to be too extreme for their blue and purple state electorates (Delaware, Nevada, and Colorado). In 2012, Tea Partiers Richard Mourdock and Todd Aiken became entangled in unfortunate comments about rape that allowed Democrats to win in red states (Missouri and Indiana). Adding to the dilemma, Greenberg and Carville find that the GOP establishment constitutes only 5 percent of the party's base voters (even as they dominate the money game).[79]

The result is to place the Republican Party in a bind. As David Frum notes, Tea Party Republicans are nostalgic "for a mis-remembered past"—forgetting the federal government's historic role in building the nation's infrastructure, creating its education system, and providing a social safety net (including Social Security and Medicare) from which they—and everyone else—benefit. The problem, notes Frum, is that nostalgia "is no basis for governing a diverse and advancing nation."[80] Political analyst Earl Ofari Hutchinson believes that the Tea Party

> casts a huge shadow over the GOP. Their fervent backers touch a deep, dark and throbbing pulse among legions of ultra-conservatives who think that President Obama and many Democrats are communists, gays are immoral, and that the health care reform law is a massive intrusion into their personal affairs.[81]

John Feehery, director of government affairs for Quinn Gillespie and Associates, agrees, writing that Tea Party groups "have become a fifth column within the Republican party, blowing up bridges, sabotaging supply lines, creating false controversies, [and] wasting valuable party resources."[82]

While Tea Partiers did not get their way in 2014—as establishment Republicans made sure that their best candidates were placed at the top of the ballots—there is no sign that the Tea Party will cease to exert its influence, especially when it comes to choosing the 2016 Republican presidential nominee. As one Tea Partier put it: "America is rising back up and getting a backbone again, and making our voices heard one way or another, whether it's Tea Party, or whatever else." A second agrees, "They are a group to be reckoned with, because if we're going to turn things around, the Tea Party's going to need to be part of it." A third added: "I thank God there's enough people getting angry now and it will have to stop. I think people realize that we're going to have to rise up and take control." As one Tea Party sympathizer concluded, "These are the kind of people the Tea Party's made of."[83]

Obama's Victory

In his 2010 book, *The Battle: How the Fight Between Free Enterprise and Big Government Will Shape America*, Arthur C. Brooks writes that young people have "exhibited a frightening openness to statism."[84] In fact, Brooks believes that the battle may already be lost, as there are a growing number of Americans who have either zero or negative income tax liability:

> President Obama plans to increase dramatically the percentage of non-payers. In early 2009, before his stimulus package was enacted into law, 38 percent of Americans were estimated to have zero or negative income tax liability. (Negative taxes are paid by people receiving refundable tax credits and similar subsidies from the government, such as the Earned Income Tax Credit). After President Obama's budget stimulus and tax changes, this proportion will increase to almost 47 percent. . . . Very soon it is clear that nonpayers will outnumber the payers. We will eventually reach a threshold beyond which most Americans have no incentive to defend free enterprise, because it is so far from their interest to do so. The young sympathizers of socialism today may be the grown-up defenders of socialism tomorrow.[85]

In 2012, Barack Obama used this prevailing pessimism to his benefit. Historically, presidential elections are won by optimists, not dour naysayers. Ronald Reagan provides ample proof of this point. Reagan biographer Lou Cannon perceptively noted that Reagan's optimism "was the essential ingredient of an approach to life that had carried Reagan from the backwater of Dixon to fame as a sports announcer and then to the stages of Hollywood and of the world." Cannon added, "the feeling that 'everything is going to be all right' . . . would be his most distinctive quality as president."[86]

Such optimism is lacking among today's top GOP strategists and thinkers. One reason is a prevailing pessimism among voters. In 2014, 48 percent said they expected life for the next generation of Americans to be *worse*—only 22 percent thought things would improve.[87] Still, Americans want their presidents to believe in a brighter future—not one dominated by the survival of the fittest, or one where people get something for nothing. Unfortunately for the GOP, its 2012 presidential nominee, Mitt Romney, lacked Reagan's distinctive optimism. Attuned to pessimists like Arthur Brooks, Romney made his infamous comments about the "47 percent," noting that these people should be written off to Republican entreaties:

> [They, the 47 percent of non-taxpayers] believe that they are victims, who believe the government has a responsibility to care for them, who believe that they are entitled to healthcare, to food, to housing, to you-name-it. That's an entitlement. And the government should give it

to them. And they will vote for this president no matter what. . . . These are people who pay no income tax. My job is not to worry about those people. I'll never convince them that they should take personal responsibility and care for their lives.[88]

According to one survey, 55 percent had a negative reaction to Romney's comments.[89]

But to Republicans (especially Tea Partiers), disparaging a dependent 47 percent resonated. As one put it, "That's the sort of subculture that the Democrats are creating is that sense of entitlement, because they want us dependent on them."[90] Thus, Republicans have a pessimistic view of the direction of the country, which leaves them "worried," "discouraged," "scared," and "concerned."[91] While there are many good reasons to feel this way—an anemic economic recovery, stagnant wages, trouble overseas, and a president who may be out of his depth—Republicans have a different reason for their concern. Despite Barack Obama's anemic poll ratings (rivaling, in some places, those of George W. Bush in his second term), Republicans believe that Obama has already *won*. As Greenberg and Carville report:

> To them, Obama has imposed his agenda and Republicans in Washington let him get away with it. The country is sure that gridlock has won the day, but Republicans see a president who has fooled and manipulated the public, lied, and gotten the secret socialist agenda done.
> The Republican base thinks they face a victorious Democratic Party that is intent on expanding government to increase dependency and therefore electoral support. It starts with food stamps and unemployment benefits; expands further if you legalize the illegal immigrants; but insuring the uninsured through the Affordable Care Act will dramatically expand the number of those dependent on government. They believe these policies are part of an electoral strategy—not just a political ideology or economic philosophy. If Obamacare is fully implemented, the Republican party may be lost forever.[92]

One means by which Republicans think Obama can claim victory is his use of executive orders. Even though the number of such orders are *fewer* than previous presidents (including George W. Bush), Obama's reliance on his pen rattles Republicans.[93] As one Tea Party sympathizer put it:

> When Congress is gone . . . he just does an Executive Order. He's going to get anything he wants. And there's nobody there that will have the guts enough to stand up to him. There's so many secret things that go on—that are—bills are passed and regulations are passed—we never knew about.[94]

Especially galling to Republicans are measures designed to help minorities that Obama has unilaterally approved. In 2012, Obama signed an executive order known as Deferred Action Against Childhood Arrivals. Following the failure of the DREAM Act in 2010, Obama decided to take unilateral action that directed the Department of Homeland Security to refrain from enforcing immigration laws when it came to underage children who entered the United States illegally. Obama's action proved popular with Hispanics, and he won 71 percent of their votes in 2012.[95] After the 2014 midterm elections, Barack Obama signed executive orders allowing up to five million undocumented immigrants to remain free of prosecution if they lived in the United States for five years, had a child who was American-born, and had no criminal history. Republicans dubbed Obama an "emperor" and vowed to fight. But many believe the battle was already lost, since GOP congressional leaders were far more interested in governing than confronting the president.

Others see a kind of "vast left-wing conspiracy" (to paraphrase Hillary Clinton) that has empowered the federal government to take unprecedented steps to intrude into the lives of individuals. As one Tea Partier explained:

> He's turned the government into a spy agency on us. . . . [They are] setting up an organization and a machinery that can control and spy on every asset of our lives, and control it. And once it's infiltrated with all of the little webs . . . you won't be able to undo it.[96]

This pessimism has even penetrated into the comments of several Republican leaders, among them former vice presidential nominee Paul Ryan:

> We are reaching a fiscal tipping point. The moral tipping point is, before too long we could become a society we were never intended to be. We could become a society where the net majority of Americans are takers, not makers.[97]

Such sentiments among conservative right-wingers are hardly new. As Richard Hofstadter wrote in 1964, "the modern right wing . . . feels dispossessed: America has been largely taken away from them and their kind, though they are determined to try to repossess it and to prevent the final destructive act of subversion."[98]

It is not only the expansion of government and presidential authority that bothers Republicans, it is the sense that even on cultural matters the country has moved in a different direction. Gay marriage is reaching a turning point where it may become universal throughout the United States very soon. Abortion is a settled issue, with majorities agreeing with Bill Clinton that the procedure should be "safe, legal, and rare." Marijuana is legal in the states of Colorado and Washington, with more states poised to act.

The coming end of the culture wars leaves many Republicans believing that they are on the losing side of history. As one put it: "We're having to realize that we're going to be in a very politically incorrect minority pretty soon."[99] David Frum agrees: "At a time when the need to broaden the party's appeal seemed overwhelmingly compelling, Republicans narrowed their appeal to the most ideological fragment of the conservative base." The solution, says Frum, is that twenty-first century conservatism "must become economically inclusive, environmentally responsible, culturally modern, and intellectually credible."[100]

Unfortunately, there are few signs that Republicans are poised to move away from their longing for a nostalgic past. While the party can administer thumpings from disgruntled voters dissatisfied with Barack Obama (as happened in 2010 and 2014), it remains unable to translate these wins into a coherent strategy for governance. In many ways, the present-day Republican plight is reminiscent of the Democrats in the 1980s. Back then, Democrats realized that they had become the minority party in presidential politics and needed to reform themselves. While they could capitalize on the discontents of the moment, it was not until Bill Clinton came along that the Democrats began to possess both the intellectual firepower and the willingness to abandon old New Deal nostrums. Only when Republicans undergo a similar metamorphosis will they be able to make inroads with today's presidential electorate—much in the same way that Dwight D. Eisenhower recognized that the Republicans were in the minority and that their brand needed refurbishing. That means having a GOP leader with the intellectual resources that allow him or her to rethink old positions, which involves a certain type of dynamic thinking. It also means that such a leader be granted a degree of latitude by the party base. Until then, Republicans will remain locked in a kind of perverse conservative straightjacket they have created for themselves.

Notes

1 Quoted in Thomas B. Edsall, *Building Red America: The New Conservative Coalition and the Drive for Permanent Power* (New York: Basic Books, 2006), 67.
2 Quoted in Joe Scarborough, *The Right Path: From Ike to Reagan, How Republicans Once Mastered Politics—and Can Again* (New York: Random House, 2013), 5.
3 Quoted in Garry Wills, *Reagan's America: Innocents at Home* (Garden City, New York: Doubleday, 1987), 286.
4 Quoted in E.J. Dionne, Jr., *Why Americans Hate Politics* (New York: Simon and Schuster, 1991), 170.
5 Ibid., 171.
6 Dwight D. Eisenhower, State of the Union Address, Washington, D.C., February 2, 1953.
7 Fred I. Greenstein, *The Hidden-Hand Presidency: Eisenhower as Leader* (New York: Basic Books, 1982), 51–52.

8 Dwight D. Eisenhower, Acceptance Speech, Republican National Convention, San Francisco, August 23, 1956.
9 Arthur Larson, *A Republican Looks at His Party* (New York: Harper and Brothers, 1956), 14.
10 See John Kenneth White, *Still Seeing Red: How the Cold War Shapes the New American Politics* (Boulder: Westview Press, 1997), 112.
11 Dwight D. Eisenhower, "Statement by the President Upon Signing the National Defense Education Act," September 2, 1958. In *Public Papers of the Presidents of the United States: Dwight D. Eisenhower* (Washington, D.C.: U.S. Government Printing Office, 1959), 224.
12 Dwight D. Eisenhower, *Mandate for Change: The White House Years, 1953–1956* (Garden City, New York: Doubleday and Company, 1963), 549.
13 "Speeches by Eisenhower, Nixon," *New York Times*, November 7, 1956, 12.
14 Larson, *A Republican Looks at His Party*, 10.
15 Cited in Vincent J. and Vee Burke, *Nixon's Good Deed: Welfare Reform* (New York: Columbia University Press, 1974), 127.
16 Ibid.
17 Ibid.
18 Bill Clinton, *My Life* (New York: Alfred A. Knopf, 2004), 594.
19 Ibid.
20 From Andrew Jackson to Dwight Eisenhower, only four presidents had to confront either a House or a Senate controlled by the opposition party: Zachary Taylor in 1848, Rutherford B. Hayes in 1876, James Garfield in 1880, and Grover Cleveland in 1884.
21 Quoted in Doris Kearns, *Lyndon Johnson and the American Dream* (New York: New American Library, 1976), 146–147.
22 Richard Nixon, Victory Speech, November 6, 1968. See https://www.youtube.com/watch?v=v3xT-lSIC7A. Accessed November 2, 2014.
23 Barry M. Goldwater with Jack Casserly, *Goldwater* (New York: Doubleday, 1988), 109.
24 Larson, *A Republican Looks at His Party*, 19.
25 Richard M. Scammon and Ben J. Wattenberg, "Is This the End of an Era?," *Public Opinion*, October/November 1980, 11.
26 George F. Will, "No More Jury Duty," *Washington Post*, January 19, 1989, A-27.
27 "Moving Right Along? Campaign '84's Lessons for 1988: An Interview with Peter Hart and Richard Wirthlin," *Public Opinion*, December/January 1985, 60.
28 David Frum, *Why Romney Lost and What the GOP Can Do about It* (Newsweek ebook, published online, 2012).
29 Daniel Patrick Moynihan, "Of 'Sons' and Their 'Grandsons,'" *New York Times*, July 7, 1980, 15.
30 See John Kenneth White, *The New Politics of Old Values* (Hanover, New Hampshire: University Press of New England, 1988), 60.
31 Cited in Jonathan Alter, *The Center Holds: Obama and His Enemies* (New York: Simon and Schuster, 2013), 73.
32 Daniel Patrick Moynihan, "The Paranoid Style in American Politics Revisited," *The Public Interest*, Fall 1985, 112.
33 Edsall, *Building Red America*, 5.
34 Moynihan, "The Paranoid Style in American Politics Revisited," 126.
35 Richard Hofstadter, "The Paranoid Style in American Politics," *Harper's*, November 1964, 82.
36 Aaron B. Wildavsky, "The Goldwater Phenomenon: Purists, Politicians, and the Two-Party System," found in Norman L. Zucker, ed., *The American Party*

Process: Readings and Comments (New York: Dodd, Mead and Company, 1968), 445, 446.

37 Hofstadter, "The Paranoid Style in American Politics," 86.

38 Barry M. Goldwater, Acceptance Speech, Republican National Convention, San Francisco, July 16, 1964.

39 Cited in Theodore H. White, *The Making of the President, 1964* (New York: Atheneum Publishers, 1965), 208.

40 Ibid., 228.

41 Ibid., 229.

42 Jennifer Rubin, "Jim DeMint's Destruction of the Heritage Foundation," *Washington Post*, October 21, 2013.

43 Cited in Alter, *The Center Holds*, 73.

44 Arthur C. Brooks, *The Battle: How the Fight Between Free Enterprise and Big Government Will Shape America's Future* (New York: Basic Books, 2010), 1.

45 See https://www.youtube.com/watch?v=4bA9m3IG99s. Accessed November 3, 2014.

46 See https://www.youtube.com/watch?v=ObVnA0nIx_s. Accessed November 3, 2014, and Aaron Blake, "Priebus: Romney's Self-Deportation Comment Was 'Horrific,'" *Washington Post*, August 16, 2013.

47 See https://www.youtube.com/watch?v=tJPKQ3UQsIc. Accessed November 3, 2014.

48 See https://www.youtube.com/watch?v=ASQNITVweLo. Accessed November 3, 2014.

49 Edsall, *Building Red America*, 36.

50 Cited in Republican National Committee, *Growth and Opportunity Project* (Washington, D.C.: Republican National Committee, December 2012), 5.

51 Ibid., 6.

52 Ibid., 54.

53 Frum, *Why Romney Lost*.

54 David Frum, "Crashing the Party: Why the GOP Must Modernize to Win," *Foreign Affairs*, September/October 2014.

55 Cited in Republican National Committee, *Growth and Opportunity Project*, 5.

56 Quoted in Stanley Greenberg and James Carville, memo, "Inside the GOP: Report on the Republican Party Project," June 12, 2014, 23.

57 See John J. Pitney, Jr., "Asymmetric Warfare: Supporters and Opponents of President Obama," in Steven E. Schier, ed., *Transforming America: Barack Obama in the White House* (Lanham, Maryland: Rowman and Littlefield, 2011), 121–142.

58 Barack Obama, Commencement Address, University of Michigan, Ann Arbor, May 1, 2010.

59 Ibid.

60 Cited in Frum, *Why Romney Lost*.

61 Ibid.

62 "Shields and Brooks," *PBS NewsHour*, broadcast, August 1, 2014.

63 Frum, *Why Romney Lost*.

64 See https://www.youtube.com/watch?v=wcvSjKCU_Zo. Accessed November 1, 2014.

65 See https://www.youtube.com/watch?v=uZSlOifcEo4. Accessed November 1, 2014.

66 Mark Meckler and Jenny Beth Martin, *Tea Party Patriots: The Second American Revolution* (New York: Henry Holt and Company, 2012), 23.

67 Kate Zernike, *Boiling Mad: Inside Tea Party America* (New York: Times Books, Henry Holt and Company, 2010), 180.

68 Quoted in Theda Skocpol and Vanessa Williamson, *The Tea Party and the Remaking of Republican Conservatism* (New York: Oxford University Press, 2013), 46.

69 Ibid.

70 Greenberg and Carville, "Inside the GOP," 19.

71 Ibid.

72 Edison Media Research and Mitofsky International, exit poll, November 2, 2010.

73 For more on this see John Kenneth White, "Caught between Hope and History: Obama, Public Opinion, and the 2010 Elections," in Steven E. Schier, ed., *Transforming America: Barack Obama in the White House* (Lanham, Maryland: Rowman and Littlefield Publishers, 2011), 43–62.

74 NBC News/*Wall Street Journal*, poll, October 25–28, 2013. Text of question: "Now I'm going to read you the names of several public figures, groups, and organizations, and I'd like you to rate your feelings toward each one as very positive, somewhat positive, neutral, somewhat negative, or very negative. . . . The Republican party." Very positive, 6 percent; somewhat positive, 16 percent; neutral, 24 percent; somewhat negative, 23 percent; very negative, 30 percent; don't know/not sure, 1 percent.

75 NBC News/*Wall Street Journal*, poll, October 25–28, 2013. Text of question: "Now I'm going to read you the names of several public figures, groups, and organizations, and I'd like you to rate your feelings toward each one as very positive, somewhat positive, neutral, somewhat negative, or very negative. . . . The Tea party." Very positive, 9 percent; somewhat positive, 12 percent; neutral, 20 percent; somewhat negative, 13 percent; very negative, 34 percent; don't know/not sure, 12 percent.

76 Edison Research, exit poll, November 4, 2014.

77 Greenberg and Carville, "Inside the GOP," 2.

78 Ibid.

79 Ibid.

80 Frum, *Why Romney Lost.*

81 Quoted in Chuck McCutcheon, "Future of the GOP: Can the Republicans Gain More Minority Support?," *CQ Researcher*, October 24, 2014, 893.

82 John Feehery, "Do Tea Party Groups Have Too Much Influence Over the GOP?," *CQ Researcher*, October 24, 2014, 905.

83 Greenberg and Carville, "Inside the GOP," 19.

84 Brooks, *The Battle*, 30.

85 Ibid., 21–22.

86 Lou Cannon, *President Reagan: The Role of a Lifetime* (New York: Simon and Schuster, 1991), 26, 226.

87 Edison Research, exit poll, November 4, 2014.

88 ABC News, "Romney Stands By 'Entitled' Obama Supporters in Leaked Video," September 17, 2012.

89 Pew Research Center, "Romney's 47 Percent Comments Criticized, But Many Say Also Overcovered," press release, October 1, 2012.

90 Greenberg and Carville, "Inside the GOP," 14.

91 Ibid., 32.

92 Ibid., 2.

93 See the American Presidency Project, http://www.presidency.ucsb.edu/data/orders.php. Accessed May 30, 2015. Through May 20, 2015, Barack Obama has issued 206 executive orders to George W. Bush's 291.

94 Greenberg and Carville, "Inside the GOP," 9.

95 Edison Research, exit poll, November 6, 2012.

96 Greenberg and Carville, "Inside the GOP," 10.
97 Quoted in Frum, *Why Romney Lost.*
98 Hofstadter, "The Paranoid Style in American Politics," 81.
99 Greenberg and Carville, "Inside the GOP," 16.
100 Frum, *Why Romney Lost.*

Chapter 5

Why the Republican Party Is Necessary

"The country needs a vibrant Republican Party."
Lindsey Graham, South Carolina Republican U.S. senator

Alone in a dark, dank, and unfinished White House in the early winter months of 1801, an angry president received his successor with the cry, "You turned me out!" Attempting to calm the distraught John Adams, Thomas Jefferson tactfully replied,

> I have not turned you out, Mr. Adams. . . . In consequence of a division of opinion existing among our fellow-citizens, as to the proper constitution of our political institutions, and of the wisdom and propriety of certain measures . . . that portion of our citizens that approved and advocated one class of these opinions and measures selected you as their candidate . . . and their opponents selected me. If you and myself had been inexistent, or for any cause had not been selected, other persons would have been selected in our places; and thus the contest would have been carried on, and with the same result, except that the party which supported you would have been defeated by a greater majority, as it was known that, but for you, your party would have carried their unpopular measures much further than they did.[1]

The 1800 presidential campaign waged by Federalist candidate John Adams and Democratic-Republican nominee Thomas Jefferson was more than a personal battle between two giants. Amidst the personal invective hurled at the two men by their rabid supporters, their political disagreements involved an age-old question that neither could fully resolve: "What is the proper role of the federal government versus that of the states?" Answers to this perpetual dilemma could not be found in the U.S. Constitution, and attempts to resolve the issue during the George Washington administration came to naught. Indeed, the Washington presidency had been rendered asunder on this very issue, with Treasury Secretary Alexander Hamilton and Secretary of State Thomas Jefferson taking opposite sides and both ultimately leaving the cabinet.

Hamilton and his followers argued that liberty must be paired with authority so that economic interests (including Hamilton's own) could be protected. For Hamilton and his partisans, this meant a powerful presidency, as he so famously advocated in *The Federalist Papers*: "Energy in the executive is the leading character in the definition of good government."[2] By having a strong national government, with an energetic president at its epicenter, Hamilton hoped any expressions of local interests would be muted. To make his point, Hamilton professed that any pronouncement of either a local or regional preference was "mischievous," adding:

> Mutual wants constitute one of the strongest links of political connection. . . . Suggestions of an opposite complexion are ever to be deplored, as unfriendly to the steady pursuit of one great common cause, and to the perfect harmony of all parts.[3]

Richard Henry Lee, author of the resolution calling for independence from Great Britain, correctly observed that Hamilton "calculated to make the states one consolidated government."[4]

Thomas Jefferson and his partisans were wary of Hamilton's motives and opposed him at every turn. Jefferson's devotion to liberty, coupled with his disdain of an all-too-powerful federal government, was captured in his famous warning: "Were we directed from Washington when to sow, and when to reap, we should soon want bread."[5] Americans, Jefferson believed, would "surmount every difficulty by resolution and contrivance. Remote from all other aid we are obligated to invent and execute; to find means within ourselves and not lean on others."[6] For Jefferson and his partisans, the United States was a patchwork of states whose customs and local civic virtues must remain paramount. To a nation largely composed of farmers, he once declared, "Those who labor in the earth are the chosen people of God, if ever He had a chosen people, whose breasts He has made the peculiar deposit for substantial and genuine virtue."[7] With comments like these addressed to the vox populi, it was no wonder Jefferson beat Adams in 1800.

Many believed that Hamilton and his Federalist Party would ultimately fail because of Hamilton's disdain for what one writer called "the rabble—the poor, the uneducated, the average human being who, even then, made up the mass of his countrymen."[8] Franklin D. Roosevelt's depiction of Hamilton's denigration of the common man is accurate and, in fact, his Federalist Party met its demise a decade after Hamilton succumbed to the wounds inflicted upon him by Jefferson's vice president, Aaron Burr, in their infamous duel. Yet Hamilton's ideas still hold sway because Americans want the federal government to *do something* in the event of wars, economic recessions, or other exigencies. Thus, the epic battles between Hamilton nationalism and Jefferson localism endure. In his book *Jefferson and Hamilton*, Claude G. Bowers concluded: "The eighteenth century witnessed their Plutarchian battles; the twentieth century uncovers at the graves at Monticello and in Trinity Churchyard—but the spirits of Jefferson and Hamilton still stalk the ways of men—still fighting."[9]

Indeed, just when either Hamilton or Jefferson seems likely to prevail, new successors emerge to renew and carry on the fight. One such moment occurred in 1925. In a review of Bowers's book published in *The New York Evening World*, Franklin D. Roosevelt, still recovering from the effects of infantile paralysis, pronounced himself "fed up with the romantic cult" that has "surrounded the name of Alexander Hamilton," adding:

> A year ago, I took occasion in a letter addressed to more than a thousand Democratic leaders throughout the country, to refer in passing to the difference between the Jeffersonian and Hamiltonian ideals for an American method of government and to apply their fundamental differences to present-day policies of our two great parties. Immediately, many editors, including even some of the metropolitan press, launched open sneers at the mere suggestion that Jeffersonianism could, in any remote manner, bear upon the America of 1925. A materialistic press reflects a materialistic age,—but I still boil inwardly when I think of those smug writers who, wish being father to the thought, deny that the forces hostile to control of the government by the people which existed in the crisis of 1790–1800 could still be a threat in our day and land.[10]

Franklin D. Roosevelt's defense of Jeffersonian localism is striking since, as chief executive less than a decade later, he would undertake the greatest expansion of the federal government known until that time. Roosevelt's New Deal—including Social Security and the many "alphabet soup" agencies he created—gave Hamiltonian nationalism a decisive advantage. Defending himself against Republican attacks, Roosevelt tried to remain true to his Jeffersonian ideals: "We have been extending to our national life the old principle of the community. . . . [The] neighbors [now] are the people of the United States as a whole."[11] But it was Hamilton who guided Roosevelt's presidency toward a new era of energetic executives. To Roosevelt and his Democratic successors, it was now "self-evident" that pressing national problems such as "drought, dust storms, floods, minimum wages, maximum hours, child labor and working conditions in industry, monopolistic and unfair business practices cannot be handled by forty-eight separate State Legislatures, forty-eight separate State administrations and forty-eight separate State courts."[12] Indeed, the 1936 Democratic platform warned that, should it become necessary, the U.S. Constitution would be amended to allow the federal government to act in the best interests of "the family and the home."[13] That year, the Gallup poll found broad support for FDR's preference for federal action. When respondents were asked, "Which theory of government do you favor: concentration of power in the federal government, or concentration of power in the state government?," 56 percent chose the federal government; 44 percent answered state government.[14]

Yet a mere two years after FDR's landslide 1936 reelection victory, Jeffersonian localism was on the rise. A September 1938 Gallup poll found 59 percent saying FDR should pursue "more conservative" policies;[15] 61 percent thought the federal government was spending "too much";[16] just 37 percent wanted more federal spending to help businesses "out of the present slump";[17] and 63 percent favored reducing taxes on business.[18] On the eve of the 1938 elections, Roosevelt warned voters: "We have to have reasonable continuity in liberal government in order to get permanent results. . . . The voters throughout the country should remember that need for continuous liberal government when they vote next Tuesday."[19]

They didn't. In 1938, Republicans gained seventy-two House seats, seven Senate seats, and governorships in Michigan, Pennsylvania, and Ohio. According to former FDR adviser Raymond Moley, the GOP triumph represented "a comeback of astounding proportions."[20] Indeed it was, given that only two years before, Republicans had sixteen Senators (out of a possible ninety-six), and eighty-eight House members (out of a possible four-hundred-thirty-five).[21] Still, in 1940, Roosevelt won an unprecedented third term (and later a fourth)—not merely because "Dr. New Deal" had morphed into "Dr. Win the War," but because Americans wanted to preserve the fruits of the New Deal that FDR had created.

Hamilton vs. Jefferson: The Eternal Struggle

Some years ago, journalist Walter Lippmann noted that Americans do not like to choose between the two schools of thought represented by Hamilton and Jefferson:

> To be partisan as between Jefferson and Hamilton is like arguing whether men or women are more necessary to the procreation of the race. Neither can live alone. Alone—that is, without the other—each is excessive and soon intolerable.[22]

Even at his zenith, Franklin D. Roosevelt tried to preserve some combination of Hamilton and Jefferson by approving this language in the 1936 Democratic platform: "Transactions and activities which inevitably overflow State boundaries call for *both* State and Federal treatment [emphasis added]."[23]

Nonetheless, zealots siding with Hamilton and Jefferson have tried to expunge the opposite's point of view with less than satisfactory results.

Herbert Croly once argued that Hamilton "perverted that national idea as much as Jefferson perverted the American democratic idea, and the proper relation of these two fundamental conceptions one to another cannot be completely understood until this double perversion is corrected."[24] In the twentieth century, the excesses of the New Deal and Great Society were "corrected" by Ronald Reagan's skepticism of federal authority and his desire to reduce its omnipotence. The success of Reagan's challenge was captured in remarks by the late Massachusetts Democratic U.S. senator Paul Tsongas. Addressing the National Press Club in 1982, Tsongas bluntly declared that his party "should take the best of what [Reagan] did and embrace that without embarrassment," adding that when Democrats returned to the White House, "not all of the spending cuts [Reagan initiated] are going to be restored."[25] A decade later, Tsongas sought the Democratic presidential nomination, and many of his ideas were appropriated by the party's nominee, Bill Clinton, and his New Democrat followers. In 1996, Clinton famously declared, "The era of big government is over."[26]

Throughout history, most Americans have given neither Hamilton nor Jefferson a complete triumph. Instead, they have consistently preferred some amalgamation of both schools of thought. In 2014, for example, 54 percent of voters declared that government "is doing too many things better left to businesses and individuals"; only 41 percent wanted it "to do more to solve problems."[27] But shortly after the ballots were tallied, NBC News and *The Wall Street Journal* found large majorities supporting congressional action by the newly empowered Republican Congress on the following issues:

- Providing access to lower cost student loans and providing more time to those who are paying off their student loan debt (82 percent).
- Increasing spending on infrastructure projects for our roads and highways (75 percent).
- Raising the minimum wage (65 percent).
- Approving emergency funding to deal with Ebola in West Africa (60 percent).
- Addressing climate change and global warming by setting specific targets to limit carbon emissions (59 percent).
- Approving permits and building the Keystone XL pipeline that would transport oil from Canada across America to the Gulf of Mexico (54 percent).[28]

In 1964, public opinion analysts Lloyd Free and Hadley Cantril made an important discovery about the political psychology of Americans. When voters were asked about an issue in *ideological* terms, they noted that "the public tended to be quite conservative and bearish about too large an involvement for the Federal Government. Whereas when people were asked about *specific* Federal programs, they tended to support them in overwhelming proportions."[29] Their 1964 study concluded, "While the old argument about the 'welfare state' has long since been resolved at the operational level of government programs, it most definitely *has not* been resolved at the ideological level."[30]

Eventually, Ronald Reagan settled the question, as Americans have consistently opted for the ideologically conservative response (always worried that government was getting too big for its britches) while remaining operational liberals when asked about specific government programs—be they Social Security, Medicare, education, or the environment. As the late Everett Carll Ladd perceptively noted: "People may complain today that taxes are too high, that bureaucrats intrude too much, that 'the government' wastes money. But ask them what they want to do in each specific policy sector, and they reply, 'Keep going.'"[31] Even Tea Party supporters agree. When one was asked how she reconciled wanting a smaller government with being on Social Security and eventually needing Medicare, she replied: "I guess I mis-spoke. I didn't look at it from the perspective of losing things I need. I think I've changed my mind."[32]

Because the major parties often side exclusively with either Hamilton or Jefferson (but not with both), Americans often express their distaste for the two-party monopoly. According to a 2013 Fox News poll, 55 percent believe that "the two-party system is broken [and] it's time for more political parties."[33] In one sense, the public is right. Democrats are Hamilton's champions and eschew any reference to Jefferson, content to narrow their debates over just how many Hamiltonian-inspired ideas the country is willing to accept. Meanwhile, Republicans are doing a poor job of representing Jeffersonian localism—as the party is torn apart by a Tea Party faction that believes ideological purity trumps governing, while the party establishment wants to break free of an ideological straightjacket and enact a moderate, conservative agenda. Texas senator Ted Cruz expresses the former view: "What it takes is backbone, the willingness to stand and fight for principles in the face of opposition and derision."[34] Former 2012 GOP presidential candidate Jon Huntsman disagrees: "I think the Republican party has a huge opportunity to take the high ground if it were to focus on problem-solving and solutions and practical approaches. And we're completely divorced from that basic approach and ethos these days."[35] Republican strategist Alex Castellanos summarizes the public's dilemma:

> Government's failing. Nothing works. People are trapped in a room with President Obama and the Democratic party and there is a huge demand for change. They want to get out of that room. But the only door out leads to a room full of lepers—that's the Republican party.[36]

Some years ago, political scientist Clinton Rossiter observed that the two major parties were "creatures of compromise . . . vast, gaudy, friendly umbrellas under which all are invited for the sake of being counted in the next election."[37] The problem for today's Republican Party is that its umbrella keeps getting smaller and the internal arguments less friendly. Andrew Kohut, the former president of the Pew Research Center, describes the consequences of this Republican outrage:

> The outsize influence of hard-line elements of the party base is doing to the GOP what supporters of [presidential candidates] Gene McCarthy and George McGovern did to the Democratic party in the late 1960s and early 1970s: radicalizing its image and standing in the way of revitalization.[38]

Paul Ryan, the 2012 Republican vice presidential nominee, states the problem even more succinctly: "We have to be a party for everybody."[39]

Why Americans Hate Politics

While Americans occasionally respond to the allure of a third party, they always keep coming back to the two major parties largely because they keep the flames of Hamilton and Jefferson burning bright. One party usually captures the essence of Hamilton's thinking about the importance of an activist federal government with the president at its center, while the other often is the repository for Jefferson's preference for state and local decision-making. As Clinton Rossiter famously observed:

> The most momentous fact about the pattern of American politics is that we live under a persistent, obdurate, one might almost say tyrannical, two-party system. We have the Republicans and we have the Democrats, and we have almost no-one else . . . in the struggle for power.[40]

That struggle for power has involved intense competition between Hamilton and Jefferson and their heirs. Beginning with FDR, it is the Democrats who are today's Hamiltonian party. Democrats continue to look to the federal government as the primary instrument for solving today's problems. Thus, while the party continues to suffer from the overall perception of Obamacare as being too intrusive, Democrats remain committed to the singular domestic achievement of the Obama presidency. For their part, Republicans want to repeal Obamacare, even as they seek to preserve the state healthcare exchanges created by it. Senate Majority Leader Mitch McConnell promised Kentucky voters in 2014 that he would expunge Obamacare "root and branch" from the federal statutes, while at the same time preserving Kynect—the state healthcare exchange that administers Obamacare in Kentucky.[41] (Like Hamilton and Jefferson, one cannot exist without the other.) An October 2014 Fox News poll found a similar division among Americans at large: 46 percent thought Obamacare "went too far," while 49 percent maintained the law "didn't go far enough" or was "about right."[42]

Republicans under Ronald Reagan became a Jeffersonian party. Speaking on the "chicken and mashed potatoes circuit" in the 1960s, Reagan gave voice to Jeffersonian thinking long before he became president:

> Government tends to grow, government programs take on weight and momentum as public servants say, always with the best of intentions, "What greater service we could render if we only had a little more money and a little more power." But the truth is that outside of its legitimate function, government does nothing as well or as economically as the private sector of our economy.[43]

He continued to echo the same themes as a presidential candidate, telling voters on the eve of his 1980 election: "Government has grown too large, too bureaucratic, too wasteful, too unresponsive, too uncaring to people and their problems."[44]

It was by promising to weaken the federal government that Reagan and his Republican successors won the right to control it. But neither Reagan, nor the two Bushes, actually weakened the federal government. In fact, they expanded its reach in key areas of American life—especially education—precisely because the public wanted it. Indeed, what voters desire is not a false choice between a Hamiltonian or a Jeffersonian party, but some amalgamation of the two. Bill Clinton liked to illustrate America's twin commitments to the Hamiltonian and Jeffersonian ideals by calling attention to the humble penny:

> Take a penny from your pocket. On one side, next to Lincoln's portrait is a single word: "Liberty." On the other side is our national motto. It says "E Pluribus Unum"—"Out of Many, One." It does not say "Every man for himself." That humble penny is an explicit declaration—one you can carry around in your pocket—that America is about both individual liberty and community obligation. These two commitments—to protect personal freedom and to seek common ground—are the coin of our realm, the measure of our worth.[45]

Clinton's use of the humble penny illustrates the power both Hamilton and Jefferson continue to exercise in today's politics, and the frustration Americans have with both parties. As *Washington Post* columnist E. J. Dionne has observed, Americans hate politics largely because the questions they pose—questions that surround the eternal divisions between

Hamilton and Jefferson—are often artificially constructed and demand answers that voters are reluctant to give. As Dionne has so presciently noted:

> We are suffering from a false polarization in our politics, in which liberals and conservatives keep arguing about the same things when the country wants to move on. . . . Americans yearn simultaneously for untrammeled personal liberty and a strong sense of community that allows burdens and benefits to be shared fairly and willingly, apportioned through democratic decisions.
>
> In their very different ways, the Sixties Left and the Eighties Right reflected both of these honorable impulses—and all of their contradictions. The "if-it-feels-good-do-it" left rejected the imposition of conventional moral norms through force of law. The entrepreneurial right rejected the imposition of compassion through taxation and regulation. The New Left and the more conventional liberals who ran the Great Society believed that the federal government could strengthen and "empower" local communities to organize themselves and act on their own behalf, sometimes by fighting City Hall and the federal government itself on the streets and in the courts. The Eighties Right also took "empowerment" seriously and sought to give individuals and local communities more say, at the expense of the federal government and bureaucrats of all kinds.[46]

These frustrations, expressed by Dionne back in 1988, still exist. The necessity for both Hamilton and Jefferson to cohabitate in American political thought—even as they are engaged in constant battles—is reminiscent of a line spoken by a character in a Tom Robbins novel titled *Even Cowgirls Get the Blues*: "Until humans can solve their philosophical problems, they're condemned to solve their political problems over and over and over again. It's a cruel, repetitious bore."[47]

The Republican Imprisonment

The victories of Dwight D. Eisenhower, Richard M. Nixon, Ronald Reagan, and even George W. Bush happened because the GOP moderated its conservative thinking to produce an amalgam of progressive ideas and conservative governance. Moderation was required to win votes—as Dwight D. Eisenhower's Modern Republicanism and George W. Bush's formulation of "compassionate conservatism" so amply demonstrated. And with these victories, the Republican Party chose, in the words of MSNBC host Joe Scarborough, "the right path."[48] According to Scarborough, today's

Republicans should learn from their forebears and place "principled pragmatism" ahead of an ideological "reflexive purity":

> Republicans of the modern era, driven by conservatives, resonated with
> a majority of Americans when they demonstrated a genuine commit-
> ment to the ideas of greater liberty, a restrained state, social order, and
> strength abroad. These are the key conservative principles that most
> Americans agree with, have always agreed with, and will agree in the
> future. Republicans who try to use the power of the state to interfere
> in matters of personal liberty will be as doomed as the big-government
> Democrats who wanted to use the authority of government to impose
> a singular "Great Society" on all of America. Conservatives know
> that the world is made up of what Edmund Burke described as "little
> platoons"—the small towns or the city neighborhoods where happiness
> is pursued.
>   The right path to power lies in appreciating that politics isn't a science
> but an art—that America has been at her best and will be again when
> the common wisdom of the people, carefully weighed in the Madiso-
> nian scales of the Constitution, has a prime place in the governance of
> the nation. And history shows that the common wisdom of the people
> is essentially conservative in that most people want to find the right bal-
> ance between freedom and responsibility.[49]

The Death of Modern Republicanism

But the difficulty with espousing Modern Republicanism in today's highly
partisan environment is its lack of a sound defense based on principles.
Instead of promoting a GOP brand based on the need for fiscal prudence,
coupled with government activism when required, Modern Republicans
have made their arguments based on a pragmatic view that only they
could win votes from Democrats and independents. As E. J. Dionne has
pointed out, "Eisenhower's prudence was precisely what [conservative
William F.] Buckley saw as a 'blandness' designed 'to more or less please
more or less everybody.'"[50] In Dionne's words, "Modern Republicanism
amounted to little more than a *smorgasbord* of liberal and conservative
feelings."[51]

While this may be what the country wanted, political scientist Nicol C.
Rae argues that Modern Republicans allowed conservatives "to win the
intellectual argument by default."[52] Rae notes that liberal Republicans did
not attempt to challenge conservatives on principles. Instead, he writes,
their appeals were framed "in terms of personality or electability, rather
than of political principle, frequently acknowledging the validity of most
of the right's doctrines, while arguing that they would have to be modified

to win votes for the party."[53] Thus, governors Nelson A. Rockefeller of New York, William Scranton of Pennsylvania, George Romney of Michigan, and a host of historical faces from Republican contests of yore made the point that only they could win a presidential election—as each of them had done in their big, diverse states that had lots of Democrats and independents (and not so many Republicans). All lost their bids for the GOP nomination.

Today, former Florida governor Jeb Bush is making a similar case. As Bush explores a 2016 candidacy, he readily concedes that he may have to "lose the primary to win the general."[54] Following Bush's expression of interest in seeking the presidency, Matthew Dowd, a key strategist in George W. Bush's campaigns, described the hard path ahead for the younger Bush on Twitter: "Reminder folks: last Bush to run was 40 points ahead, out-raised everyone at least 5 to 1, had every endorsement, & nearly lost the nomination."[55] Today, as Dowd and others know all too well, Republicans are far less inclined to support a candidate based on armchair punditry that he or she is best positioned to win the presidency come the following November. Nonetheless, at this early stage of the 2016 contest, Jeb Bush, New Jersey governor Chris Christie, Mitt Romney, Ohio governor John Kasich, and a host of other potential candidates are not making their cases based on principles, per se. Like the Modern Republicans of years past, they are telling GOP primary voters that only they can attract Democrats and independents needed to win a general election—as they have done in their respective statewide contests.

Such arguments are exactly what the base of the Republican Party *does not* want to hear. A principal reason for this is that Republicans *do not* believe that they are the minority party—at least when it comes to presidential politics. The explanations are many. First, Republicans like to blame their previous nominees for their losses. To them, John McCain and Mitt Romney were flawed candidates who trimmed their conservative sails. Rather than running based on principles, McCain and Romney conducted campaigns designed to woo Democrats and independents. Both failed miserably at attracting Democratic support—10 percent and 8 percent respectively.[56] While McCain won only 44 percent of independents in 2008, Romney did much better, getting 50 percent of their votes four years later.[57] But the results were the same: both lost to Obama, and their races were not even close.

2014: A False Dawn

A more significant reason for Republican base voters not accepting their presidential minority status emerges from the outcomes of the 2010 and 2014 midterm elections. The 2014 results are of particular significance because they reinforce a prevailing view among many Republicans that the party is entering the 2016 contest in excellent shape. As the *Cook Political Report* notes:

- Democrats have the lowest number of U.S. Senate and House seats since 1928.
- Democrats hold fewer state legislative seats than they have since 1928.
- Republicans picked up nine seats to win their majority in the U.S. Senate. The GOP had not won more than six Senate seats since 1994 (when they picked up ten seats).
- Republicans did not lose a single incumbent senator in a primary or in the general election for the first time since 2004.
- Republicans won 57 percent of all U.S. House districts in 2014, up from 54 percent in 2012. Measured in land area, House Republicans now represent 86 percent of the nation.
- Not since Harry Truman has one party lost as many U.S. House seats in midterm elections as have Democrats in 2010 and 2014. During Truman's two midterm elections, Democrats lost 83 seats; Obama, 76 seats.
- There are no Democrats in the U.S. House from rural Appalachia, nor are there any white Democrats from the Deep South.[58]

While these numbers provide a considerable degree of reassurance to most Republicans, another perspective using the same data indicates the need for the GOP to immediately rebrand itself. Even some Republicans share this view. Conservative columnist Michael Gerson worries that following the 2014 landslides, Republicans will indulge themselves in a kind of ideological complacency: "Some parts of the Republican coalition—highly ideological members of Congress from safe districts, outside groups, and think tanks that raise funds off appeals to purity—seem content, even happy on the gentle slope of Republican decline."[59] Just as Democrats in the 1980s contented themselves with their congressional majorities—even as they dismissed Ronald Reagan as a "Teflon President" whose unpopular policies could not stick to him (or so they claimed)—Republicans point to their built-in advantages in the House; a Senate majority that will be difficult to dislodge in 2016; and the vast number of governorships and state legislative seats the party now holds. After the 2014 elections, Republicans control thirty-one governors' mansions, the most they have held since 1998. In addition, Republicans won an additional 320 state legislators in 2014, giving them control of 56.5 percent of all state legislative seats—the most since 1928.[60] With these numbers, Republicans ask, "What's wrong?"

"The Governing Trap"

To find a renewed sense of vibrancy, the Republican Party must adopt a different strategy than consistently playing to its conservative, activist base.

While Republicans may find comfort in opposing Barack Obama and the Democrats, this is not what the country wants. According to an NBC News/*Wall Street Journal* poll taken immediately after the 2014 election, 63 percent desired the winning candidates "to make compromises to gain consensus on legislation"; only 30 percent preferred that officeholders "stick to their campaign positions even if that means NO consensus on legislation."[61] But a Pew Research post-election poll found 66 percent of Republicans wanted their party to "stand up" to Obama and offer no compromises. Most strikingly, 50 percent of Republicans believe the new GOP-controlled Congress should immediately begin an impeachment investigation of President Obama.[62] Others prefer that the party do nothing and wait for the next election when, surely, Republicans will occupy every branch of the federal government. A loud voice advocating such a strategy is the influential *National Review*. Having achieved a historic victory in 2014, the editors of the conservative publication argue that Republicans should avoid "the governing trap," adding:

> A prove-you-can-govern strategy will inevitably divide the party on the same tea-party-versus-establishment lines that Republicans have just succeeded in overcoming. The media will, in particular, take any refusal to pass a foolish immigration bill that immediately legalizes millions of illegal immigrants as a failure to govern.
>
> Even if Republicans passed this foolish test, it would do little for them. If voters come to believe that a Republican Congress and a Democratic president are doing a fine job of governing together, why wouldn't they vote to continue the arrangement in 2016?[63]

Others advocate a more activist, hard-line approach. The day after the 2014 elections, Dan Holler, a spokesman for Heritage Action for America, declared:

> Just like the House majority four years earlier, the new Senate Republican majority is built on the repeal of Obamacare. And in a stark departure from conventional wisdom, nearly every newly-elected Republican Senator ran against amnesty. As we move forward, Republicans must govern as they campaigned.[64]

Jenny Beth Martin of the Tea Party Patriots was even more succinct: "You're welcome GOP. Now keep your promises."[65] This is precisely the problem: the Tea Party and its adherents do not see obstructionism as "doing nothing." For them, it *is* governing.

The Southern Imprisonment

In many ways, the Tea Party's preference for a downsized federal establishment began in 1968, when Richard Nixon made a deal with South Carolina

U.S. senator Strom Thurmond for southern support at the Republican National Convention. There the "southern strategy" was born. In return for Thurmond's support, Nixon promised to "go slow" on civil rights and appoint "strict constructionists" to the U.S. Supreme Court. These prospective justices would provide far less sweeping interpretations of the U.S. Constitution than had the liberal Warren Court (headed by Chief Justice Earl Warren). On other matters, these southern political antecedents of the Tea Party fumed over what they saw as a proliferation of black "welfare queens," and they castigated Lyndon Johnson's Great Society as a bunch of "something-for-nothing" federal programs geared toward minorities and financed by white taxpayers. Ironically, their animus toward the federal government became possible after their forebears, weighed down by the Great Depression, were saved by Franklin D. Roosevelt's New Deal. Former "have-nots" became "haves," and viewing the federal establishment through their taxpaying eyes, they saw waste, fraud, and abuse everywhere. In the years that followed, these same voters cemented their allegiance to the GOP as social and cultural issues (e.g., prayer in schools, abortion, the death penalty, and the rights of gun owners, women, and gays) became increasingly prominent.

The southern strategy worked: Dixie became a GOP fortress, as Republicans swept the South. The lone exception was Jimmy Carter, who, in 1976, won every southern state except Virginia. (Yet, even Carter *lost* the southern white vote, but he won those states due to overwhelming backing from African-Americans.) In 1992, even the first all-southern Democratic ticket since Harry Truman and Alben Barkley in 1948, Arkansan Bill Clinton and Tennessean Al Gore, could not accomplish what Carter did. While Clinton and Gore carried some southern states, all of them continued their steady march toward the Republicans and today are solid red states, including Clinton's home state of Arkansas and Gore's home state of Tennessee.[66] In a predominantly white America, the power of the southern strategy was unbeatable. And the temptation of Republicans to rely on it to secure the presidency was overwhelming. For years, Democrats tried to court southern whites without success. Political scientist Thomas F. Schaller crystalized an argument that had been building for Democrats to "whistle past Dixie." In his view, Democrats no longer needed the South to win presidential elections, as a demographic revolution allows Democrats to substitute other mega-states—especially California, Illinois, New York, and much of the industrial Midwest—as powerhouses that can overcome GOP strength in the South.[67]

Today, some of the most strident GOP voices are demanding that the party live up to the bargain engineered by Richard Nixon and Strom Thurmond in 1968—i.e., making sure that Republicans do not support programs such as Obamacare, which, in their view, is the latest example of more "something-for-nothing" government waste geared toward minorities;

securing the southern border so that the ongoing demographic transformation of the United States may be slowed or stopped; and enunciating socially conservative views, even as a "live-and-let-live" philosophy is taking hold, especially among millennials. The result is another kind of GOP imprisonment, as the southern strategy has become a fortress that the GOP cannot readily escape. Put bluntly, Republicans are locked up in the South. Their ability to win there compromises their appeal in more cosmopolitan regions of the country that are growing in electoral strength.

The result is continuing division and discord, as base Republicans prevent more pragmatic voices from healing the intraparty divisions and guiding the party toward future victories. In 2015, these intraparty squabbles may become even more bitter, since Republicans can no longer blame Senate Democrats for their troubles. Tasked with governing, pragmatic, establishment-minded congressional Republicans are likely to find themselves at odds with Tea Party-inspired legislators. Political scientists Thomas E. Mann and Norman J. Ornstein envision tough days ahead:

> Welcome to the 114th Congress, in which the warfare within the GOP will only be amplified by the party's new power. The pragmatic desire of mainstream Republicans to transcend their "party of no" label and show they can actually govern will clash with the forces that continue to pull the GOP to the right and oppose anything the president does. This fight within the party will define the new Congress nearly as much as the battles with a Democratic president. . . . If anything, the breadth and depth of the Republican victory will convince the party base—and the conservative activists, talk radio hosts and bloggers animating it—that the obstruction of the past several years worked beautifully, that they have the power and the mandate to push radical anti-government policies, and that any compromise would be abandonment and betrayal.[68]

As the 2016 GOP field takes shape, the divisions described by Mann and Ornstein are likely to emerge among the presidential candidates. Eventually, there will have to be some resolution. Just as the Democrats could not paper over their troubles during the Carter years, Republicans are likely to find themselves in a similar position should they overcome the odds and win the presidency in 2016.

What Can Be Done?

It is often said that political parties are elastic institutions—namely, that they have persevered because of their ability to bounce back from historic defeats. Historically, Republicans have validated this axiom. Having suffered five historic setbacks at the hands of Franklin D. Roosevelt and Harry Truman, the GOP went on to win seven of the ten presidential elections held between 1952 and 1988. A primary reason for this turnaround was the power of the party establishment to push back against conservative cries and nominate candidates who could win. Ever since Richard Nixon won the GOP nomination in 1968, a Republican rule of thumb developed: "To win, tack to the right in the primaries. But, once nominated, run pell-mell toward the center in the general election." Establishment Republicans hewed to this axiom, sometimes even running toward the center in the primaries in order to win votes they might not otherwise receive.

Ronald Reagan and George H.W. Bush Show the Way

A powerful example of Republicans running to the center even before they had secured the party's nomination occurred in 1980, when Ronald Reagan and George H. W. Bush were asked this question in a televised debate from Houston, Texas: "Do you think children of illegal aliens should be allowed to attend Texas public schools for free, or do you think their parents should pay for their education?" Their answers illustrate the type of pragmatic conservatism that establishment-minded Republicans want today's Republican Party to emulate, and which is necessary if it is to compete on a new demographic playing field:

Bush: "I'd like to see something done about labor needs and human needs [so] that problem wouldn't come up. Today, if those people are here, I would reluctantly say that they get whatever society is giving to their neighbors. But the problem has to be solved. The problem has to be solved. If we make illegal sometimes the labor I'd like to see legal, we're doing two things: we're creating a whole society of really honorable, decent, family-loving people that are in violation of the law and, secondly, we're exacerbating relations with Mexico. The answer to your question is much more fundamental than whether they attend Houston schools it seems to me. If they are living here, I don't want to see a group of six, seven, and eight-year-old kids living here totally uneducated and made to feel that they're living outside the law. Let's address ourselves to the fundamentals. These are good people, strong people. Part of my family is Mexican-American." [Applause.]

Reagan: "I think the time has come that the United States and our neighbor to the south [Mexico] should have a better relationship than we've ever had. And I think we haven't been sensitive enough to our size and power. There's a problem of 40 to 50 percent unemployment [in Mexico]. Now this cannot continue without the possibility arising with regard to Cuba and what it is [doing] stirring up of [sic] trouble below the border. We could have a very hostile and strange neighbor on our border. Rather than talking about putting up a fence, why don't we work out some recognition of our mutual problems, make it possible

for them to come here legally with a work permit, and then while working and earning here, they pay taxes here, and when they want to go
back, they can go back. Open the border both ways by understanding
their problems."[69]

Four years later, Reagan reiterated his position, telling voters, "I believe in
the idea of *amnesty* for those who have put down roots and who have lived
here, even though sometime back they may have entered illegally [emphasis
added]."[70]

The Party of No

Today's Republican Party would find the Reagan-Bush position on the
touchstone issue of immigration abhorrent, with Reagan using the dreaded
word "amnesty." Today the need for immigration reform is even greater
than it was during the Reagan years. In a televised address following the
2014 elections, Barack Obama stated the obvious: "Our immigration system is broken, and everyone knows it," adding:

> Families who enter our country the right way and play by the rules
> watch others flout the rules. Business owners who offer their work-
> ers good wages and benefits see the competition exploit undocumented
> immigrants by paying them far less. All of us take offense to anyone who
> reaps the rewards of living in America without taking on the responsi-
> bilities of living in America. And undocumented immigrants who des-
> perately want to embrace those responsibilities see little option but to
> remain in the shadows, or risk their families being torn apart. It's been
> this way for decades. And for decades, we haven't done much about it.[71]

To accomplish a permanent solution requires bipartisan cooperation, something that Obama has yearned for but has found incredibly elusive. Yet it is
such bipartisan cooperation that would help rebrand the GOP into something more than the party of no.

The "opposition for opposition's sake" during the Obama years raises
the question: Does the Republican establishment have enough power to
move the party back toward the "principled pragmatism" that Joe Scarborough, David Frum, and other analysts believe is crucial to winning the
presidency? When it comes to immigration reform, the answer is clearly
no. Republican House members have almost no incentives to take up the
issue—comfortable as they are in their largely all-white districts—despite its
paramount importance to their party's presidential future. In fact, their virulent opposition to any immigration bill has made this topic a kind of third
rail—joining abortion as an issue from which any deviancy is not tolerated.
Ironically, the Republican hold on the House of Representatives is one more

reason why the party finds itself in a kind of imprisonment when it comes to competing for the presidency.

Indeed, because congressional Republicans (and the base of the party that so ardently supports them) are so vehemently against immigration reform, contenders for the party's 2016 presidential nomination are likely to outdo each other in decrying Obama's executive orders—with each promising repeal as their first action once in office. While no Republican will emulate Mitt Romney in using the ill-conceived phrase "self-deport," the message to Hispanics will be the same. In short, no Republican is likely to quote either Ronald Reagan or George H.W. Bush (even Jeb Bush) when it comes to dealing with immigration, and no Republican, therefore, is likely to extricate the party from its demographic Rubik's Cube. As South Carolina senator Lindsey Graham told CNN at the end of 2014: "If we don't at least make a down payment on solving the [immigration] problem and rationally dealing with the 11 million [illegal immigrants believed to be in the U.S.], if we become the party of self-deportation in 2015 and 2016, then the chance of [Republicans] winning the White House I think is almost non-existent."[72]

A Weakened Establishment

But the GOP dilemma is even deeper. As noted in Chapter 4, Republicans have virtually no structures designed to elicit conservative ideas that go beyond the Reagan era and evoke a kind of "principled pragmatism" that will set the party on a different course. Radio talk show hosts, Internet bloggers, Fox News, and conservative think tanks remain comfortable in their echo chambers, and they fully subscribe to the notion that the party's next victory is merely days away.

This is quite unlike the Democratic Party in the 1980s that, after three consecutive presidential losses, concluded that Franklin D. Roosevelt and John F. Kennedy were history; that the New Deal was over; and, despite protests from the Left, that the party would have to move in a more centrist direction. To that end, Democrats established the Democratic Leadership Council and the Progressive Policy Institute, which set about the task of formulating policies that would appeal to voters inclined to give Democrats a hearing. Democrats decided that controlling the Congress was not enough, and they desired to be a national party that could win the presidency. That meant acknowledging their weaknesses, and using blunt language in doing so. In 1989, the Progressive Policy Institute published a report entitled "The Politics of Evasion: Democrats and the Presidency." In it, authors William Galston and Elaine Ciulla Kamarck delivered a blunt assessment of the Democrats' troubles:

> The Democratic Party's 1988 presidential defeat demonstrated that the party's problems would not disappear, as many had hoped, once Ronald

Reagan left the White House. Without a charismatic president to blame for their ills, Democrats must now come face to face with reality: too many Americans have come to see the party as inattentive to their economic interests, indifferent if not hostile to their moral sentiments, and ineffective in defense of their national security. . . .

Democrats have ignored their fundamental problems. Instead of facing reality they have embraced the politics of evasion. They have focused on fundraising and technology, media and momentum, personality and tactics. Worse, they have manufactured excuses for their presidential disasters—excuses built on faulty data and false assumptions, excuses designed to avoid tough questions. In place of reality, they have offered wishful thinking; in place of analysis, myth.[73]

No such language is heard among today's Republicans. Rather than acknowledging the party's problems, establishment figures are focused on process and technological fixes (e.g., moving the party's convention to midsummer, limiting the number of GOP presidential debates, and becoming as savvy as Democrats are in data collection). In addition, many Republican leaders think that another establishment candidate named Bush might just be the answer to what ails Republicans. But there is no evidence that either the GOP base or the electorate at large desires another Bush presidency. According to an NBC News/*Wall Street Journal* survey, 57 percent of all voters could not see themselves supporting Jeb Bush in 2016. (But 50 percent of respondents in the same poll could envision themselves backing Hillary Clinton.[74]) Republicans find themselves trapped in an era in which the party has none of the structures needed to undertake the arduous task of redefining Jeffersonian ideals for the twenty-first century.

Recent Supreme Court decisions have also weakened the power of the party establishment. The 2010 *Citizens United* case has allowed mega-millionaires to solely finance campaigns of Republican hopefuls. While at first blush this would appear to give the GOP a solid advantage in the money game, the effect has been to give marginal candidates a boost. In 2012, Foster Friess gave millions to Rick Santorum, while casino magnate Sheldon Adelson did the same for Newt Gingrich. Both millionaires single-handedly extended the political lives of these two conservative, base-appealing Republican hopefuls far beyond their expiration dates. And there is nothing to prevent other ideologically minded mega-millionaires from doing the same in 2016 (and far into the future). An old political axiom is pertinent here: "Be careful what you wish for, you might just get it." The *Citizens United* decision was cheered by establishment Republicans (including the U.S. Chamber of Commerce) because it put corporate interests first and no longer tarred their money-giving as being inherently corrupt. This 5–4 ruling was derided by the minority on the Court, three of whom were put there by Democratic presidents. As John Paul Stevens (the lone Republican dissenter appointed by Gerald R. Ford) concluded in his famous objection: "While American democracy is imperfect, few outside the majority of this Court would have thought its flaws included a dearth of corporate money in politics."[75]

The question for Republicans, then, is can they bounce back? It is often said that parties are flexible institutions, capable of absorbing big losses and quickly adapting themselves to a new future. But that old axiom may no longer hold. The effects of a strong, yet smaller, partisan base; an ideological rigidity that permits almost no dissent; and an avalanche of millions of dollars that can be used to keep ultraconservative candidacies afloat have weakened the party establishment. Remember that it took an intense effort by GOP leaders to keep conservative Robert A. Taft at bay in 1952. And this was against one of the most admired men in U.S. politics: World War Two hero Dwight D. Eisenhower. Today, the Republican establishment is in a far weaker position than it was in 1952.

While the struggles between Hamilton and Jefferson will undoubtedly endure, the question remains: "Can the Republican Party continue to be a vessel in which Jeffersonian localism can make its case?" There are the twin dangers that the Republican establishment will become politically neutered and, as that happens, the party will shrink to the interior of the country (where the electoral college votes are fewest) while Democrats remain powerful on both coasts. California is a superb example. Today, Republicans no longer actively compete in Ronald Reagan's adopted home state, and every statewide officeholder wears a Democratic label. In presidential politics, Republicans have not won the Golden State since George H. W. Bush did so a generation ago in 1988. Instead of competing for votes, Republicans board California-bound airplanes to extract money from their wealthy contributors. The effect is to create a kind of electoral forfeit. In 2014, for example, there were eight California House races that were decided by 5 percent or less, and Democrats won all of them. Remarkably, Republicans have not added a California House seat since 1998—despite their overwhelming victories in 2010 and 2014.[76]

"We Have to Be Great"

Recently, South Carolina's Lindsey Graham addressed the dissatisfaction many voters feel with today's politics. His prescription is a simple one: "The country needs a vibrant Republican party."[77] While the need for vibrancy is apparent, how to achieve it remains elusive. David Frum writes that while Republicans can overcome their present troubles, "The ominous question for Republicans is how much time will the overcoming take?"[78]

Certainly, by continuously playing to their conservative base, Republicans are likely to find that their victories will be Pyrrhic ones. In the short term, should the GOP adopt a continued strategy of confrontation with Obama (as the base of the party so earnestly desires), or do nothing and wait for better times, the 2014 election (just like 2010) will prove to be a "false dawn." In 2014, voter turnout was a meager 36.4 percent—the lowest since 1942, a year when the country was at war and voters were either distracted or unable to vote.[79]

While Republican activists can have an outsized influence on midterm results—where the shape of the electorate is skewed toward Republican wins—Democrats can concentrate on presidential elections where a rising tide lifts all Democratic boats. The result is an inborn flaw in U.S. politics, as the structure of elections favors Democrats at the *presidential* level while Republicans dominate *congressional* contests. Voter turnout in presidential elections (around 60 percent) far outweighs midterm election turnouts (approaching 40 percent). A rising Democratic electorate of young voters, minorities, and single women is much more likely to cast ballots in presidential years—when, they say, their votes *really count*—as opposed to midterm contests that lack clarity at the top of the ticket. Republicans, meanwhile, can employ their activist conservative base in midterm elections to gin up their supporters and make sure they get the party's message. As Barack Obama has observed:

> Democrats have a congenital defect when it comes to our politics, and that is we like voting during presidential years and during the midterms we don't vote. And so you already have lower voting totals during the midterms, and it's our folks that stay home.[80]

At the same time, Republican National Chairman Reince Priebus acknowledges that his party faces tough challenges ahead. Speaking at a Christian Science Monitor breakfast shortly after the 2014 results were tallied, Priebus was seized by a moment of candor:

> We've got a long way to go to be ready for 2016. We've got to be about perfect as a national party to win a national cultural vote in this country. I think the Democrats can be good and win, but we have to be great.[81]

Being "great" means Republicans have to do a much better job of gaining an audience with a rising Democratic electorate of minorities, single women, and young voters. Jeb Bush and Clint Bolick summarize the current Republican imprisonment, noting that the party is living on "borrowed time," adding,

> Republicans will face an ever shrinking base—and ultimately extinction—if they continue to alienate the voters they lost in great numbers in 2012, including single women, blacks, and gays. But nothing is more inexplicable than the failure to reach out to immigrants generally, and Hispanics specifically, given that they cherish traditional

American ideals. How are we to save the country if not for the newcomers brought here by their devotion to those ideals?[82]

The Democratic Party's demographic advantages, especially among Hispanics, will be decisive in the upcoming presidential battle. But in the short period of time between Election Day 2014 and the installation of the 114th Congress the following January, Republicans have hurt their chances by their vehement opposition to Barack Obama's executive orders giving amnesty to millions of illegal immigrants. Speaker John Boehner's reaction was harsh: "By ignoring the will of the American people, President Obama has cemented his legacy of lawlessness and squandered what little credibility he has left."[83] Kentucky senator Rand Paul declared that he would not "sit idly by and let the President bypass Congress and our Constitution."[84] Obama's retort was simple, yet effective: "Pass a bill."[85]

Like the condemned prisoner on the eve of an execution, what Republicans may need is another defeat to concentrate the mind. After three consecutive losses in the 1980s, Democrats rebounded to win the presidency—but only after a serious attempt to rebrand themselves. Republicans, today, are in similar need of such a rebranding. But would-be Republican reformers face significant challenges from a party base that is more bent on luxuriating in ideological comfort within its own echo chambers. Overcoming this complacency will not be easy.

While Hamilton and Jefferson will undoubtedly continue to exert their influence—just as they have done for more than two centuries—the question is, what vessels will be used to extend their dialogue into the twenty-first century? Democrats seem comfortable with Hamilton's idea of an enlarged federal bureaucracy with a powerful president at its center. Indeed, the real debate within the Democratic Party today is just how much of Hamilton's ideas should Democrats adopt? Hillary Clinton, like her husband, is inclined to try to merge Hamilton and Jefferson, while Bernard Sanders and Elizabeth Warren are leading calls on the Left for a more powerful federal government that can exercise even more authority over what they see as an unregulated business sector. It is the Republicans, however, that seem most endangered as the vessel that can espouse Jefferson's ideals of local civic virtue and decentralized decision-making. The need to do so makes the Republican Party (or some version of it) a political necessity. But the long-term future of the party is in doubt—imprisoned by activists who do not see the necessity for change and a party establishment that makes an unwinnable argument for electability, even as its authority is weakened. Whether this imprisonment is either a short-term or a long-term sentence is unknown. But what seems clear is that the Republicans lack an escape plan. One can presume that the Republican Party will play a big part in our nation's political future. The question is, "How do they get back into the game?"

Notes

1 Quoted in Claude G. Bowers, *Jefferson and Hamilton: A Classic Study of America's Greatest Antagonists* (Boston: Houghton, Mifflin Company, 1966 edition), 489–490.
2 Alexander Hamilton, "Federalist Number 70," found in Alexander Hamilton, John Jay, and James Madison, *The Federalist* (New York: Random House, The Modern Library edition, 1941), 454.
3 Quoted in Morton J. Frisch, ed., *Selected Writings and Speeches of Alexander Hamilton* (Washington, D.C.: American Enterprise Institute, 1985), 316.
4 Quoted in Edward Meade Earle's introduction to Hamilton, Jay, and Madison, *The Federalist*, xiii.
5 Quoted in Richard Reeves, *The Reagan Detour* (New York: Simon and Schuster, 1985), 19.
6 Quoted in Ted Morgan, *FDR: A Biography* (New York: Simon and Schuster, 1985), 365.
7 Ibid., 38.
8 Franklin D. Roosevelt, "Jefferson and Hamilton," *New York Evening World*, Review of Claude B. Bowers, *Jefferson and Hamilton*, November 16, 1925.
9 Bowers, *Jefferson and Hamilton*, 511.
10 Roosevelt, "Jefferson and Hamilton."
11 Quoted in Reeves, *The Reagan Detour*, 43.
12 Democratic National Platform, 1936, as reprinted in the *New York Times*, June 26, 1936, 1.
13 Ibid.
14 Gallup poll, January 20–25, 1936. Text of question: "Which theory of government do you favor: concentration of power in the federal government or concentration of power in the state government?" Federal government, 56 percent; state government, 44 percent.
15 Gallup poll, September 25–30, 1938. Text of question: "During the next two years, would you like to see the Roosevelt administration become more conservative or continue along present lines?" More conservative, 59 percent; continue along present lines, 33 percent; no opinion, 8 percent.
16 Gallup poll, December 25–30, 1938. Text of question: "Do you think the Federal Government is spending too much, too little, or about the right amount of money at this time?" Too much, 61 percent; too little, 10 percent; about right, 29 percent.
17 Gallup poll, March 17–22, 1938. Text of question: "Do you think government spending should be increased to help get business out of its present slump?" Yes, 37 percent; no, 63 percent.
18 Gallup poll, March 25–30, 1938. Text of question: "In your opinion, which will do more to get us out of the depression: increase government spending, or reduce taxes on business?" Increase government spending, 15 percent; reduce taxes on business, 63 percent; no opinion, 21 percent; both (volunteered), 1 percent.
19 Franklin D. Roosevelt, "Radio Address on the Election of Liberals," November 4, 1938. See http://docs.fdrlibrary.marist.edu/php11438.html. Accessed November 16, 2010.
20 See Andrew E. Busch, "The New Deal Comes to a Screeching Halt in 1938," Ashbrook Center, May 2006 editorial. See http://www.ashbrook.org/publicat/oped/busch/06/1938.html. Accessed November 22, 2010.
21 The 75th Congress was composed as follows: Senate: Democrats, 76 seats; Republicans, 16 seats; 2 Farmer-Labor Party; 1 Progressive; 1 independent.

House of Representatives: Democrats, 334 seats; Republicans, 88 seats; 8 Progressives; 6 Farmer-Labor Party.

22 Quoted in James Reston, "Liberty and Authority," *New York Times*, June 29, 1986, E-23.

23 Democratic National Platform, June 26, 1936.

24 Herbert Croly, *The Promise of American Life* (New York: Archon Books reprint, 1963), 29.

25 Paul E. Tsongas, speech, National Press Club, Washington, D.C., October 5, 1982.

26 Bill Clinton, State of the Union Address, Washington, D.C., January 23, 1996.

27 Edison Media Research, exit poll, November 4, 2014. Text of question: "Which is closer to your view? Government should do more to solve problems. Government is doing too many things better left to businesses and individuals." Government should do more, 41 percent; government is doing too many things, 54 percent.

28 NBC News/*Wall Street Journal*, poll, November 14–17, 2014.

29 Quoted in Charles W. Roll and Albert H. Cantril, *Polls: Their Use and Misuse in Politics* (Cabin John, Maryland: Seven Locks Press, 1972), 123.

30 Ibid., 124.

31 Everett Carll Ladd, Jr., *Where Have All the Voters Gone?* (New York: W. W. Norton, 1982), 28.

32 Quoted in Kate Zernike, *Boiling Mad: Inside Tea Party America* (New York: Times Books, Henry Hold and Company, 2010), 9.

33 Fox News, poll, October 20–22, 2013. Text of question: "Please tell me whether you agree or disagree with each of the following statements. The two-party system is broken. It's time for more political parties." Agree, 55 percent; disagree, 42 percent; don't know, 3 percent.

34 Quoted in Chuck McCutcheon, "Future of the GOP," *CQ Researcher*, October 24, 2014, 891.

35 Ibid., 895.

36 Quoted in Philip Rucker, "Stage Is Set for Election Drama," *Washington Post*, October 19, 2014, A-1.

37 Clinton Rossiter, *Parties and Politics in America* (Ithaca, New York: Cornell University Press, 1960).

38 Quoted in McCutcheon, "Future of the GOP," 891.

39 Ibid., 893.

40 Rossiter, *Parties and Politics in America*, 3.

41 Quoted in Seth McLaughlin, "Obamacare Repeal Pressure Building on Mitch McConnell, John Boehner," *Washington Times*, November 2, 2014. See http://www.washingtontimes.com/news/2014/nov/2/obamacare-repeal-pressure-building-on-mitch-mcconn/?page=all. Accessed December 18, 2014.

42 Fox News, poll, October 25–27, 2014. Text of question: "Which of the following best describes how you feel about the new (2010) health care law, also called Obamacare—do you think the health care law went too far, didn't go far enough, or is it about right?" Went too far, 46 percent; didn't go far enough, 26 percent; about right, 23 percent; too soon to tell (volunteered), 2 percent; don't know, 3 percent.

43 Ronald Reagan with Richard G. Huebler, *Where's the Rest of Me?* (New York: Duell, Sloan, and Pearce, 1965), 303.

44 Ronald Reagan, "A Vision for America," television broadcast, November 3, 1980.

45 Quoted in E. J. Dionne, Jr., *Our Divided Political Heart: The Battle for the American Idea in an Age of Discontent* (New York: Bloomsbury, 2012), 71.

46 E. J. Dionne, Jr., *Why Americans Hate Politics* (New York: Simon and Schuster, 1991), 31, 330.

47 Quoted in John Kenneth White, *The New Politics of Old Values* (Hanover, New Hampshire: University Press of New England, 1988), 144.

48 Joe Scarborough, *The Right Path: From Ike to Reagan, How Republicans Once Mastered Politics—and Can Again* (New York: Random House, 2013), passim.

49 Ibid., xiii–xiv.

50 Dionne, *Why Americans Hate Politics*, 172.

51 Ibid., 175.

52 Ibid.

53 Ibid.

54 "Joy Division: Jeb Bush and 2016," *The Economist*, December 20, 2014.

55 Quoted in Dan Balz, "Jeb Bush: Front-runner, Underdog, or Both?," *Washington Post*, December 18, 2014, A-4.

56 Edison Media Research, exit polls, November 4, 2008, and November 6, 2012.

57 Ibid.

58 "40 Interesting Facts about the 2014 Election," *Cook Political Report*, December 19, 2014.

59 Michael Gerson, "The Downside of Victory for Republicans," *Washington Post*, October 21, 2014, A-17.

60 "40 Interesting Facts about the 2014 Election."

61 NBC News/*Wall Street Journal*, poll, November 14–17, 2014. Text of question: "Do you want the candidates that were elected to office this year to make compromises to gain consensus on legislation, or stick to their campaign postures even if that means NO consensus on legislation?" Make compromises, 63 percent; stick to their campaign positions, 30 percent; depends (volunteered), 2 percent; not sure, 5 percent.

62 See Stan Greenberg, James Carville, and Page Gardner, "Tuesday and What It Tells Us about 2016," Democracy Corps, memo, November 7, 2014.

63 "The Governing Trap," *National Review Online*, editorial, November 5, 2014.

64 Quoted in David Nather, "It's On: Battle for the Soul of the GOP," *Politico*, November 5, 2014.

65 Ibid.

66 Clinton and Gore carried Arkansas, Louisiana, Georgia, and Kentucky.

67 Thomas F. Schaller, *Whistling Past Dixie: How Democrats Can Win Without the South* (New York: Simon and Schuster, 2006), passim.

68 Thomas E. Mann and Norman J. Ornstein, "The Party of Now What?," *Washington Post*, November 9, 2014, B-1.

69 Reagan-Bush presidential debate, Houston, Texas, April 23, 1980. See https://www.youtube.com/watch?v=YfHN5QKq9hQ. Retrieved March 7, 2014.

70 Reagan-Mondale presidential debate, Kansas City, Missouri, October 21, 1984.

71 Barack Obama, Address to the Nation, Washington, D.C., November 21, 2014.

72 Jeremy Diamond, "Graham: 2016 Hinges on Immigration," CNN, December 28, 2014.

73 William Galston and Elaine Ciulla Kamarck, "The Politics of Evasion: Democrats and the Presidency," Progressive Policy Institute, September 1989, 1.

74 NBC News/*Wall Street Journal*, poll, December 10–14, 2014. Text of question: "Next, I'm going to mention a number of people who might consider running for president in 2016. For each one, please tell me, yes or no, whether you could see yourself supporting that person for president in 2016. If you don't know the name, please just say so." Jeb Bush: Yes, could see self supporting, 31 percent; no, could not see self supporting, 57 percent; don't know name, 8 percent; not sure, 4 percent. Hillary Clinton: Yes, could see self supporting, 50 percent; no, could not see self supporting, 48 percent; don't know name, 1 percent; not sure, 1 percent.

75 *Citizens United v. Federal Election Commission*, 2010, No. 08–205, 90.
76 Cited in "40 Interesting Facts about the 2014 Election."
77 Quoted in McCutcheon, "Future of the GOP," 897.
78 Ibid., 891.
79 Domenico Montanaro, Rachel Wellford, and Simone Pathe, "2014 Midterm Election Turnout Lowest in Seventy Years," *The Morning Line*, November 10, 2014.
80 Quoted in Paul Steinhauser and Adam Aigner-Treworgy, "Obama: Democrats 'Don't Vote' in Midterms," CNN, May 9, 2014. See http://politicalticker.blogs.cnn.com/2014/05/09/obama-democrats-dont-vote-in-midterms/. Accessed November 28, 2014.
81 Quoted in David Cook, "GOP Party Chairman: Obama Executive Amnesty Is 'A Nuclear Threat,'" *Christian Science Monitor*, November 7, 2014.
82 Jeb Bush and Clint Bolick, *Immigration Wars: Forging an American Solution* (New York: Threshold Editions, Simon and Schuster, 2013), 200, 223.
83 Quoted in Eric Bradner and Jedd Rosche, "Republicans Hammer Legal Case Against Obama on Immigration," CNN.com, November 21, 2014.
84 Ibid.
85 Obama, Address to the Nation, November 21, 2014.

Bibliography

Selected Books

ABC News. *The '84 Vote*. New York: American Broadcasting Company, 1985.

Alter, Jonathan. *The Center Holds: Obama and His Enemies*. New York: Simon and Schuster, 2013.

———. *The Promise: President Obama, Year One*. New York: Simon and Schuster, 2010.

Ambrose, Stephen E. *Nixon: The Triumph of a Politician, 1962–1972*. New York: Simon and Schuster, 1989.

Baker, Peter. *The Breach: Inside the Impeachment and Trial of William Jefferson Clinton*. New York: Scribner, 2000.

Barrett, Laurence I. *Gambling with History: Reagan in the White House*. Garden City, New York: Doubleday and Company, 1983.

Bowers, Claude G. *Jefferson and Hamilton: A Classic Study of America's Greatest Antagonists*. Boston: Houghton, Mifflin Company, 1966 edition.

Brewer, Daniel Chauncey. *The Conquest of New England by the Immigrant*. New York: G. P. Putnam and Sons, 1926.

Brooks, Arthur C. *The Battle: How the Fight Between Free Enterprise and Big Government Will Shape America's Future*. New York: Basic Books, 2010.

Brooks, David. *On Paradise Drive: How We Live Now (And Always Have) in the Future Tense*. New York: Simon and Schuster, 2004.

Brown, Peter. *Minority Party: Why Democrats Face Defeat in 1992 and Beyond*. Washington, D.C.: Regnery Gateway, 1991.

Buchanan, Patrick J. *The Death of the West: How Dying Populations and Immigrant Invasions Imperil Our Country and Civilization*. New York: St. Martin's Press, 2002.

———. *The Greatest Comeback: How Richard Nixon Rose from Defeat to Create the New Majority*. New York: Crown Forum, 2014.

Burke, Vincent J., and Vee Burke. *Nixon's Good Deed: Welfare Reform*. New York: Columbia University Press, 1974.

Burns, James MacGregor. *Roosevelt: The Lion and the Fox*. New York: Harcourt, Brace, and World, 1956.

———. *Running Alone: Presidential Leadership JFK to Bush II*. New York: Basic Books, 2006.

Burns, James MacGregor, and Georgia J. Sorenson. *Dead Center: Clinton-Gore Leadership and the Perils of Moderation*. New York: Scribner, 1999.

Bush, Jeb, and Clint Bolick. *Immigration Wars: Forging an American Solution*. New York: Threshold Editions, Simon and Schuster, 2013.

Califano, Joseph A. *A Presidential Nation*. New York: W.W. Norton, 1975.

Cannon, Lou. *President Reagan: The Role of a Lifetime*. New York: Simon and Schuster, 1991.

Clinton, Bill. *My Life*. New York: Alfred A. Knopf, 2004.

Clinton, Hillary Rodham. *Hard Choices*. New York: Simon and Schuster, 2014.

Committee on Political Parties. *Toward a More Responsible Two-Party System*. New York: Rinehart Books, 1950.

Coontz, Stephanie. *Marriage, a History: From Obedience to Intimacy or How Love Conquered Marriage*. New York: Viking, 2005.

Cose, Ellis. *Color-Blind: Seeing Beyond Race in a Race-Obsessed World*. New York: HarperCollins, 1997.

Croly, Herbert. *The Promise of American Life*. New York: Archon Books, reprint, 1963.

Deaver, Michael K. *A Different Drummer: My Thirty Years with Ronald Reagan*. New York: HarperCollins, 2001.

DeFrank, Thomas M. *Write It When I'm Gone*. New York: G.P. Putnam and Sons, 2007.

Dionne, E.J., Jr. *Our Divided Political Heart: The Battle for the American Idea in an Age of Discontent*. New York: Bloomsbury, 2012.

———. *Why Americans Hate Politics*. New York: Simon and Schuster, 1991.

Divine, Robert A. *Foreign Policy and U.S. Presidential Elections, 1952–1960*. New York: New Viewpoints, 1974.

Edsall, Thomas B. *Building Red America: The New Conservative Coalition and the Drive for Permanent Power*. New York: Basic Books, 2006.

Eisenhower, Dwight D. *Mandate for Change: 1953–1956*. Garden City, New York: Doubleday and Company, 1963.

Etzioni, Amitai. *The Monochrome Society*. Princeton: Princeton University Press, 2001.

Fernandez, Ronald. *None of the Above: Immigrants, Fusions, and the Radical Reconfiguration of American Culture*. Ann Arbor: University of Michigan Press, 2007.

Ford, Gerald R. *A Time to Heal: The Autobiography of Gerald R. Ford*. New York: Harper and Row Publishers, 1979.

Frisch, Morton J., ed. *Selected Writings and Speeches of Alexander Hamilton*. Washington, D.C.: American Enterprise Institute, 1985.

Frum, David. *Why Romney Lost (and What the GOP Can Do About It)*. Newsweek ebook, 2012.

Goldman, Peter, and Tony Fuller. *The Quest for the Presidency, 1984*. New York: Bantam Books, 1985.

Goldwater, Barry M., with Jack Casserly. *Goldwater*. New York: Doubleday, 1988.

Greenstein, Fred I. *The Hidden-Hand Presidency: Eisenhower as Leader*. New York: Basic Books, 1982.

Halperin, Mark, and John Heilemann. *Double Down: Game Change 2012*. New York: Penguin Press, 2013.

Hamilton, Alexander, John Jay, and James Madison. *The Federalist*. New York: Random House, The Modern Library edition, 1941.

Heilemann, John, and Mark Halperin. *Game Change: Obama and the Clintons, McCain and Palin, and the Race of a Lifetime.* New York: Harper Collins, 2010.

Henry, William A., III. *Visions for America: How We Saw the 1984 Election.* Boston: Atlantic Monthly Press, 1985.

Hughes, Emmet John. *The Living Presidency.* New York: Coward McCann and Geohegan, 1973.

Huntington, Samuel P. *Who Are We? The Challenges to America's National Identity.* New York: Simon and Schuster, 2004.

Jordan, Hamilton. *Crisis: The Last Year of the Carter Presidency.* New York: Berkley Books, 1983.

Kearns, Doris. *Lyndon Johnson and the American Dream.* New York: New American Library, 1976.

Kennedy, John F. *A Nation of Immigrants.* New York: Harper and Row Publishers, 1964.

Klein, Joe. *The Natural: The Misunderstood Presidency of Bill Clinton.* New York: Doubleday, 2002.

Klinkner, Philip A. *The Losing Parties: Out-Party National Committees, 1956–1963.* New Haven: Yale University Press, 1994.

Kusnet, David. *Speaking American: How the Democrats Can Win in the Nineties.* New York: Thunder's Mouth Press, 1992.

Ladd, Everett Carll. *Where Have All the Voters Gone? The Fracturing of America's Political Parties.* New York: W. W. Norton, 1982.

Larson, Arthur. *A Republican Looks at His Party.* New York: Harper and Brothers, 1956.

Lowi, Theodore J. *The Personal President: Power Invested, Promise Unfulfilled.* Ithaca, New York: Cornell University Press, 1985.

Maraniss, David. *First in His Class: The Biography of Bill Clinton.* New York: Simon and Schuster, 1995.

McWilliams, Wilson Carey. *Beyond the Politics of Disappointment? American Elections, 1980–1998.* New York: Chatham House Publishers, 2000.

Meckler, Mark, and Jenny Beth Martin. *Tea Party Patriots: The Second American Revolution.* New York: Henry Holt and Company, 2012.

Mieczleoski, Yanek. *Gerald Ford and the Challenges of the 1970s.* Lexington: University Press of Kentucky, 2005.

Morgan, Ted. *FDR: A Biography.* New York: Simon and Schuster, 1985.

Morrison, Donald. *The Winning of the White House, 1988.* New York: Time, 1988.

Nixon, Richard M. *RN: The Memoirs of Richard Nixon.* New York: Grosset and Dunlap, 1978.

Obama, Barack. *The Audacity of Hope: Thoughts on Reclaiming the American Dream.* New York: Crown Publishers, 2006.

———. *Dreams from My Father: A Story of Race and Inheritance.* New York: Times Books, 1995.

O'Neill, Thomas P., with William Novak. *Man of the House: The Life and Political Memoirs of Speaker Tip O'Neill.* New York: Random House, 1987.

Porter, Kirk H., and Donald Bruce Johnson. *National Party Platforms: 1840–1968.* Urbana: University of Illinois Press, 1970.

Quayle, Dan. *Standing Firm: A Vice Presidential Memoir.* New York: HarperCollins, 1994.

Reagan, Ronald, with Richard G. Huebler. *Where's the Rest of Me?* New York: Duell, Sloan and Pearce, 1965.

Reeves, Richard. *The Reagan Detour.* New York: Simon and Schuster, 1985.

Regan, Donald T. *For the Record: From Wall Street to Washington.* San Diego: Harcourt Brace Jovanovich, 1988.

Rogin, Michael. *Ronald Reagan, the Movie and Other Episodes in Political Demonology.* Berkeley: University of California Press, 1987.

Roll, Charles W., and Albert H. Cantril. *Polls: Their Use and Misuse in Politics.* Cabin John, Maryland: Seven Locks Press, 1972.

Rossiter, Clinton. *Parties and Politics in America.* Ithaca, New York: Cornell University Press, 1960.

Santorum, Rick. *It Takes a Family: Conservatism and the Common Good.* Wilmington, Delaware: ISI Books, 2005.

Scammon, Richard M., and Ben J. Wattenberg. *The Real Majority.* New York: Coward-McCann, Inc., 1970.

Scarborough, Joe. *The Right Path: From Ike to Reagan, How Republicans Once Mastered Politics—and Can Again.* New York: Random House, 2013.

Schaller, Thomas F. *Whistling Past Dixie: How Democrats Can Win Without the South.* New York: Simon and Schuster, 2006.

Schattschneider, E. E. *Party Government.* New York: Rinehart and Company, 1942.

Schier, Steven E. *Transforming America: Barack Obama in the White House.* Lanham, Maryland: Rowman and Littlefield, 2011.

Skocpol, Theda, and Vanessa Williamson. *The Tea Party and the Remaking of Republican Conservatism.* New York: Oxford University Press, 2013.

Sorensen, Theodore C. *Kennedy.* New York: Harper and Row, 1965.

Stockman, David A. *The Triumph of Politics: Why the Reagan Revolution Failed.* New York: Harper and Row, 1986.

Swarns, Rachel. *American Tapestry: The Story of the Black, White, and Multiracial Ancestors of Michelle Obama.* New York: HarperCollins, 2012.

Taylor, Paul. *The Next America: Boomers, Millennials, and the Looming Generational Showdown.* New York: Public Affairs, 2014.

Thomas, Evan, Karen Breslau, Debra Rosenberg, Leslie Kaufman, and Andrew Murr. *Back from the Dead: How Clinton Survived the Republican Revolution.* New York: Atlantic Monthly Press, 1997.

Todd, Chuck. *The Stranger: Barack Obama in the White House.* New York: Little Brown and Company, 2014.

von Damm, Helene. *Sincerely, Ronald Reagan.* Ottawa, Illinois: Green Hill Publishers, 1976.

Warren, Elizabeth. *A Fighting Chance.* Henry Holt and Company, 2014.

Wattenberg, Ben J. *The Birth Dearth.* New York: Pharos Books, 1987.

White, John Kenneth. *Barack Obama's America: How New Conceptions of Race, Family, and Religion Ended the Reagan Era.* Ann Arbor: University of Michigan Press, 2009.

———. *The New Politics of Old Values.* Hanover, New Hampshire: University Press of New England, 1988.

———. *Still Seeing Red: How the Cold War Shapes the New American Politics*. Boulder: Westview Press, 1997.

———. *The Values Divide: American Politics and Culture in Transition*. Washington, D.C.: Congressional Quarterly Press, 2003.

White, John Kenneth, and John C. Green, eds. *The Politics of Ideas*. Lanham, Maryland: Rowman and Littlefield, 1995.

White, John Kenneth, and Matthew R. Kerbel. *Party On! Political Parties from Hamilton and Jefferson to Today's Networked Age*. New York: Oxford University Press, 2012.

White, John Kenneth, and Jerome M. Mileur, eds. *Challenges to Party Government*. Carbondale: Southern Illinois University Press, 1992.

White, Theodore H. *The Making of the President, 1964*. New York: Atheneum Publishers, 1965.

Wilcox, Clyde. *The Latest American Revolution? The 1994 Elections and Their Implications for Governance*. New York: St. Martin's Press, 1995.

Williams, Kim M. *Mark One or More: Civil Rights in Multiracial America*. Ann Arbor: University of Michigan Press, 2006.

Wills, Garry. *Reagan's America: Innocents at Home*. Garden City, New York: Doubleday, 1987.

Wirthlin, Dick, with Wynton C. Hall. *The Greatest Communicator: What Ronald Reagan Taught Me about Politics, Leadership, and Life*. New York: John Wiley and Sons, 2004.

Wolfe, Alan. *Moral Freedom: The Impossible Idea That Defines the Way We Live Now*. New York: W. W. Norton, 2001.

Zernike, Kate. *Boiling Mad: Inside Tea Party America*. New York: Times Books, Henry Holt and Company, 2010.

Zucker, Norman L. *The American Party Process: Readings and Comments*. New York: Dodd, Mead and Company, 1968.

Selected Articles

ABC News. "Romney Stands By 'Entitled' Obama Supporters in Leaked Video." September 17, 2012.

Ahrens, Frank. "Disney's Theme Weddings Come True for Gay Couples." *Washington Post*, April 7, 2007.

Aigner-Treworgy, Adam. "GOP's Cantor: 'We Have to Deliver.'" CNN.com, November 3, 2010.

Alter, Jonathan. "A Man Not of His Time." *Newsweek*, November 4, 1996.

———. "Playing the Gipper Card." *Newsweek*, February 1, 1999.

Balz, Dan. "Jeb Bush: Front-runner, Underdog, or Both?" *Washington Post*, December 18, 2014.

———. "Picking Up Votes in a Maze of Ideals." *Washington Post*, October 5, 1998.

Barnes, Fred. "Campaign '88: Bush's Mandate." *New Republic*, November 14, 1988.

Berke, Richard L. "Republicans End Silence on Troubles of President." *New York Times*, March 1, 1998.

Blake, Aaron. "Priebus: Romney's Self-Deportation Comment Was 'Horrific.'" *Washington Post*, August 16, 2013.

Bolger, Glen, and Neil Newhouse. "Congrats GOP! Now Here's a Reality Check." *Washington Post*, November 2, 2014.

Bordelon, Brendan. "McConnell Warns Obama on Amnesty: 'Like Waving a Red Flag in Front of a Bull.'" *National Review Online*, November 5, 2014.

Bradner, Eric, and Jedd Rosche. "Republicans Hammer Legal Case Against Obama on Immigration." CNN.com, November 21, 2014.

Broder, David S. "Factions, Competing Ideologies Challenge Coalition Builders." *Washington Post*, November 7, 1996.

———. "A Prescient Assessment of Reagan." *Washington Post*, December 9, 1992.

Broder, John M. "Latino Defeats Incumbent in L.A. Mayor's Race." *New York Times*, May 18, 2005.

Burge, Kathleen. "Gays Have Right to Marry Supreme Judicial Court Says in Historic Ruling." *Boston Globe*, November 19, 2003.

Cannon, Lou. "Why the Band Has Stopped Playing for Ronald Reagan." *Washington Post*, December 21, 1986.

Clarity, James F., and Warren Weaver, Jr. "Briefing: Conversion Rites," *New York Times*, October 21, 1985.

CNN/AllPolitics. "Burton Draws Fire for Clinton 'Scumbag' Remark." April 22, 1998.

CNN.com. "Wilson Funds Reach $1 Million after 'You Lie' Cry, Aide Says." September 12, 2009.

Cohn, D'Vera. "Area Soon to Be Mostly Minority." *Washington Post*, March 25, 2006.

Cook, David. "GOP Party Chairman: Obama Executive Amnesty Is 'A Nuclear Threat.'" *Christian Science Monitor*, November 7, 2014.

Cook Political Report. "40 Interesting Facts about the 2014 Election." December 19, 2014.

Coontz, Stephanie. "For Better, For Worse; Marriage Means Something Different Now." *Washington Post*, May 1, 2005.

Diamond, Jeremy. "Graham: 2016 Hinges on Immigration." CNN, December 28, 2014.

Dowd, Maureen. "A Popular President." *New York Times*, July 19, 2014.

The Economist. "Joy Division: Jeb Bush and 2016." December 20, 2014.

Fahrenthold, David A., Rosalind S. Helderman, and Jenna Portnoy. "What Went Wrong for Eric Cantor?" *Washington Post*, June 11, 2014.

Feehery, John. "Do Tea Party Groups Have Too Much Influence Over the GOP?" *CQ Researcher*, October 24, 2014.

Finnegan, Michael, and Mark Z. Barabak. "Villaraigosa Landslide: Voter Discontent Helps Propel Challenger to a Historic Victory." *Los Angeles Times*, May 18, 2005.

Fleischer, Ari. "What the GOP Must Do to Win in 2016." *Washington Post*, November 5, 2014.

Freedman, Samuel G. "Why Bob Dole Can't Be Reagan." *New York Times*, October 27, 1996.

Frum, David. "Crashing the Party: Why the GOP Must Modernize to Win." *Foreign Affairs*, September/October 2014.

Fuller, Matt. "Obama Calls Cantor After Day of Immigration Sparring." *Roll Call*, April 16, 2014.

Germond, Jack W., and Jules Witcover. "GOP Gains of Five Governors Possible in 1986." *National Journal*, December 14, 1985.

Gerson, Michael. "The Downside of Victory for Republicans." *Washington Post*, October 21, 2014.

———. "The Reagan Time Warp." *Washington Post*, November 4, 2014.

Gillespie, Edward. "Populists Beware: The GOP Must Not Become an Anti-Immigrant Party." *Wall Street Journal*, April 2, 2006.

Harwood, John. "Shut Out of White House, GOP Looks to Democrats of 1992." *New York Times*, July 4, 2014.

Hofstadter, Richard. "The Paranoid Style in American Politics." *Harper's*, November 1964.

Hornblower, Margot. "Millions View Colorful Shower in Honor of Refurbished Statue." *Washington Post*, July 5, 1986.

Hu, Winnie. "New York City Libraries Struggle to Meet Demand for English-Language Classes." *New York Times*, August 7, 2014.

Huffington Post. "Steve King: Most Dreamers Are Hauling 75 Pounds of Marijuana Across the Desert." July 23, 2013.

Ingraham, Christopher. "Whites Uneasy at Idea of Mostly Minority U.S." *Washington Post*, August 13, 2014.

Joyce, Amy. "For Gays, Some Doors Open Wider." *Washington Post*, September 24, 2006.

Kengor, Paul. "The Great Forgotten Debate." *National Review Online*, May 22, 2007.

King, Wayne. "Republican Inroads Put Texas on Edge." *New York Times*, February 21, 1985.

Kludt, Tom. "Boehner Thought Steve King Was an 'Asshole' for 'Cantaloupes' Comment." *Talking Points Memo*, January 17, 2014.

Ladd, Everett Carll. "Why Carter Will Probably Win." *Fortune*, July 28, 1980.

Lee-St. John, Jennine. "Viewpoint: Civil Rights and Gay Rights." *Time.com*, October 25, 2005.

Mailer, Norman. "By Heaven Inspired." *New Republic*, October 12, 1992.

Mann, Thomas E., and Norman J. Ornstein. "The Party of Now What?" *Washington Post*, November 9, 2014.

McCutcheon, Chuck. "Future of the GOP: Can the Republicans Gain More Minority Support?" *CQ Researcher*, October 24, 2014.

———. "Ronald Reagan Remains a GOP Icon." *CQ Researcher*, October 243, 2014.

McLaughlin, Seth. "Obamacare Repeal Pressure Building on Mitch McConnell, John Boehner." *Washington Times*, November 2, 2014.

Milbank, Dana. "Can Rand Paul Save the GOP?" *Washington Post*, November 2, 2014.

Morrow, Lance. "Yankee Doodle Magic: What Makes Reagan So Remarkably Popular a President?" *Time*, July 7, 1986.

Moynihan, Daniel Patrick. "Of 'Sons' and Their 'Grandsons.'" *New York Times*, July 7, 1980.

———. "The Paranoid Style in American Politics Revisited." *The Public Interest*, Fall 1985.

Nather, David. "It's On: Battle for the Soul of the GOP." *Politico*, November 5, 2014.

National Review Online. "The Governing Trap." November 5, 2014.

Nelson, Lars-Erik. "The Republicans' War." *New York Review of Books,* February 4, 1999.

New York Times. "Democratic National Platform, 1936." June 26, 1936.

New York Times. "Excerpts from Interview with Clinton on Goals for Presidency." June 28, 1992.

New York Times. "For Liberty's 100th Year, The Biggest Party Ever." July 6, 1986.

New York Times. "The 1992 Campaign: Transcript of 2nd TV Debate Between Bush, Clinton, and Perot." October 16, 1992.

New York Times. "Speeches by Eisenhower, Nixon." November 7, 1956.

New York Times. "State Political Parties Are Playing a New Role." June 16, 1985.

Newsweek. "How Bush Won: The Inside Story of Campaign '88." November 21, 1988.

Newsweek. "An Interview with Bush." January 30, 1988.

Palin, Sarah. "It's Time to Impeach Obama." *Breitbart News,* July 8, 2014.

Porter, Eduardo, and Michelle O'Donnell. "Facing Middle Age with No Degree and No Wife." *New York Times,* August 6, 2006.

Public Opinion. "Face-Off: A Conversation with the Presidents' Pollster, Patrick Caddell and Richard Wirthlin." December/January 1980.

Public Opinion. "Moving Right Along? Campaign '84's Lessons for 1988: An Interview with Peter Hart and Richard Wirthlin." December/January 1985.

Reston, James. "Liberty and Authority." *New York Times,* June 29, 1986.

Roberts, Sam. "A Generation Away, Minorities May Become the Majority in the U.S." *New York Times,* August 14, 2008.

———. "It's Official: To Be Married Means to Be Outnumbered." *New York Times,* October 15, 2006.

Roosevelt, Franklin D. "Jefferson and Hamilton." *New York Evening World,* November 16, 1925.

Rubin, Jennifer. "Jim DeMint's Destruction of the Heritage Foundation." *Washington Post,* October 21, 2013.

Rucker, Philip. "Stage Is Set for Election Drama." *Washington Post,* October 19, 2014.

Scammon, Richard M., and Ben J. Wattenberg. "Is This the End of an Era?" *Public Opinion,* October/November 1980.

Schneider, William. "The Democrats in '88." *Atlantic Monthly,* April 1987.

———. "Half a Realignment." *The New Republic,* December 3, 1984.

Schwartzman, Paul. "In Virginia's 10th Congressional District, GOP Struggles to Woo Minority Voters." *Washington Post,* July 20, 2014.

Schwarz, Hunter. "Obama Presidency Is One for the Textbooks." *Washington Post,* August 27, 2014.

Schwarzenegger, Arnold. "Schwarzenegger: GOP Take Down That Small Tent." *LATimes.com,* May 6, 2012.

Shabad, Rebecca. " 'Shame on Us' for Not Passing Immigration Reform, Graham Says." *The Hill,* November 23, 2014.

Sidey, Hugh. "A Conversation with Reagan." *Time,* September 3, 1984.

Silva, Mark. "GOP Chairman: 'Message Received.' " *Washington Post,* November 9, 2006.

Sink, Justin. "Poll: Boehner Lawsuit a 'Political Stunt.' " *The Hill,* July 14, 2014.

Slevin, Peter. "Town's Eye View of Immigration Debate." *Washington Post,* April 3, 2006.

Steinhauser, Paul, and Adam Aigner-Treworgy. "Obama: Democrats 'Don't Vote' in Midterms." CNN, May 9, 2014.

Thomas, Evan. "The Small Deal." *Newsweek*, November 18, 1996.

Thurber, Jon. "Witty Reagan Aide and Gun Control Advocate, James S. Brady." *Washington Post*, August 5, 2014.

Time. "Gays on the March." September 8, 1975.

Traub, James. "Is (His) Biography (Our) Destiny?" *New York Times Magazine*, November 4, 2007.

Vozzella, Laura. "McAuliffe Signs East Sea Bill That Pitted Korean Americans Against Japan." *Washington Post*, April 2, 2014.

Weintraub, Bernard. "For Ronald Reagan, the Ceremonies Stir Pride and Patriotism." *New York Times*, July 5, 1986.

———. "Notebook: Reagan Amid 'All the Hoopla.'" *New York Times*, July 6, 1986.

Will, George F. "No More Jury Duty." *Washington Post*, January 19, 1989.

Wilson, James Q. "A Guide to Reagan Country: The Political Culture of Southern California." *Commentary*, May 1, 1967.

———. "Reagan and the Republican Revival." *Commentary*, October 1980.

Woodward, Bob, and Peter Baker. "Behind Calm Air, President Hides Rage Over Starr." *Washington Post*, March 1, 1998.

Selected Interviews

Bush, George H. W. CNN interview, June 15, 1992.

Frank, Barney. Interview with John Kenneth White. Washington, D.C., December 20, 2000.

"Ronald Reagan and David Brinkley: A Farewell Interview." ABC News, December 22, 1988.

Wirthlin, Richard B. Interview with John Kenneth White. Washington, D.C., November 22, 1988.

Selected Polls

ABC News, exit poll, November 6, 1984.

ABC News/*Washington Post*, polls, 2013–2014.

CBS News/*New York Times*, exit poll, November 4, 1980.

CBS News/*New York Times*, polls, 2013–2014.

CNN/Opinion Research Corporation, polls, 2013–2014.

Decision/Making/Information, polls, 1984–1987.

Edison Media Research, exit poll, November 4, 2014.

Edison Media Research and Mitofsky International, exit poll, November 4, 2008.

Edison Media Research and Mitofsky International, exit poll, November 2, 2010.

Edison Research, exit poll, November 6, 2012.

Fox News, polls, 2013–2014.

Gallup Polls, 1936–2014.

NBC News/*Wall Street Journal*, polls, 1998–2014.

Princeton Survey Research Associates, polls, 2012.

Quinnipiac University, polls, 2014.

Selected Speeches

Buchanan, Patrick J. Speech to the Republican National Convention. Houston, August 17, 1992.

Bush, George H.W. Acceptance Speech. Republican National Convention, New Orleans, August 18, 1988.

Bush, George W. State of the Union Address. Washington, D.C., January 20, 2004.

Carter, Jimmy. Address to the Nation. Washington, D.C., July 15, 1980.

Clinton, Bill. Acceptance Speech. Democratic National Convention, Chicago, August 29, 1996.

———. Commencement Address. Portland State University, Portland, Oregon, June 13, 1998.

———. Election Eve Address. NBC Broadcast, November 2, 1992.

———. Remarks Following the House of Representatives Vote on Impeachment. Washington, D.C., December 19, 1998.

———. State of the Union Address. Washington, D.C., January 24, 1995.

———. State of the Union Address. Washington, D.C., January 23, 1996.

Eisenhower, Dwight D. Acceptance Speech. Republican National Convention, San Francisco, August 23, 1956.

———. State of the Union Address. Washington, D.C., February 2, 1953.

———. Statement by the President Upon Signing the National Defense Education Act. Washington, D.C., September 2, 1958.

Goldwater, Barry M. Acceptance Speech. Republican National Convention, San Francisco, July 16, 1964.

Johnson, Lyndon B. Remarks at the Signing of the Immigration Bill. Liberty Island, October 3, 1965.

———. Remarks to the American Committee on Italian Migration on the Occasion of the Termination of the National Origins Quota System. Washington, D.C., July 1, 1968.

Kennedy, John F. Remarks to Delegates to the 18th Annual American Legion Boys Nation. Washington, D.C., July 24, 1963.

Landon, Alfred M. Text of Governor Landon's Milwaukee Address on Social Security. Milwaukee, September 27, 1936.

McDaniel, Chris. Concession Speech. Hattiesburg, Mississippi, June 24, 2014.

Obama, Barack. Address to the Nation. Washington, D.C., November 21, 2014.

———. Commencement Address. University of Michigan, Ann Arbor, May 1, 2010.

———. Keynote Address. Democratic National Convention, Boston, July 27, 2004.

Quayle, Dan. Address to the Commonwealth Club of California. San Francisco, May 19, 1992.

Reagan, Ronald. Acceptance Speech. Republican National Convention, Detroit, July 17, 1980.

———. Address to the Nation on Independence Day. New York Harbor, July 4, 1986.

———. Announcement Speech. Los Angeles, November 13, 1979.

———. Radio Address to the Nation on the Observance of Mother's Day. Washington, D.C., May 7, 1983.

———. Remarks at the Republican National Convention. New Orleans, August 15, 1988.

———. Remarks on Arrival at West Lafayette, Indiana. West Lafayette, Indiana, April 9, 1987.

———. Remarks to Members of the Republican National Committee and the Reagan-Bush Campaign Staff. Dallas, August 24, 1984.

———. State of the Union Address. Washington, D.C., January 26, 1982.

———. State of the Union Address. Washington, D.C., January 25, 1984.

———. State of the Union Address. Washington, D.C., February 6, 1985.

———. State of the Union Address. Washington, D.C., February 4, 1986.

———. A Time for Choosing. Los Angeles, October 27, 1964.

———. A Vision for America. Television broadcast, November 3, 1980.

Roosevelt, Franklin D. Radio Address on the Election of Liberals. Washington, D.C., November 4, 1938.

Sasso, John. World Trade Center Club Speech. Boston, January 19, 1989.

Stevenson, Adlai. A Purpose for Modern Woman. Commencement Address. Smith College, Northampton, Massachusetts, June 6, 1955.

Tsongas, Paul. National Press Club Speech. Washington, D.C., October 5, 1982.

Other Printed Matter

Batalova, Jeanne. "Asian Immigrants in the United States." Migration Information Service, May 24, 2011.

———. "Immigrants in the Armed Forces." Migration Information Service, May 15, 2008.

Busch, Andrew E. "The New Deal Comes to a Screeching Halt." Ashbrook Center, May 2006.

Cook, Rhodes. "Gay Marriage Ban and the Bush Vote in 2004." *The Rhodes Cook Letter*, May 2005.

Democratic Party Platform, 1992. Washington, D.C.: Democratic National Committee.

Democratic Party Platform, 1996. Washington, D.C.: Democratic National Committee.

Flora, Jan L., Claudia M. Prado-Meza, and Hannah Lewis. "After the Raid Is Over: Marshalltown, Iowa, and the Consequences of Worksite Enforcement Raids." Immigration Policy Center Report, January 2011.

Galston, William, and Elaine Ciulla Kamarck. "The Politics of Evasion: Democrats and the Presidency." Progressive Policy Institute, September 1989.

Greenberg, Stan, and James Carville. "Inside the GOP: Report on the Republican Party Project." Democracy Corps Memo, June 12, 2014.

———. "Inside the GOP: Why Boehner Is Halting Immigration Reform." Democracy Corps Memo, February 2, 2014.

———. "Why the GOP Really Hates the Immigration Executive Order." Democracy Corps Memo, November 21, 2014.

Greenberg, Stan, James Carville, and Page Gardner. "Tuesday and What It Tells Us about 2016." Democracy Corps Memo, November 7, 2014.

Greenberg Quinlan Rosner Research. "Coming of Age in America, Part II," press release. September 2005.

Hoeffel, Elizabeth M., Sonya Rastogi, Myoung Oak Kim, and Hasan Shahid. "The Asian Population, 2010." U.S. Census Bureau, Washington, D.C., March 2012.

Jones, Nicholas A., and Jungmiwha Bullock. "The Two or More Races Population, 2010." U.S. Census Bureau Briefs, September 2012.

Lofquist, Daphne. "Same-Sex Couple Households." U.S. Census Bureau Report, September 2011.

Montanaro, Domenico, Rachel Welford, and Simone Pathe. "2014 Midterm Election Turnout Lowest in Seventy Years." *The Morning Line*, November 10, 2014.

Passel, Jeffrey S., and D'Vera Cohn. *U.S. Populations Projections: 2005–2050.* Pew Research Center report, February 11, 2008.

Passel, Jeffrey S., D'Vera Cohn, and Ana Gonzalez-Barrera. "Population Decline of Unauthorized Immigrants Stalls, May Have Reversed." Pew Research Center Hispanic Trends Project, press release, September 23, 2013.

Pew Research Center. "Romney's 47 Percent Comments Criticized, But Many Say Also Overcovered." Press release, October 1, 2012.

Popenoe, David. *The Future of Marriage in America.* Rutgers University, National Marriage Project, 2007.

Popenoe, David, and Barbara Dafoe Whitehead. *Should We Live Together?: What Young Adults Need to Know about Cohabitation before Marriage.* Rutgers University, National Marriage Project, 2002.

Republican National Committee. *Growth and Opportunity Project.* Washington, D.C.: Republican National Committee, December 2012.

Republican National Platform, 1980. Washington, D.C.: Republican National Committee, 1980.

Ryan, Camille. "Language Use in the United States, 2011." U.S. Census Bureau, American Community Survey Reports, August 2013.

Saad, Lydia. "Best President? Lincoln on Par with Reagan, Kennedy." Gallup press release, February 11, 2009.

U.S. Census Bureau. "Most Children Younger than Age One Are Minorities, Census Bureau Reports." Press release, May 17, 2012.

Vespa, Jonathan, Jamie M. Lewis, and Rose M. Kreider. "America's Families and Living Arrangements, 2012." U.S. Census Bureau, report, August 2013.

Walters, Nathan P., and Edward N. Trevelyan. "The Newly-Arrived Foreign-Born Population of the United States, 2010." U.S. Census Bureau, American Community Survey Reports, November 2011.

Whatley, Monica, and Jeanne Batalova. "Indian Immigrants in the United States." Migration Policy Institute, press release, August 21, 2013.

Wilcox, W. Bradford, ed. *The State of Our Unions: Marriage in America, 2011.* Charlottesville, VA: National Marriage Project, 2011.

Wirthlin, Richard B. "Final Report of the Initial Actions Project." January 29, 1981.

———. *Reagan for President: Campaign Action Plan.* June 29, 1980.

Wood, Robert G., Sarah Avellar, and Brian Goesling. "Pathways to Adulthood and Marriage: Teenagers' Attitudes, Expectations, and Relationship Patterns." Report to the U.S. Department of Health and Human Services, October 2008.

Index

20283792R00096

Printed in Great Britain
by Amazon